Transcend Your Inner Bully

Transcend Your Inner Bully

Live Free of Guilt and Negative Self-Talk

Salee Reese, LCSW

Advance Praise

"An engaging, well-written book to help readers silence their inner critic. Reese offers multiple case examples and experiences as well as effective, easy-to-understand strategies for getting relief."

—Beverly Engel, LMFT, author of *Freedom at Last: Healing the Shame of Childhood Sexual Abuse*

"An absolute *must-read*! There's literally a gem on every page. You'll learn multiple activities and perspectives that will change the course of your life as well as master amazing tools to assess your inner true self and triumph over your Inner Bully. Don't hesitate – buy this book!"

—Kristina Hallett, PhD, AAPB, author of *Banish Burnout - Create Motivation from the Inside Out*

"Salee has created a powerful map to change the destructive pattern of self-criticism. I strongly recommend this book to anyone who finds self-criticism a habit. You will be very glad you did."

—Lynn D. Johnson, PhD, author of *Enjoy Life! Healing with Happiness.*

"For a very long time, people have grasped for language to describe those critical messages that stir inside us and often squash our potential. Down through the years, these negative, self-defeating messages have been variously labeled internal saboteurs, tapes, or harsh internal critics. Salee Reese's term, Inner Bully, is as good as any because these negative internal messages leave us feeling intimidated, belittled, and reluctant to walk around unimpeded on the playground of life. This book will help readers identify their inner bullies and, most importantly, learn how to defy them. It's a helpful addition to the negative self-talk literature."

—Alan E. Godwin, Psy.D

"A gentle treatise on how we emotionally hurt ourselves that will inspire you to free yourself from self-imposed harsh judgment. This reader-friendly, step-by-step handbook helps us understand how our self-criticism started, and how to stop our automatic negative thoughts from beating us up. Practice the truths the author speaks, weight will be lifted and your self-esteem will grow and flourish."

—Wayne M. Gerard, LCSW, DCSW,
Diplomate in Clinical Social Work

Table of Contents

1   Introduction

1   Chapter One
     Hostage to an Inner Bully

7   Chapter Two
     The Little Girl Who Was Me

19   Chapter Three
     Know the Enemy

25   Chapter Four
     How to Spot Your Inner Bully

49   Chapter Five
     Guilt: The Good, the Bad ... and Is It All Ugly?

65   Chapter Six
     The Birthing of Your Inner Bully

77   Chapter Seven
     How to Debunk, Defy, and Disempower
     Your Inner Bully

101 Chapter Eight
     The Glittering Truth About You

115 Chapter Nine
     Life in the Command Module: Making Change Stick

129 Chapter Ten
     Ditch Perfection: Go Easy on Yourself

135   CHAPTER ELEVEN
       Heed the Call to Self-Protect: It's How We Love Ourselves

155   CHAPTER TWELVE
       Roadblocks: Why We Stay and Endure

167   CHAPTER THIRTEEN
       Perceive Your Parents Through Fresh Eyes

177   CHAPTER FOURTEEN
       When Inner Bullies Pop Up in Relationships

191   CHAPTER FIFTEEN
       Going Forward – What to Expect

197   CHAPTER SIXTEEN
       Wallow in Freedom!

205   APPENDIX ONE
       Self-Evaluation Exercise (SEE)

207   APPENDIX TWO
       The Inner Bully and Addiction

211   ACKNOWLEDGMENTS

215   ABOUT THE AUTHOR

For my clients

Your stories expanded my consciousness,
my knowledge, and my heart – and I thank you for that.

Introduction

I never thought I was a bully
until I saw how I speak to myself.
I think I owe myself an apology.
—ANITA MOORJANI, *DYING TO BE ME*

Would you willingly hang out with a shaming, abusive bully who makes you feel small, worthless, and incompetent?

Well, of course not! you're thinking. *I'd dump that monster in two seconds!* But the sad truth is that you are carrying that monster with you everywhere you go, day and night. And you've willingly given it space right inside your own head.

I'm talking about what's commonly referred to as the inner critic: the voice within that relentlessly criticizes how you look and what you say, do, or think. Author Michael Singer, in his book *The Untethered Soul*, calls this unfriendly menace the "inner roommate." In so doing, Singer likened the critical inner voice to an annoying roommate who won't let you have a moment to yourself – and ohhh, the nonstop commentary. It's usually cranking out an array of endless criticisms – especially about you.

The term "inner critic" is well known and well understood, so I'll use it occasionally throughout this book – but there are times when that label falls short. This voice isn't just critical, it's also judgmental and condemning. It tells you that whatever you do or don't do is wrong, yes, but it also tells you *how bad you are for it*. It badgers, demeans, and engages in brutal name-calling, and it launches these attacks with the relentlessness of a tennis ball machine. It's *intent is to* hurt you and make you feel bad. It's a bully. And so, I'll primarily be using the term "Inner Bully."

I've been a psychotherapist for thirty-five years, and I continue to be floored by both the damage the Inner Bully inflicts and its far-reaching effects. It saps its victims of energy, motivation, self-esteem, and it robs their souls of sunshine – and it does it while flying under the radar, masquerading as reason or truth. Few people would put up with such flagrant mistreatment at the hands of another, but when it comes to this insidious voice within, many are helpless to separate themselves from it and question its judgment. In clinical terms, this kind of gaslighting and insensitive treatment is categorized as psychological abuse.

So what gives the Inner Bully this megadose of power? Simple: guilt.

I'm not talking about healthy guilt – the kind that arises from having hurt someone's feelings, or forgetting a friend's birthday, or eating your kid's Halloween candy and claiming it was stolen. I'm talking about toxic guilt, the kind that gets in the way of healthy functioning and stops us from making good decisions, taking chances, or creating positive change in our lives.

Toxic guilt eats away at emotional health and self-worth. It leads to stress, anxiety, and depression. I've seen it stop clients from speaking up or sharing their real thoughts in all arenas of their daily life, including within their relationships. Toxic guilt is often at the root of why people overextend and sacrifice themselves unrealistically and to a degree that's detrimental to their overall well-being – even including their physical health. Toxic guilt hinders a person's innate capacity to self-protect, leaving them vulnerable to toxic people and external bullies.

Those driven by the Inner Bully are typically consumed by guilt. They see themselves as selfish if they don't run themselves ragged or yield to the whims of the cruel voice within. Their guilt can turn them into people-pleasing (and Inner Bully-pleasing) doormats, vulnerable to being walked on and taken advantage of. The inner critic and its potent stew of toxic guilt drives people to seek some kind of unattainable perfection.

But wait, you say. Isn't feeling guilty the result of having a conscience? Isn't a conscience a *good* thing?

Yes. Yes. Yes. A conscience is a good thing. But what I'm talking about isn't a conscience. A conscience is a spiritual, uplifting moral guide. And your Inner Bully is just the opposite – it's critical and demoralizing. A conscience invites you to be a better person. But your demoralizing Inner Bully tells you you'll *never be* a better person.

Ouch.

If you're taunted by an Inner Bully, you'll find yourself self-blaming, self-criticizing and self-sacrificing. You dim your light to avoid shining, you feel unworthy of the good things in life, you endure way too much, you submit too often, and you surrounded yourself with people who can't love you right.

You also have a disproportionate concern for the needs and feelings of others while ignoring your own. Perhaps you have difficulty saying no, or advocating for what you want. Perhaps you're struggling with addiction.

Most debilitating of all these symptoms is self-loathing, not loving the wonder that you are – in fact, not even seeing it! Modern life can be a lonely one, but nothing tops the loneliness we feel when we're estranged from our very self.

Now no one, including me, is entirely immune to the relentless harangue of the Inner Bully, as you'll see later in the book. But with awareness and some tools to fight it, we can take back our lives and reclaim the inside of our heads as ours alone.

Consider this book a beacon for guiding you out of the murky darkness of toxic guilt. The enemy within will be rendered impotent as you learn how to stare it down and attain control over your own choices and actions.

Do you deny yourself the joys of life? Are you hounded by past regrets? Do you apologize for things when you don't really need to? Are you driven to achieve perfection? Do you go through bouts of unhinged guilt? Are you *compelled* to appease others or to make them happy?

If you answered yes to any of the questions above, I wrote this book for you.

Chapter One

Hostage to an Inner Bully

Anytime we beat ourselves up mentally, it's abuse.
And if it's wrong to be abusive to others,
why is it okay to be abusive to ourselves?

—SALEE

You are under attack by an internal enemy. Its commanding presence overshadows and dims your real self. It spreads its influence by manipulating your self-concept and recruiting you in its relentless drive to punish you. Eventually, it steals your ability to feel joy, discouraging you from pursuing it and convincing you that you are no longer worthy of it. Without an internal revolution, its incessant deprecating remarks will continue to "make sense." You'll find yourself agreeing with it and gaining a twisted sort of satisfaction from joining forces with it.

Like a malignancy gone wild, that monster within will, left unchecked, have its way in destroying your connection to your truest self. One day, you wake up and realize this enemy has taken possession of your life. On that day, you hear yourself screaming: "I want it back!"

This book is designed to empower you to face it down and win dominion over it.

Your Inner Bully is that taunting, judgmental inner voice that finds something wrong with nearly everything you do. It condemns you for wasting your time, wasting your food, and wasting your life. It calls you a loser when you fail and an egotist when you enjoy your successes. It ridicules you for not exercising enough *even when you are exercising enough*. It snickers maliciously when you make mistakes and belittles you for losing things, being late, or for taking some time off. It criticizes you for disappointing others and labels you as selfish when you do something for yourself. It even judges you for doing what it's doing: judging.

In the eyes of the Inner Bully, you're fatally flawed, and it's impossible to get perfect enough to fix that.

Brooke

One of my clients, thirty-nine-year-old Brooke, is an excellent example. Unhealthy guilt, the kind that's oversized and unwarranted, paralyzes her. The purpose of healthy guilt is to awaken us. It empowers us to do some healthy soul-searching, correct our behavior, and make amends. But guilt shouldn't be a club we use for beating ourselves up. In Brooke's case, unhealthy guilt keeps her from trying new things – testing her wings, so to speak. Guilt keeps her world narrowed and unfulfilling.

Before Brooke and I explored her childhood to look for clues that would explain where her unhealthy brand of guilt took root, I taught her about Inner Bullies. I told her that an Inner Bully is a critical inner voice that chops away at our self-esteem and well-being without us even being aware of it. And for that reason, the Inner Bully's ability to deflate and sabotage us goes unchecked.

We didn't get very far into our session before Brooke became aware of her own Inner Bully, a fact made clear to me when she blurted out some deeply felt frustration: "I want to do something with my life but anything I come up with gets shot down! My Inner Bully tells me: 'You're not good enough. You'll fail at it.'"

Digging a little deeper, she shared this:

> *I feel guilty if I'm not perfect. My father expected us to be perfect at everything. We had to be perfect at sports, get perfect grades, and be perfect at playing an instrument. I remember him grabbing my sister's flute from her and beating her with it because she didn't*

meet his expectations. The house had to be perfect. The car had to be perfectly clean. We weren't allowed to play in our yard because it had to look perfect. We had to dress in nice clothes for school because we had to look perfect. As a family, we had to portray the perfect image. The list is endless. Trying to be perfect is exhausting! It makes me nervous to try anything. I always feel I'm going to make the wrong decision. There's no way to escape feeling like a failure!

Almost all of us can relate to Brooke. We may not have experienced the same childhood but, like Brooke, we have our own personal internal bully.

This nasty brute hangs out in your head, badgering, scolding, bossing, and shaming you. Common assaults go like this: "You're too sensitive." "You're insensitive," "It's your fault." "How could you be so stupid?" "What's wrong with you?"

This degrading treatment begins the moment you get out of bed: "You should've gotten up earlier! Are you ignoring all you have to do?! You stayed up too late as usual. Will breakfast be granola bars for the kids ... again!? Your hair's a mess. Don't forget to contact Jonathan today. He expects a call, you know. You're such a slacker."

Making matters worse, your Inner Bully is notorious for giving you conflicting messages. For example, while rushing to get ready, it instructs you to skip breakfast, but once you're out the door, driving down the road, it chastises you for doing so. You can't win!

Once we're fully convinced that we're bad, unlovable, or worthless, our defenses collapse. We simply cannot shield ourselves from the ongoing barrage of internal assaults.

And isn't it understandable that such ongoing badgering would tempt any one of us – desperate for relief – to seek out some form of addiction in order to escape? Yep, it's understandable. Alcohol, drugs, food, social media, and packed schedules are a few of the popular distractions of our time. Even suicide can start to seem like an attractive alternative. When we're consumed with shame, both the world on the inside and the world on the outside are hostile places. Why stay?

Stay. Because that Inner Bully can be defeated.

Being held hostage by toxic guilt is similar to wandering through a murky swamp, eyes fixed straight ahead, desperate for any speck of daylight revealing the pathway for getting out. You've existed in that foul, smelly place for what feels like eons. You've even thought of it as home. But it's toxic and inhospitable, and you're spent. It's time to leave it. How? This book will answer that question for you.

Everyone who has lived in one of those dark places has their own swamp-story to tell. During my thirty-five years as a psychotherapist I've listened to several. In the pages to come, I'm going to share many of those stories with you – changing names and some insignificant details, as I have with Brooke. In essence, you'll get to be the proverbial fly on the wall, listening in on therapy sessions, experiencing the journeys others have taken through their swamp.

I have also included examples from my own swamp journey: what it was like there and how I got free. Like many, I have a personal history with my own Inner Bully. We go way back. It came on the scene when I was a small child, and its impact was close to unbearable at times. The good news is that my less-than-ideal childhood served as a major catalyst in my decision to make psychotherapy my career. Helping to free people from the stranglehold of their internal abusers has been a driving passion for me.

In this book, I portray unhealthy, toxic guilt as a distinct entity, separate from the self. It *is,* in fact, separate because it bears no resemblance to our True Selves.

Transcend Your Inner Bully is about the power a ruthless internal bully has over your well-being and how it impacts – negatively – every arena of your life. By reading the following chapters, you'll learn how to get the upper hand.

If you have trouble liking and forgiving yourself, receiving praise, asking for what you want, believing you're valuable, and worthy of love and protection, then this book is for you. Read on and say hello to freedom. Before long, you won't be just looking at it with your nose and hands pressed against the window. You'll be living there!

Chapter Two

The Little Girl Who Was Me

Our childhood follows us like a shadow throughout our lives, weaving its pattern into the fabric of our day-to-day living.

—SALEE

A few years back, while walking through a crowded department store, I noticed a little girl standing directly in my path several yards in front of me. She had to be about four years old. As I got closer, her mother aggressively yanked her out of the way while harshly scolding her: "You're in everyone's way! That's rude!"

The image of that crushed little girl, who was sobbing as one does when severely heartbroken, is still imprinted in my mind. In the fleeting seconds during which that event took place, had I given voice to the heavy, sick feeling in my soul, I would have said to that mother, *Oh, I wish you hadn't bludgeoned your little girl's self-esteem on my account. And do you have any idea the amount of hate you just injected into her?*

But in that brief and unexpected moment, I didn't know what to say. In an attempt to counter the mother's harshness, I tried to meet the little girl's eyes while smiling reassuringly, but my efforts were unsuccessful. Her head was buried in her coat, an understandable response to being subjected to shame and embarrassment.

I'm fairly certain this little girl's mother loves her and believes that it's her job to teach her daughter how to behave in public. Yes, as parents, it is our duty to plant the seeds of respectful social conduct, but we do that best by showing, not just telling. If I want my child to be respectful and sensitive to others, I must exhibit those qualities myself. The mother in the department store wasn't modeling the respect and sensitivity she was expecting her child to demonstrate.

A better approach – and far more effective – would have been for the mother to gently pull the little girl to her side saying, "Sweetie, let's move out of the way, so other people can get through."

That would have been positive and productive – seizing the moment as an opportunity for teaching. But in the scenario I witnessed, the little girl learned more about fearing her mother's anger than about the courtesy of not blocking aisles. She also learned that innocence can be deemed unforgivable and deserving of a harsh tongue-lashing.

My own experience with shame took place at about the same age. I lived on a quiet street lined with trees and pretty houses. My favorite possession of all time was my tricycle! I loved riding it on the sidewalk out in front of our house. That bike and I were welded together. I was happy and oh-so-free on that bike. But then things took an unexpectedly sad turn. My parents decided to buy the house across the street. On moving day, we all shared the job of hauling our things across the street. I remember carrying small items and feeling happy to be part of the action.

But something didn't feel good. My bike didn't come with us, and I didn't know why. I still don't know why. What I do know is how horrible I felt when, shortly after we got settled in, I saw another little girl riding it. Her name was Phyllis. She and her family had moved into our old house.

Seeing Phyllis on my bike provoked an uncontrollable sense of injustice. Barely noticing the other people standing around, I marched right across the street and without the least bit of hesitation, I hit her. Phyllis started crying. Mom, appearing out of nowhere, grabbed me by the arm and began berating me on the spot. I cried. I remember it was a very hard cry – the cry of being deeply wounded and misunderstood. But that didn't matter. What mattered to my mother was that I had hurt someone else. I was all alone, suffering silently in my grief and my shame. I felt Mom was more connected to Phyllis than she was to me.

That's what shame does to you. It disconnects you from everybody else – from the world and especially from those who matter to you.

It also disconnects you from you. That's what happened to me too.

Something severe takes place inside the child who is being scolded, shamed, or yelled at. The door to their parent's heart is abruptly slammed shut. Whether that's true or not is immaterial. It's what it *feels like* to the child. But parents don't normally look at it that way. They view their stormy reaction as justified, and wave it off as momentary and insignificant. But to the child, those few seconds are an eternity that leaves them in a state of extreme psychological distress. In some cases, depending on the severity and frequency of the shaming, it can be traumatizing.

Where does this lead? Out of sheer desperation, that child will do almost anything to reestablish a bond and a sense of security with their parent. Because of the child's innate position of utter dependence, they can't afford to have their parent mad or unresponsive to their needs.

So they conform, which is generally the only apparent option available to them. They learn to appease, they learn to "be good," and they learn to self-sabotage. They bury their true feelings and become master pretenders, pretending even to themselves.

For me, as the years wore on, my mother's manner of shaming manifested in varying ways. Sometimes it came in the form of detached coldness, harsh slaps across the face, enraged spankings, or angry stares. But no matter how it manifested, it was clear to me that she felt justified in unleashing her fury and disapproval. In her mind, it was totally deserved. And since I could never really put a finger on what was so awful about what I had done, I became convinced I was the awful thing. I was guilty for being me.

There were no expressions of remorse, reconnecting on an emotional level – the kind of healing elements and practices I teach parents to do with their kids. A warm touch or a spontaneous hug from her was a rare occurrence. That just wasn't who she was. My attempts to get love from her – to feel wanted and cherished by her – were refused or ignored. And there wasn't anything I could do to change that. Small gestures, like tidying up the house while she was gone, delighted her. They won me her gratitude and a warm approving smile, but they had no lasting effect.

I will say this: as I got older, starting in my late teens, we connected on an intellectual level. That was nice. And I gained much from her breadth of knowledge.

Looking back, I can see that Mom's general demeanor in the home can best be described as smoldering irritation. Although that wasn't the case one hundred percent of the time, it was enough to cause Dad, me, and my two sisters to lie low. That was the safest option. No one wanted to be her target. Her eruptions and attacks weren't pleasant.

Interestingly, at no point did we all talk about our common experience. It would have helped, perhaps reducing the sense of isolation and tempering some of the shame. Maybe I would have been less inclined to take it personally. Maybe.

For some reason, Mom seemed happier outside the home. She was always jovial and chatty when she came home from work. And certain outings with her, such as shopping excursions, could actually be joyful events. Fun, even.

Once I became an adult, and could see with clearer eyes, I realized that my mother was a very unhappy woman – unhappy in her marriage and unhappy in her domestic role. She wasn't happy with her life. Period. There's no doubt in my mind that she would have found focusing on a career far more rewarding. She held down office jobs, but they were limiting. There was more to her, and it wasn't getting tapped – not fully – not at work and certainly not on the domestic front. I recollect her avid interest in history, political science, world religions, and different cultures. She read and watched programs on those topics and would passionately share what she learned with the rest of us. No question, my mother would have been perfectly suited as the head of some history or sociology department somewhere.

A nurturer she was not. She knew this and at times she conveyed genuine regret for what her kids were missing out on. "I'm not the hugging, cookie-baking type," she would say apologetically.

Our father was the nurturer but, for the most part, he remained disconnected – isolated in his alcohol-bubble. He was no antidote to my mother's toxicity. He could have been, but he wasn't.

Painful as it was at times, my childhood planted the seeds for what grew into my life's work.

In my senior year in high school, I just happened to take a class in psychology. That class proved to be a turning point for me. It was a validating experience, making me realize that what I was feeling was real. I began acquiring the knowledge

I needed to see myself and my family in a whole new light. It was both freeing and illuminating! I started to question my automatic patterns of thinking – especially about myself.

Yep, the field of psychology was for me, not only as a tool for healing myself, but for helping others heal. My career was born.

The pain I experienced as a child also gave me the determination to be a better parent. I remember telling myself: *I won't be making the same mistakes my parents did. Nope, it won't happen.* I vowed that my children would never go to bed with the same horrible feelings about themselves that I had. They would grow up feeling loved, and they would grow up convinced they were lovable human beings who were *worthy* of love.

Even with my training and experience, I wasn't always certain I was getting it right. My worry over causing lasting psychological damage was unwavering. But reassurance came after an incident with my oldest son, Rod, who was sixteen at the time.

He accidentally broke a vase, and it triggered an instantaneous, irate response on my part. Catching myself almost immediately, I apologized, telling him, "Rod, that was wrong of me to yell at you. You didn't deserve that."

Being apologetic under such circumstances wasn't unusual for me. It became absurd, actually. I followed him around like a puppy, checking his psychological pulse incessantly. My fears of being like my mom drove me to do that.

He appeared comforted and went on, unaffected, about his business. But I wasn't convinced, so, as was typical of me, I just had to ask, "Are you sure you're okay?"

Generally, he would reassure me with a matter-of-fact nod. But this time was different. He walked right over to me, looked me straight in the eyes, and uttered these words: "Mom, you never had to be a perfect mom. The thing that mattered was that it mattered to you."

Magically, sixteen years' worth of parental guilt and anxiety lifted from my shoulders. Giddy with relief, I recall saying, "Rod, I needed to hear that when you were a baby!"

Before Rod's words, I hadn't understood that my good intentions were actually visible to my children. And unbeknownst to me, healing was taking place – on the spot.

I learned something important that day: Sincere regret in the form of a heartfelt apology nullifies shame.

Being tethered to shame isn't all that rare. Unless you grew up with perfect parents, perfect siblings, perfect everybodies – or unless you landed on a perfect planet – you'll end up lugging around a chunk of shame: archaic debris left over from an imperfect childhood. Such rubble may be affecting your life more than you realize.

Vanessa

When I began working with Vanessa, shame was something she felt on a regular basis. The house was never clean enough, she didn't exercise or diet enough, she wasn't a good enough wife, and she didn't give Carson – her baby – enough of her time.

Her Inner Bully was the culprit, and it followed her wherever she went. After hanging out with friends, heckling thoughts like *Maybe I wasn't nice enough* or *Maybe I talked too much* would torment her for hours.

Vanessa was convinced she wasn't worthy of love. In her eyes, she had zero value as a human being. But I believed otherwise. In one of our sessions, she showed me a photo she had taken of Carson gazing at her with loving, happy eyes. That told me volumes. I couldn't resist commenting, "Well, you're certainly doing something right!"

Unlovable? Lacking value? Hmmm. Vanessa's negative self-appraisal just wasn't adding up. She was just too warm-hearted, too caring, too sensitive to be a member of that club. She clearly didn't meet the criteria.

So where did the self-loathing and irrational guilt originate? Self-loathing wasn't something Vanessa was born with. It was learned.

When we were babies, we had no innate sense of disgust with ourselves. If our rattle fell to the ground, we didn't berate or despise ourselves. We didn't suffer shame over it – shame isn't even a reality to babies. So the incident didn't become an indictment against our character, and we weren't left with the sense of being a bad baby … or a bad person.

Clearly, we have a lot to learn from babies!

Yet as adults, many of us, just like Vanessa, lug around a truckload of accumulated guilt – the excessive, irrational, unhealthy kind. It's overkill. Yes, self-scrutiny can be a good thing, and sometimes guilt is warranted, like the guilt for being nasty to a store clerk, or losing something we borrowed. But we shouldn't agonize over those things. Learn from the life lesson, and move on.

Vanessa endured severe punishments as a child, and she was a target of ongoing critical and condemning messages. If we're treated this way repeatedly, a negative view of ourselves develops – a corrupted self-concept. We may be convinced we're detestable. In fact, the thought of being worthy of love, being accepted, even cherished, can seem utterly unfathomable.

The crux of Vanessa's problem was that she bought into a lie, and hidden from her consciousness is an Inner Bully that keeps spouting that lie.

The answer: go after the Inner Bully.

Questionnaire

Inner Bullies are extremely hard to recognize. The self-talk that drives many of us is so subtle and constant that we're usually oblivious to it. So the best way to discover Inner Bullies is by pinpointing the signs. This means noticing how they affect us.

The following questionnaire is designed for that purpose: to help you detect your Inner Bully by identifying how it is impacting you. Answering yes to any of the questions should raise your suspicions about its presence. Most likely, it means your Inner Bully is operating just beneath the surface, undermining you.

- Are you amazed when someone tells you they love you?
- Would you rather wither and shrink than shine?
- Does shining make you feel pompous or like you're being a show-off?
- Do you feel compelled to apologize when it's clearly not your fault?
- Do you push yourself to do, do, do?

- Does taking care of yourself seem selfish?
- Do you tend to overvalue others and undervalue yourself?
- Do you get uneasy if the people around you aren't happy?
- Are you uncomfortable taking time for yourself?
- Do you have difficulty turning down an invitation?
- Do you struggle with receiving compliments?
- Are you never satisfied with your achievements?
- Are you always unhappy with your appearance?
- Is it okay to spend money on others but not yourself?
- Do you feel it's wrong to be forgiving of yourself?
- Do you think you're lazy if you're not busy all the time?
- Do you avoid leaving someone because it might hurt their feelings?
- Would you rather be rejected than do the rejecting?
- Are you afraid of hurting someone's feelings or appearing disrespectful if you say what you really think?
- Do you automatically assume that most everything is your fault?
- Do you obsess about all the clothes hanging in your closet that don't get worn?
- Do you yearn for a nurturing relationship but feel unworthy of one?
- When you're sick, do you feel compelled to go to work even if losing income isn't a factor?
- Do you dwell on past regrets?
- Do you feel that no matter how much you do or how hard you try, it's never enough?
- Do you label yourself a bad parent?

- Is it easier to list your flaws than your finer qualities?
- Is it impossible for you to relax in your home if things aren't neat?
- Does telling people no give you the guilts – is it just easier to give in?
- Do you feel selfish asking someone to pay what they owe you?
- Do you get mad at yourself for making mistakes?
- Are you compelled to clean your plate?
- Do you take on a lot that you shouldn't?
- Do you feel responsible if your attempts to rescue someone don't work?
- Are you troubled by leaving dishes in the sink?
- Are you inclined to exhaust yourself – sacrificing your own needs – to avoid letting someone down?

If you found yourself nodding while reading the list above, it's very likely you have an Inner Bully that constantly tears you down, and like Vanessa, you're buying into its lies. The good news: if you bought into a lie, you can also buy into the truth. Vanessa did, and I'll show you the same process that worked for her.

Chapter Three

Know the Enemy

You can't conquer an enemy you can't see.

—SALEE

Most of us have a part of our brain that observes our own behavior. But the observers lodged in our brains are neither objective nor compassionate. They're more likely to be judgmental, always reminding us that we are not good enough. And so we criticize ourselves, judge ourselves, work harder, sleep less, or push our loved ones more... all in an effort to somehow be okay.

Most people I know assume that the judge is accurate! ... Generally that critical voice is seen as one who has power and wisdom.

—DANIEL GOTTLIEB, *LEARNING FROM THE HEART*

If that critical voice we carry around lacks objectivity, wisdom, and compassion, then why do we give it so much weight? Such prominence and power are undeserved. We must realize that any voice that's less than kind and loving has no business hanging out in our brain.

The critical voice that Gottlieb speaks of above has been given various labels over the years, including inner critic, inner judge, inner bully, and inner shamer. And then there's that term Michael Singer coined the "inner roommate," who lives with you and critically narrates your very existence.

If the inner voice were an actual roommate, Singer says, you would have terminated that relationship a long time ago. But not so with the one who takes up residence in your head. That roommate is tolerated. Why is that?

I believe a major reason most of us tolerate the Inner Bully is because it escapes detection. It has a way of creeping up on you with cat feet – it wouldn't escape notice otherwise. Let's face it, you're not likely to chase it down the road, begging it to come home with you. No, it worms its way in when you're not looking, then sits around waiting for opportunities to accost you. It attacks you for letting food go bad, losing your keys, forgetting someone's birthday, missing an exit, ignoring your dog, neglecting your emails, or buying the wrong box of cereal for your family.

Singer points out that "you don't generally notice it occurring because you don't step back from it. You're so close that you don't realize that you're actually hypnotized into listening to it."

Meg, a former client you'll learn more about later on, couldn't agree more. "It's something you don't even realize is there," she says, "but it rules your life." By the way, Meg, I'm happy to report, became an expert at *stepping back from it.*

And as for ruling your life, yes, it does. In fact, it can wreak a world of havoc on your happiness and psychological well-being. Round the clock, the Inner Bully chips away at your self-esteem with a steady onslaught of critical and unfair jabs. It dedicates itself to making you feel small. It belittles, badgers, intimidates, and bosses you around. And don't count on it being kind. Ever! That will never happen. In fact, it does everything it can to make you as miserable as possible.

Where does that leave you? Feeling beat up most the time. That's why we call our little monster an "Inner Bully." As we all know, bullies beat people up – and they delight in doing so. As Meg implies, we mindlessly bow and pay homage to this insulting presence. We give it more power and authority, in fact, than we give our own intellect. That's sheer absurdity on our part! Why? Because that hostile intruder is not a conscience, it's not a moral guide – it's not even intelligent! Later on, you'll learn that it's not mentally balanced either ... *you* are, but it isn't.

Here's an important fact: just as we learn to erect boundaries against toxic people, we must learn to do the same with our toxic enemy within – the bully we haul around wherever we go. That's why it's vital that we become aware of it. It's important to reiterate that we can't correct what we don't detect, and we can't conquer or protect ourselves against an enemy we can't see.

Becoming conscious of our Inner Bully's presence is essential for getting free of its stranglehold. In this chapter, you'll be developing an awareness of its existence and learning to recognize when and how it's impacting you. Without this awareness, you remain a helpless puppet to the thing.

The best way to begin this journey is to simply start observing your feelings. As you know, depending on the circumstances, your feelings will fluctuate throughout any given day. Sometimes they can be categorized as good feelings and, at other times, not so good.

Good feelings foster an overall sense of well-being. That's something young children seem to have a handle on. Ever notice that they're happy most the time? Of course, that can change rather abruptly, especially when they're denied something they want, or if they get hurt, or if their ice cream falls off the cone. But invariably, they snap back to a good feeling place again.

As for us adults, life's restrictions and ongoing curve balls impacts our happy, too. And, by the way, those curve-ball episodes seem to be commonplace and have a way of knocking us off balance ... but only for a while. It appears that a general sense of emotional well-being is a human default setting. In fact, that good feeling state can serve as a gauge. When things are off – when we're not in a good feeling state – we know something's not right. Our physical well-being offers a good comparison. When things are off, we get alerted almost immediately in the form of discomfort or pain. It forces us to stop and pay attention. We ask ourselves, *Hey, what's going on?*

So when you're feeling bad emotionally, stop and pay attention. Ask yourself what's going on. "Why do I feel this way?" It could be rooted in a disappointment, a frustration, or one of life's many ice cream cone incidents. Or perhaps those "bad emotions" are an indication that your Inner Bully is hard at work. That's not always the case, but feeling bad should alert you to that possibility.

If I make a mistake or do not accomplish my task as efficiently as possible, I often feel very anxious as if I am being watched and criticized.

—PETE WALKER,

COMPLEX PTSD: FROM SURVIVING TO THRIVING

Yes, anxiety can be a clue that your Inner Bully might be lurking behind the scenes somewhere. Guilt, shame, depression, and rage can be clues too.

The same is true if you feel compelled to be perfect, please others, or bite off more than you can chew. Other telltale signs include feeling haunted by past regrets, driven by "shoulds," and controlled by obligations. Holding yourself back or suppressing yourself are other indicators. Do you keep quiet rather than speak up? Do you water yourself down or become smaller around other people?

Any of these signs, and more, can serve as indicators that you're dealing with an underlying, undermining Inner Bully. Do keep in mind, though, that it's natural to experience bad feelings, even without an Inner Bully. If you're a human being, negative feelings come with the territory. They turn problematic when their frequency or intensity cause you to suffer. That's when you know you're dealing with an Inner Bully. You feel tormented, miserable, compelled, driven, compromised, or stifled. Indisputably, those things have a happiness-deadening effect on us humans.

Right along with being aware of your feelings, it's important to become aware of the thoughts you're having at any given time. Thoughts ignite emotions. I'll give you an example. If someone you know fails to respond to a text, your emotional response will likely be dictated by how you interpret that event. In other words, your thoughts will play a key role in the emotions that get triggered in you. Your thoughts will affect your happy.

Ponder this for a moment: Thoughts are essentially composed of words, and words, whether they originate from somewhere outside yourself or from inside your own skull, are extremely powerful. Let's say someone's words – aimed at you – convey that you're irresponsible or perhaps inadequate in some way. Maybe they imply that you're a liar or that your sister is the "bright" one in the family, or that your brother is more successful than you. Your well-being will understandably take a hit. It will also take a hit if those very same demeaning remarks originate from inside your head. It matters little where the words come from. The negative effects will likely be identical.

Feelings and thoughts. Recognizing these are your first baby steps to unmasking and neutralizing your Inner Bully. It's going to take some practice, so why not get started right now?

Chapter Four

How to Spot Your Inner Bully

Awareness is the greatest agent for change.

—ECKHART TOLLE

To help augment your awareness skills, I'll offer a sampling of ways Inner Bullies invade our psyches. Although the ways they manifest are boundless, I narrowed the list down to those I hear most often from my clients and also those I relate to personally. My hope is that this chapter will empower you to begin to spot your Inner Bully at work.

As you begin reading the examples, I urge you to jot down the ones that mirror your own experience.

Shining Makes You Feel Guilty

What if a ray of sunlight
– feeling guilty for its brightness –
purposely dims itself? Who loses out? We all do!

—SALEE

Do you have a tendency to dim yourself? That is to say, do you feel guilty if you feel proud or good about yourself? Are you inclined to present yourself as less than who you really are – less bright, less capable, less talented?

Imagine that you're walking along a trail, and you spot an unusual and stunning butterfly. Perched on a small branch, its richly colored wings and exquisite gracefulness invite you to pause and absorb the wonder before you. But suddenly something baffling and disturbing happens. The butterfly tucks its wings in tightly, concealing its beauty. Guessing the butterfly was frightened by your presence, you continue on your walk. Several minutes later, unable to put the butterfly's strange behavior out of your mind, you return to that same spot. Your heart sinks at what you see. The butterfly still hasn't untucked its wings. You walk away ... sad.

How many of us, like the butterfly, conceal our beauty – dim our light, so to speak – and hide our true nature and worth? Shouldn't our heart sink over that too?

So why do we dim *our* light? Because if we give ourselves permission to shine, just a wee bit, the taunting critical voice within – our Inner Bully – will get activated.

Take Holly. When she first came to see me, she was depressed and didn't know why. As she talked about her life and how unfulfilled she felt, I began to suspect that her unhappiness stemmed from self-suppression.

Dimming does that to people.

Growing up, Holly got approval for being the model child. "Out of all my siblings," she said, "I was expected to be perfect." To her, this meant acting like a little lady: never raising her voice, never being rowdy, never getting messy, always being well-behaved, and always getting good grades.

Expressing her natural buoyancy, her individuality, even her own thoughts – displaying her lovely wings in all their grandeur – was frowned upon by her parents.

"I learned that I'd be liked if I fit their mold," she said.

But winning her parents' approval came with a price. Not only was she a prisoner in her own skin but also she believed those efforts made her siblings despise her. She recalled a painful moment when a sister lashed out at her: "You've always been the good one, the perfect one, the smart one!"

Feeling guilty for her shining attributes, and believing they offended others, she concluded that it was best to play small.

In time Holly grew up and left home, but she still wasn't free to "untuck her wings." She was a blind captive to the programming she'd received and adopted as a child. "I purposely avoid having an air of authority or appearing smart," she said. "If I display confidence, it means I'm being conceited. The words *Who do you think you are, young lady?* still ring in my head, so I keep a low profile wherever I go."

What a pity. Holly loses out, but so do others. Like all of us, she has unique gifts to share with the world.

It was important for her to see that tucking in her wings benefits no one, and how sad it would be if the Mother Theresas and the Einsteins of the world had done that. What if Gandhi had hidden his powerful belief in peace? What if the guy who happens to be really good at fixing the office photocopier hid his abilities and stood by while everyone around him experienced hair-pulling frustration? What if the woman who was a natural-born leader sat back and watched those less adept run the meeting, guide others, initiate change, or lead a nation?

In our sessions, Holly learned that depression is an indicator, just like a headache or stomachache can be. It informs us that something's not quite right and that we need to do something about it. In some cases, the cause for depression is purely physical. But depression may also be direct feedback from our innermost essence telling us that we're not fulfilling our true nature. We forfeit life-fulfillment and happiness when we squelch our True Self.

If you want to see your Inner Bully in action, or lure it out into the open, dare to say these words out loud: "I'm a marvelous person and deserving of love." Did that get a rise out of your Inner Bully? Most likely it did. Here's a list of common things Inner Bullies say:

- "Who the hell do you think you are?"
- "The word marvelous describes other people, not you."
- "You don't deserve that label – you haven't earned it."
- "You're a fraud."
- "You've got a big head."
- "No one could ever love you ... you don't deserve it."

What did yours say? Pay close attention to how you feel immediately after saying the words aloud.

Compliments Make You Squirm

People who live under their Inner Bully's thumb are compelled to reject compliments. They shrug them off. That's because being complimented triggers guilt. One client put it this way: "I feel guilty if I feel good about myself so when someone gives me a compliment, I must shoot it down."

Compliment-deniers pacify their Inner Bully by refusing to accept their own self-worth.

You can tell when your Inner Bully is at work when a compliment elicits a thought like:

- What the heck!
- You don't deserve that compliment!
- That person was lying!
- They didn't really mean it.
- Get over yourself!

What does yours say? What do you think the moment you hear a compliment?

You're Driven to Be Perfect

Perfectionism is self-abuse of the highest order.

—ANNE WILSON SCHAEF, PSYCHOLOGIST AND AUTHOR

What's behind the drive to be perfect? What's the underlying motive? One of my clients provided the *perfect* answer: "If I'm perfect, I won't feel shame."

It's probably safe to say that our drive to be perfect is in many cases aimed at silencing our Inner Bully. After all, Inner Bullies feast generously on our flaws.

Perfectionism manifests in multiple ways. For you, it might be putting a lot of effort into your physical appearance or the appearance of your home, the lawn, or your car. Or maybe you have to be perfectly organized, with everything in its place. If that's the case, you find yourself constantly clearing away clutter both at home and at work. Perhaps you expend exhaustive energy getting a perfect score, completing projects perfectly, or writing the perfect paragraph (just ask me). Maybe you feel you have to be a perfect parent, a perfect manager, a perfect health care worker, or a perfect lumberjack.

There's nothing wrong with striving and wanting things to be just so. There can even be joy in chasing after perfection and expending the required energy. It only becomes problematic if your inner peace is dependent upon attaining it. That is, if you're unable to relax or transition comfortably to something else.

Expecting the impossible is a form of self-torture, and that's what perfection is: impossible. When it comes to life here on planet Earth, imperfection is simply built in. The skater – no matter how well-trained – will fall. The car – no matter how fussed over – will get dinged. The plan – no matter how polished – will be altered. Count on it.

But knowing this fact about life doesn't keep us from being hard on ourselves for the errors we make. Ironically, many people find it easy to forgive others but are hard-pressed to forgive themselves. This shouldn't be the case – forgiveness is forgiveness, right? Why be discriminating?

In his slim, insightful book *The Four Agreements,* Don Miguel Ruiz sums up what perfectionism leads to: "Not being perfect, we reject ourselves."

It's true. How many of us are self-rejecting when we fail to get a perfect performance review, when we lose our keys for the billionth time, or when we fail to keep a perfectly neat house while raising perfectly behaved and – of course – perfectly happy children?

Toni, a successful businesswoman, told me she's terrified of making a mistake. "The stress eats me alive," she said. "I'm convinced that people will think less of me if they know I'm not perfect. I'm also afraid people will look at me differently if my hair doesn't look perfect or if I'm not dressed just so. I'll know I've made progress when I no longer worry if someone shows up when my dishes aren't done."

So yes, perfectionism can be a form of self-abuse if we're harsh with ourselves for failing to make the impossible happen.

How does your Inner Bully push you to be perfect? How does it ride you? Is it kind and understanding when you make mistakes, take breaks, or fail to do something perfectly? Do you have to look a certain way or act a certain way? What if you don't? What does that Inner Bully of yours say?

It Feels Wrong to Spend Money on Yourself

Ironically, you probably have no trouble
spending money on others.

—SALEE

Here's a look at how my own Inner Bully gets its hooks into me. One day, I was reaching for a bowl in the back of my cupboard. I wasn't looking for a particular bowl, but a particular size. I just so happened to grab one I had forgotten all about. I had purchased it at an art festival a long time ago.

For me, it's not unusual to feel guilty about buying something that has no justification other than the fact that it delights me. It may be a clothing item of some sort – shoes are a big one – a piece of jewelry, or something arty, like pottery. Typically, I tuck it away somewhere – waiting for the guilt to wear off. It does in due time but initially my punishment entails being denied the joy of the thing. I'm not supposed to enjoy it – God, no! I see where the delayed enjoyment serves to appease my Inner Bully. After all, my penance must be served for having done wrong. It grins over its power!

How does your Inner Bully discourage you from spending money on yourself? What does it say?

You Push Yourself to Do, Do, Do

When I walk in the door and see a pile of clothes,
my thoughts don't go to: Gee, I should relax with a book.

—JULIE

The next time you catch yourself obsessing over your mile-long to-do list, I encourage you to pay attention to what your Inner Bully might be up to. I assure you, it won't be off somewhere taking a leisurely nap. Hardly. It'll be fully energized and poised to attack.

For example, let's say you successfully check ten items off your to-do list by mid-afternoon and decide to sit down and relax. Will that be okay with your Inner Bully? Or maybe you choose to take a little stroll out in nature. Will it be cool with that? Or what if someone invites you out for some fun? Will it be understanding? The answer is simple. Probably not. Count on it hounding you. And if you're not on high alert, your Inner Bully will replace you as the decision-maker – stealing your will and dictating what you will do with your time.

Here's the irony of it all: You will never be able to check everything off your to-do list. If that's not true, then you're residing on a different planet characterized by a radically different reality system! No, the list never ends, and the nagging bully never shuts up. And if you let it sit in the captain's chair, life's enjoyment will be put on hold – permanently. And what will you have at the end of your life? You'll still have that stupid to-do list and the memory of a boring and meaningless existence.

Don't let that happen to you!

You Think You're Selfish,
Though You're Far from It

You always put the other person first,
to your own detriment, and wonder why you're
unhappy, unfulfilled, cranky, and exhausted!

—SALEE

"I was grumpy when I got up and then I took it out on my kids," Lori said. "I was just lazy and didn't want to get up."

Lori had a good excuse for wanting to stay in bed a little bit longer. She's a nurse and had worked late the night before. Needing her rest was fully warranted. But the voice inside her head told Lori she "ought to" spring out of bed every morning glowing like a Disney princess and surrounded by chirping birds and hopping pink bunnies. Regardless of what else might be happening in her life, she should be there for everyone who needs her. And that's everyone!

Sacrificing herself for others is a common theme for Lori in every arena of her life. Saying no – or saying yes to herself – seems selfish and heartless to her. "I can't let people down," she insists.

A browbeating Inner Bully is the enemy here, and it's clearly the driving force behind Lori's failure to set personal boundaries. It's also responsible for her exhaustion and eventual grumpiness. She's caught in a vicious cycle: her grumpiness leads to unfounded, unhealthy guilt. which leads to overextending herself, which leads to exhaustion, which leads to grumpiness.

You're Certain Your Partner
Is Putting You Down – All the Time

I always feel a set of eyes on me –
watching and judging me.

—MONICA

Monica was referring to her husband, but she could have just as easily been talking about her Inner Bully. Without realizing it, we can project our Inner Bully onto others. If my Inner Bully is critical of me for a messy house, guess what? I'll automatically assume that the person I live with has that exact same attitude.

You Can't Say No

If you have trouble saying no,
you're probably a dedicated people-pleaser.

—SALEE

You find yourself saying yes to all requests despite your plans, wants, and even your needs. Such self-desertion can make a person resentful, depressed – or both! Perhaps you're afraid of hurting someone's feelings so you hold back from saying what you really feel and what you really want. In short, you betray yourself. You end up being a prisoner in your own skin. Unhappiness is the byproduct of suppressed existence, a life that's stalled because a diminished self occupies the driver's seat.

When I first started seeing Meg, "stalled" described her life – and it also described a particularly agonizing experience. Because she didn't want to hurt her mother-in-law's feelings, she needlessly sat in Chicago traffic for what seemed to be hours. Not exactly Meg's idea of a wonderful day.

Planted in the driver's seat, she silently broiled. Her irritation didn't stem from her two passengers, her husband and mother-in-law. Instead, she was furious with herself. Getting trapped in traffic had been ohhhh soooo avoidable because Meg was adept at driving in Chicago traffic, maneuvering skillfully and comfortably through the endless maze of tangled highways.

So what went wrong? She failed to assert herself. Although she had the wheel, she let others "drive." Meg's traffic experience illustrates how things can and do go wrong when we shrink and take on a passive role. Such behavior impairs our ability to take charge when a situation calls for solid leadership or an expression of expertise.

Limping when fully capable of walking upright is an act of self-betrayal. It's felt at the soul level – a sickened feeling deep within. It was this anguish that prompted Meg to seek help. In our counseling session, she conveyed that she typically abandons the driver's seat in all areas of her life. The result is frustration in her relationships and a general dissatisfaction with how her life takes shape.

When you submerge yourself to satisfy others
– you divorce you.

—SALEE

When we can't say no, we put up with things we shouldn't, we resist saying things we should, and we participate in situations we should avoid. We are powerless.

And sometimes we even eat what we shouldn't! Rae was a prime example. She's been embracing healthier eating lately. "I gave up gluten, dairy, and sugar … and I feel better!" she said proudly. Sure, her restaurant options are limited, but she's learned where to go and what works for her. Unfortunately, life has an uncanny way of presenting us with challenges as soon as we make a strong decision to overhaul ourselves in some way. Rae is no exception. A while back, some of her relatives made plans to celebrate her birthday. They chose a nice restaurant and made the reservations. But the restaurant they chose was on her no-no list. Gluten, dairy, sugar … all over the menu!

She had plenty of time to suggest another venue, but guilt got in her way. You might say it sabotaged her truer self. "It was their gift to me," she said. "I just couldn't disappoint them."

That's what guilt can do to us – it makes us not matter to ourselves.

"So who got disappointed instead?" I asked.

"Ahh," she said. "Me! – of course."

Disappointment was only one part of it. She went into detail about how the meal impacted her physically the next day.

Clearly, Rae's birthday was less than it could – and should – have been. Any consideration for her own needs went by the wayside. That Inner Bully of ours bullies us into saying yes even when our health, happiness, or integrity might be sacrificed.

You're a Human Doormat

End your career as a doormat. In fact, take that doormat,
chop it up, saute it, and have it for breakfast!

—SALEE

When I started seeing Denny, he was deep into his doormat career. Like several others I've already mentioned, he had an Inner Bully who would randomly break out into a chant that went like this: "*Others come first, others come first....*"

That message was Denny's script, formed in childhood, and it dictated how he "should" function in life – his rules for living. Scripts sculpt our interactions with the world around us. They impact how we act and think and what we believe.

Denny summed up his script in one sentence: "The way I feel good about myself is by being a good guy. Doing for others." So without giving it a second thought, he would dutifully put others first even if it was at his own expense. No surprise, being taken advantage of was a common occurrence for him.

In one of our sessions, he explained how John, an acquaintance of his, needed a phone. So Denny offered to sell his own phone to him at an extremely low cost. He reassured John that he could pay him later. Weeks went by without a word from John. Finally, when they ran into each other somewhere, John paid Denny a small portion of what he owed, although there was no mention of future payments.

"What kind of feelings are you having?" I asked.

"I wanted to do the right thing," he said.

"Yes, I hear that Denny, but how do you *feel* about it on the emotional level?"

He lowered his eyes. "In all truth, I feel disrespected and used," he muttered.

So, in light of Denny's experience, I have to ask the question: Is it right to let others take advantage of you? How do others learn the same morals you were taught if you rob them of that opportunity?

You Gravitate Toward People Who Don't Love or Treat You Right

Why is that? You don't feel worthy of love and respect. Not only that, you tend to be drawn to people who echo your Inner Bully. Call it familiar territory.

This was true for Kari. While growing up, she heard, over and over again, the same three messages:

"Always be nice."

"Always put the other person first."

"It's better to give than receive."

When I first started seeing Kari, she was busy obeying her Inner Bully – being nice to everyone but herself. To do otherwise meant subjecting herself to lots of internal hounding. So when others mistreated or took advantage of her, they got a free pass because their treatment of her simply echoed the Inner Bully in her head. Her relationship with her live-in boyfriend, Paul, was a prime example. Before he moved in, they agreed that he would pay her

$350 a month. At first he did just that, but then he began slacking off. Internally, she would be fuming. Her stomach was all knotted up, and she often had trouble sleeping. But despite all the distress, she wouldn't confront him. I asked her why.

"Asking for the money makes me feel greedy and guilty," she said.

Surprised by that answer, I had to ask: "Okay, let me see if I've got this right. He's exploiting you, and *you* feel greedy and guilty?"

The irony was just too obvious for either one of us to ignore. We both laughed.

I went on. "And somehow, it would be wrong of you to hold him responsible for what he originally agreed to do … right?"

More laughing.

I knew that Kari's laughter was a way of dealing with an uncomfortable truth. She needed that for now. It served as a necessary cushion.

"And you understand," I continued, "that what he's doing to you isn't exactly *nice* … right?"

"Mmm," she said, as her mood began to shift.

"And he's certainly not putting you first … right?"

She nodded uneasily.

"And maybe he doesn't share your other standard: that it's better to give than to receive. Right?"

Kari suddenly became more animated. "No! Not at all. He's being rude!"

Ahhh, the picture had come into clear focus for her.

She spent the next several minutes expressing her frustrations – including the sick feeling in the pit of her stomach from forfeiting and deserting herself over and over again. She had to admit that her continual acceptance of Paul's disrespect sounded a bit crazy when she said it out loud.

That's because it is! *And* it clearly illustrates how senseless and self-sabotaging our allegiance to our Inner Bully can be.

Guilt Blocks You from Ending a Relationship

The reasons for wanting to leave can vary. Perhaps you've been enduring an abusive relationship – physically, emotionally, or both. Or perhaps you have a sense – a knowing – that it's over, and you don't have a clue why that thought is sitting in the middle of your brain. Physically, you're still in that situation, but your spirit has moved on.

No one plans for that to happen. It just does, and usually your consciousness is the last to know. By the time your awareness catches up, some part of you has already boarded the train and left the station. You know you should cut the cord, but your Inner Bully stands poised in the doorway, arms folded and tapping its foot. What's it telling you? That you're a self-centered, heartless quitter.

You Avoid People

If I'm not around people, I won't be doing
the wrong thing. My Inner Bully sleeps.

—SHANNA

Shanna was sad because she didn't have any friends. But in her case, she was already fully aware of the demeaning voice inside her head. "Interacting with peers is way too stressful for me," she explained. "My Inner Bully won't leave me alone. It critiques me constantly."

It told her things like, "Why did you say that?" "That was stupid," and "That was rude."

Besides being mentally harassed when she's around peers, she was also convinced that no one would ever truly *want* to be her friend, anyway.

"I'm just not friendship material," she insisted.

"I can't buy that," I countered. "Look … you're warm, respectful, interesting, fun, easy to relate to..."

She cut me off midway through the sentence. "Stop! My Inner Bully is going crazy right now!"

"What's it telling you?" I asked.

"That everything you're saying is untrue!" she said.

"I don't think your Inner Bully is happy unless you feel bad about yourself. Am I right?"

"Yessss! You are so right!"

I paused for a second.

"Hmmm … I don't think you would mind if I listed off negative qualities about you."

She nodded vigorously, saying. "No question! That would be a whole lot more comfortable for me to hear!"

You Have a Chronic Case of Low Self-esteem

You're such an idiot. You're selfish.
You're rude. You can't do anything right!
—INNER BULLY

Such internalized messages would chip away at anyone's self-esteem!

You Always Clean Your Plate

My own Inner Bully
tells me it's wrong to waste food.
—SALEE

Dad's words echo in my head yet today: *Clean your plate!*

I'm sure those very same words were something he heard repeatedly as a child while growing up in the era of the Great Depression. Food was scarce. No one could afford to take food for granted.

But as a child, I didn't have that perspective. I just obeyed. And when I was old enough to leave home, my Inner Bully picked up where Dad left off. At that point, I *obeyed* my Inner Bully. And guess what? I started gaining some unwanted pounds. No surprise.

What a sorry state of affairs. My Inner Bully dictated how I ate. Reason didn't. My body's natural signals of fullness had no bearing. My bully's orders overpowered such signals. Later on, you'll learn how I silenced my Inner Bully, and you can learn to silence yours too.

Self-love Is a Foreign Concept

Your bully doesn't want you to start loving yourself.
Loving yourself would put it out of a job.

—SALEE

Marti was being her usual witty self when she uttered these words: "The bad thing about not liking myself is not being able to get away from myself. I can't just go into the next room."

What's sad about that statement? She meant it. Equally sad is the fact that a multitude of people feel exactly the same way. They're solidly convinced that as human beings they are fundamentally tarnished – just not lovable. They can't even comprehend the concept of self-love. It seems foreign, even wrong.

How can that be? How does that happen?

As far as I know, babies aren't born with self-contempt or even an Inner Bully. Does it enter a baby's mind that she might be crying too loudly or burdening her parents with yet another dirty diaper? Hardly. If we don't like who we are it's something we acquired after being here awhile.

What to Do, What to Do?

Most likely, some of the examples above hit home. That's a good thing. It means you're gaining ground on becoming an awareness geek. You've been able now to look back and see some of your Inner Bully's footprints in your past. But remember, our goal is to drag that Inner Bully out into the open, take away its invisibility cloak. What we'd really like to be able to do is call it out right on the spot, as soon as it opens its ugly mouth. With that in mind, here are a few things to start practicing.

Begin by identifying your feelings as they shift around throughout any given day. Notice when you're immersed in good feelings and when they shift to negative. Get into the habit of pressing the "pause" button whenever you feel your emotions rise or fall significantly. Record when that happens and describe the circumstances, along with any comments your Inner Bully might be making. For example, let's imagine that you write: *I felt good until my brother called and said he needed a babysitter. Suddenly I felt weighed down with a sense of obligation. I didn't feel I had a choice.* My thoughts: There you go again, just thinking of yourself.

Keep in mind that any particular incident isn't problematic if it's not part of a pattern. When I say "pattern," I'm not referring to a pattern your brother may have of asking you to babysit, but rather your pattern of feeling obligated and your inability to say no. It's a problem you have in general – not just with your brother.

Next, look for ways *your* Inner Bully shows up in *your* life. You can use this chapter as a starting point, but don't let my examples limit you. Make a list of what you've discovered thus far.

Now ask yourself what would happen internally if you refused to obey your Inner Bully? How would it impact you emotionally? For instance, how would you feel if you let yourself shine or let yourself really absorb a compliment? What if you didn't get a perfect score, a perfect grade, a perfect review? Can you walk away from an unfinished or imperfect task? What if you let your dishes pile up? What if you simply sat down and did nothing? What if you told someone you wanted to end the relationship? What if you got really good at saying no? What if you put yourself first? What if you were in Meg's situation and told your backseat driver mother-in-law, "No worries. I've got this," while breezing through Chicago traffic?

When I asked Meg that question, she told me she would be consumed with guilt. Her response isn't all that unusual. Guilt frequently gets in our way when we try to do the right and smart thing. Yes, guilt can govern our actions and have more power over us than common sense or logic. Let's suppose Meg refused to surrender her power to her mother-in-law (who, ironically, had zero experience driving in Chicago), would guilt be called for? Would it be warranted? Nope. The guilt would be a product of a malfunctioning conscience. I think that could stand repeating. When we feel bad about things that are wildly inappropriate to feel bad about, our conscience is malfunctioning.

And who just so happens to be the maestro of that malfunctioning conscience of yours? Your Inner Bully – that stealthy, undermining, and critical voice hanging out in the shadows of your unconscious mind. Regard it as the personification of a malfunctioning conscience.

You now know you have an Inner Bully, and a completely understandable response could easily be: "I want it gone! Enough already! I'll just smash it to smithereens like the unwelcome cockroach it is!" But that won't work with the bully. Why not? Because it fights back. How? With guilt. The bully's arsenal is guilt – unrelenting guilt. The kind Meg said she would be consumed with if she refused to surrender her power to her mother-in-law.

This is a good time to talk about guilt. There are two kinds, and understanding the not-so-good type will help expose your Inner Bully so you can stop giving it your power.

Chapter Five

Guilt:
The Good, the Bad ...
and Is It All Ugly?

*Guilt can be a valuable emotion when it emerges from a
healthy conscience. But guilt gone amok is a parasite that
sucks the life out of its host. It dims the very light within
that loves life. It deadens a once-alive spirit. That brand
of guilt demands a sacrificial offering – your soul.*

—SALEE

Just as we have good and bad bacteria and good and bad cholesterol, we also have good and bad guilt. It's essential to know the difference between the two so we can get smart at catching that Inner Bully of ours red-handed.

Good guilt is the healthy side of guilt. It's that uncomfortable feeling we get when we have done something wrong, like breaking the law or violating an ethical code. It also guides us in making wise choices.

Bad guilt, in contrast, doesn't guide. It belittles, shames, and tortures. It's unhealthy. I think we can all agree that anything that belittles, shames, and tortures us is toxic to our overall well-being – punching some massive holes in any good feelings we might have.

Bad guilt is similar to an autoimmune disorder in which the body savagely attacks itself, but in this case, it leaves the person riddled with the disease of shame. Carl Jung refers to shame as a "soul-eating emotion." I can see why. It poisons how we see ourselves, breeding chronic self-disgust and self-loathing. It spawns depression, feelings of inferiority, and unrelenting self-condemnation. It can create an unhealthy need to be perfect and to please others. More often than not, it's a driving force behind addiction. (For a deeper dive into the connection between unhealthy guilt and addiction, you'll want to check out Appendix Two, written by my son Tavis. He writes not only as licensed mental health and addiction therapist, but as someone walking the recovery road himself.)

Bad guilt permeates and impacts every aspect of your life. It snakes its way into your relationships, follows you to work, and colors how you parent.

Because bad guilt cripples your capacity to care for yourself, you're left vulnerable and defenseless against both the external bullies that come into your life as well as that one sinister internal bully who's managed to take up permanent residence in your head. It's the voice of toxic guilt. You carry it with you wherever you go.

Good guilt, on the other hand, is a positive emotion that serves as a moral compass. We must admit, a healthy dose of guilt keeps us civilized. It prompts us to adjust our behaviors and strive to be a better version of ourselves. It's quite the opposite of bad guilt, which rips away at our self-worth, undercuts our confidence, and tramples our spirit. Bad guilt is toxic to our mental health and happiness – corrosive to our very essence. Instead of being a valuable tool and ultimately self-enhancing, it's self-destructive.

With good guilt, we retain the capacity to look tenderly at ourselves. Not so with the toxic side of guilt, or bad guilt. Good guilt works for us, not against us. For instance, good guilt helps us set and keep goals for ourselves. It cultivates discipline, nudging us to exercise most days, eat right, and make choices that align with our values and principles. In that sense, it protects us from distressing consequences – outcomes we'd rather avoid.

Good guilt is a self-monitoring system. We use it to critique and supervise our own conduct. To be exact, it's how we parent ourselves. Whenever we exhibit positive restraint and self-control, blame it on good guilt. It serves as a braking system for our impulses, and a beacon for adhering to moral codes. It wakes us up to our effect on the world around us and redirects us to be more thoughtful and kind. Our capacity for good guilt allows us to harness our otherwise unchecked animal instincts and impulses. We need it for establishing and maintaining ethical standards and social order. Without it, all the world would resemble an overpopulated cage of monkeys at the local zoo.

According to psychologist Alan Godwin, author of *How to Solve Your People Problems*, whenever we go against our morality, we have what he calls a "cringe response." So we might find ourselves cringing whenever we cheat, lie, steal, or cause distress in another person – or distress in an animal, for that matter. Godwin maintains that a cringe response is rooted in a healthy conscience and that it's based on "an ability to be bothered by personal wrongness."

It wouldn't be uncommon to have a cringe response soon after gossiping about another person, or after being rude to somebody. The same would hold true if we needlessly broke a promise or turned a blind eye to an obvious wrong. The truth is, such things *should* make us squirm inside. It's a sign that a healthy conscience is functioning well. Our conscience is what motivates us to make improvements and assume responsibilities that we might otherwise ignore.

Do keep in mind that although cringing is the manifestation of regret and remorse, it arrives without self-condemnation. It isn't punishing. It isn't tormenting. It's sheer *awareness.* That's big. In fact, your ability to cringe is profoundly significant. It means you're tuned in to your moral or spiritual center. Some call it the *soul* or *higher self*. It's also your True Self – who you really are. The late Wayne Dyer, renowned author and speaker on self-development, used the term "infinite self."

You'll have the chance to explore the meaning of the True Self and then reconnect with your True Self later on in this book.

In contrast, bad guilt *is* self-condemning, punishing, and tormenting. How does it do that? Through the voice in your head: your Inner Bully. And by the way, bad guilt and your Inner Bully aren't even in the same solar system as your spiritual center. Think about it. How can a demeaning experience be linked to spirituality? It can't. How can a spiritual experience be devoid of good feelings? It can't.

Bad guilt snuffs out good feelings, and that makes it almost impossible to think tenderly about yourself. It can even leave you wondering if you have a right to exist. One of my clients expressed it this way: "Sometimes I can feel I don't deserve the air I breathe."

Many people might be incapable of imagining that degree of guilt. But, like an autoimmune disease, bad guilt is destructive to our essence. It can cause us to despise who we are. That's more than unfortunate – it's abominable! It's a form of suffering, an agony no one should ever have to endure.

I don't know about you, but to me if something produces that kind of suffering – or any degree of suffering, for that matter – it cannot be based on what we understand to be spiritual.

For example, I had a client tell me that at an early age she came to understand that the only way to please her mom was to feel bad about herself. "So even today, I feel guilty if I don't feel bad about myself."

That's suffering!

Then there's Camille, who said: "I'm afraid if I'm really myself, say what I think, choose what I really want, love will be taken from me. My parents kept me in line by withdrawing their love if I was true to myself."

That's suffering!

"My mother shamed me for crying," Camille continued. "She belittled me for it." So, for years and years, Camille judged herself whenever she cried even a little.

That's suffering also!

One of my other clients, Garth, said this in one of our sessions: "I'm always waiting for punishment, so if things are going well, I'm uneasy. I'm not comfortable at all. This sounds strange but when I get hurt, I feel a sense of relief, and I even say to myself, *There – it happened.*"

That's suffering!

Jayla told me she experiences unhealthy guilt "by reliving something I wish I had never done. The very thing I'd like to erase from my brain gets replayed over and over and over. It's maddening! I can't stop thinking of what I could have done differently."

That's suffering!

Lori's boss wanted her to pay $250 of her own money to attend a conference that was two hours away. Lori declined, saying she just couldn't afford it. Her boss understood, but that didn't erase Lori's guilt. "I still feel guilty because I couldn't come up with the money," she said.

That's suffering!

Each of these people have something in common: When I began seeing them, they were entrapped by an Inner Bully – the personification of bad guilt. Self-compassion and realistic thinking didn't direct their lives. Unhealthy, toxic, and senseless guilt did.

Here's the untarnished truth: Your conscience is malfunctioning if it's irrational, if it's toxic, if it attacks your goodness and never lets you forget your mistakes

We have a word for this self-destructive mental state: *shame.*

Good or healthy guilt is fleeting – you cringe momentarily about something you *did* or *didn't* do and then you move on. Shame, on the other hand, is a perpetual, frozen state of bad guilt. Mistakes and wrongs are unpardonable, and a prolonged period of being consumed by bad feelings seems only fitting. It feels right. Guilt-wallpaper describes your normal. It's everywhere and constant.

My thoughts turn to fifty-two-year-old Kate. Getting pregnant as a teenager had resulted in unbearable shame. "In my mind, I had done something unforgivable," she said. Feeling compelled to redeem herself, she vowed "to become ultra-responsible. This meant getting good grades, enduring any and all hard work without ever complaining."

With the baby's father out of the picture, Kate shouldered full responsibility. She got a part-time job and went to college full time. While working on her degree as a special education teacher she got married and had three more children. Undeterred, she plowed through and got the degree.

Thirty-five years later Kate was – once again – tormented by guilt. This time for wanting to leave the career she worked so hard to get. In my office, she broke down in tears. "I simply cannot walk into that classroom anymore!" She described the dread and panic attacks while driving to work, the seemingly out-of-the-blue crying spells, the sleepless nights, her stomach pain, and constant headaches.

"I've lost my will to teach," she explained. She talked about the ever-increasing class sizes and the "impossible" demands placed on teachers. "It's just become too much!"

Kate's earlier vow to become an ultra-responsible person – enduring hard work and never complaining – was getting the best of her. Reason and love for herself wasn't driving her. Guilt was – the unhealthy, toxic, senseless kind. And regrettably, when we do things from that space, we ignore the bigger picture, including what we truly want and what's right for us. Bad guilt warps our better judgment. Reason is sacrificed.

As I stated earlier, guilt has its place. The discomfort of guilt is beneficial in that it nudges us to do better. Yes. All good. But we don't need to suffer to make that happen. Discomfort is enough. We don't need an attacking conscience to make us strive to do better. Shame, in fact, interferes with that process. The noise of self-chastisement obscures clear-eyed introspection. The awful heaviness of shame makes ordinary self-reflection and self-monitoring unbearable. In fact, facing up to the slightest mistake merely confirms our belief that we are detestable.

A Warped Sense of Who You Are

Shame burrows its way to the very core of your being and stains how you see yourself. It becomes your identity. It dirties you so bad, you can't like yourself anymore.

—Salee

Shame is a cold, concrete cell where the walls exude disdain for you.

That describes what my shame feels like to me. Where did it originate? There's no question my mother played a major role. She was irritated with me most of the time, and there was no on or off switch. I couldn't do anything to change it. To be steeped in that climate day in and day out is to walk around believing there is something fundamentally wrong with you. In John Bradshaw's book *Bradshaw on the Family*, he writes: "Guilt says I've *done* something wrong; shame says there *is* something wrong with me. Guilt says I've *made* a mistake; shame says I *am* a mistake. Guilt says what I *did* was not good; shame says I *am* no good."

Of course, when he made mention of guilt, he was referring to the healthy kind. Such guilt is related to specific acts. Shame, on the other hand, is related to identity – our self-concept, our idea of who we are. A shame identity is an outgrowth of bad guilt that has morphed into a belief that we're fatally flawed.

Think about this: If you're told over and over again that an object is red when in fact it's lime green, you start to believe it. By the same token, if you're told over and over again that you're a bother, you will start to believe that too. While sitting on a park bench one day, I heard a mother convey that very message to her small son while she was talking on her cell phone: "Go away! Can't you see I'm talking to someone!"

If that scenario is a common occurrence between that mother and her little boy, then there is little doubt that his Inner Bully is already taking shape. It's just a matter of time before it will be telling him – on a regular basis – that he's unimportant and unworthy of having close connections with other people. Unfortunately, he will have internalized his mother's message along with her attitude toward him. He will believe she's right.

Inner Bullies don't create shame. They merely perpetuate what we've come to believe about ourselves. They reinforce our negative self-concept – our shame identity – by unremittingly replaying and recycling the negative debris that initially formed our shame identity in the first place.

You met Vanessa earlier in Chapter Two. She was the young mother who had trouble liking herself. When she and I started working together, I asked her to describe how she saw herself. Here's what she said: "I see myself as awkward, ugly, annoying, dumb, dirty, needy, repulsive."

How sad. Even sadder is the fact that she's married to a man who thinks the world of her! But that did nothing to change her self-perception, not one iota. She was convinced he was either lying or deluding himself. She even said, "If he loves me, there's something wrong with *him*."

People with a shame identity don't feel that they can be loved. Deep within their being, they carry the iron-clad mistaken belief that they're not worth caring about.

Shame is an intensely painful feeling or
experience of believing that we are flawed and
therefore unworthy of love and belonging.
—Brené Brown

Shaming a child is usually expressed verbally – but not always, as you're discovering in this book. It can occur with disdainful glances, silent treatments, and withholding love. So it's no surprise, when considering all the ways that shaming occurs, that children who are the targets of it have an overwhelming sense of being unlovable. And as if this weren't tragic enough, they tend to blame themselves. They feel responsible for being rejected. They even feel responsible for being shamed. How is that possible? Because, deep down, they believe they're damaged goods. So flawed, in fact, that the thought of being deserving of unconditional love and acceptance is totally unfathomable to them. In a nutshell, shame erases a person's sense of intrinsic goodness.

Depressed? Suspect Your Inner Bully

Experiencing good or healthy guilt is akin to falling into a mud puddle and quickly getting out. But with bad or unhealthy guilt, we take up residence in that puddle. In a very short time it morphs into a manure pit.

—SALEE

For some, depression is just that: a manure pit. Like many plagued with depression, Brad lived a tormented existence. Shame was his place of residence. His suffering touched me so profoundly, in fact, I was moved to write this poem about him:

Crippled

I know a man who is crippled
by a self-image
a self-image he picked up in his childhood days.
It stuck.
His father and mother gave it to him.
It's not who he is – but it's who he believes he is.

Repeatedly, in their actions and words,
they conveyed to him that he was:
irresponsible
unimportant
uninteresting
inadequate
and ... a disappointment.

The crippled part of him is his belief.

I first met Brad when he was forty-one. Sitting in my office, downcast and looking defeated, he told me he desperately wanted relief from his depression, something he had been struggling with since childhood. Therapy and medications had helped over the years, but only temporarily. Some days were better than others. On good days, he did what he loved doing most: helping other people. His daughter described him as one of those people "who would gladly give you the shirt off their back." He especially enjoyed being a father. He helped his children with their homework, cooked for them, took them camping, showed them how to ride their bikes. He even went roller skating with them.

But on his down days, he retreated from all social contact. His depression was so incapacitating he couldn't even pull himself out of bed. Those days tortured Brad. His shame and regret ran deep because he couldn't be the father he wanted to be.

It's true, depression renders a person immobile in many cases, and if that person happens to be a parent, the problem is compounded a thousandfold. At one point, Brad tried to convince me that he was a bad father because of his depression.

"No you're not!" I insisted. "Bad fathers don't care if they're bad or not. And listen, dammit, your heart is bigger than your depression, and your kids *feel* that!"

Shame and depression often go hand in hand. Self-shaming actually feeds depression. So on the days that Brad couldn't get out of bed, when he had trouble functioning normally, he was hounded by the voice in his head that told him – repeatedly – that he was a failure and a worthless burden on everyone. It also echoed something he frequently heard as a child: "I'm very disappointed in you. You should be ashamed of yourself." That voice, now internalized, never lets up. It is vicious.

Depression distorts the truth and lacks any degree of self-love and understanding. So in our therapy sessions, I tried to help Brad look warmly at himself. I remember a particular time when I emphasized that depression wasn't something he willfully chose for himself.

"Am I right about that?" I asked.

He nodded.

"So there you go Brad. You're innocent!"

The hint of a smile broke through that dark cloud of his. "It really helps to hear that," he said. Then dropping his head he added, "Though when it comes to depression, most of the world says to snap out of it."

Sad to say, he's right. The world isn't very sympathetic toward depression. Or even sadness, for that matter. We expect people, including ourselves, to be positive, productive, and happy all the time. So unrealistic.

But Brad wasn't really focused on how the world viewed depression. His focus was on how his *parents* viewed his depression. Instead of offering sympathy and understanding, they shamed him for it. "It's never been okay to be down," he said. They've always said things like: "You're just being lazy," "Oh, suck it up," "It's not that bad," and "Get over it!"

Having his feelings discounted was a common occurrence. He was the youngest of five kids. "I got picked on a lot," he said. "Sometimes it even got brutal, but my parents would never defend me. My father would just shrug and tell me in so many words to tough it out." Brad shook his head. "I felt so alone and helpless."

Brad lacked the love and support he desperately hungered for and needed. Without it, he understandably assumed that his parents were tacitly approving of how his siblings treated him.

"To me, it meant they were in agreement with them," he said. "My parents just shrugged it off, and that told me there had to be something very wrong about me. So I came to believe that anything bad that happened to me was deserved."

It was clear to me that Brad's depression was compounded by shame, and obviously, the internalized demeaning messages of shame played a big role in immobilizing him.

Marti, the witty client I mentioned before, expressed her frustrations with her parents like this:

"The day my parents met was the worst day of my life. It was all downhill from there."

How can a person hearing that not spontaneously crack a smile, or even laugh? Too bad her humor contains a nugget of sad truth.

Chapter Six

The Birthing of Your Inner Bully

We don't come out of the womb with an Inner Bully.
It's something we acquire after we've been here a bit.

—SALEE

Now that you've become aware of your Inner Bully and are capable of spotting it and feeling its effects, it's time to examine its origins. Where did it come from? What gives rise to an Inner Bully?

The first thing to understand is that the human brain is powerfully programmable, so as small children, we operated very much like the average kitchen sponge. We absorbed everything, both good and bad – especially the messages we received from our parents.

We were also well-trained, just as pets are trained: through punishment and reward. If we conformed to the expected behavior, we were rewarded. We were even told, "You're a good girl," or "You're a good boy." The opposite message was given if we didn't conform: "You're bad!" "You're a disgrace!" "Where are your manners?" "You're such an embarrassment!" "We raised you better than that." "Shame on you!"

It wasn't just our parents. We also soaked up stuff from every other significant person in our growing up years, including grandparents, aunts, uncles, siblings, teachers, and coaches.

Perhaps you were told things like: "You're so stupid." "Stop being a baby." "You're a slob!" "You could have done better." "I'm so disappointed in you." "You're fat." "That's selfish!"

The list goes on.

Messages like these became the script material for our Inner Bully, who echoes the words we heard as a child. Over time, those messages got etched into our brain and established our core belief about ourselves. For the most part, that early training falls under the heading of *innocent indoctrination*. I call it that because most parents blindly mimic how their parents programmed *them*. I just cannot believe that many parents out there actually want to implant their children with a hostile, browbeating nag.

Our Inner Bully echoes more than just words, though. Christine Ann Lawson captures it in one sentence in her book, *The Borderline Mother:* "Children see themselves as reflected in the mirror of their parents' eyes."

Yes! And if that reflection is a positive one, children will tend to have a tender, accepting, and caring attitude toward themselves. On the other hand, if that reflection is negative, they're likely to form a negative self-concept.

Our early years were the spawning ground for our self-worth, self-esteem, and sense of self. We soaked it all in during those formative, early years, and we were completely incapable of questioning our parents' objectivity. At that young age, we couldn't begin to entertain the thought that our parents might have been wrong or incapable of parenting well. We considered them all-knowing. We lacked the ability to assess our parents' behavior as good or bad, or to tell whether their perceptions of us were distorted. We just assumed they were correct. And, by the time we reached adulthood, we were solidly conditioned.

One day I witnessed a heart-sinking exchange between a father and son:

"Hey Dad, what's Grandpa's phone number?" the son asked.

"What's the matter with you?" The father fired back. "You know the number. You call it all the time! Are you a retard?"

If it pained me to be a witness to such harshness, I can only imagine its impact on his son.

I remember my strong urge to ask the father how he would like his son to feel about himself in the years to come. Like most fathers, he would probably have said that he wanted his son to have a positive view of himself, to possess high aspirations, and to feel competent and confident enough to make those aspirations a reality. I would then ask: Do you think your current treatment of him is planting those seeds?

I wish I'd had the opportunity to ask Brad's parents that same question.

As you can see, a child's Inner Bully, along with their self-perception, is shaped by a combination of things – not just what they were told, but *how* they were talked to. For example, the following words spoken to my child could carry very different messages depending on my attitude: "You didn't put the milk away." My tone could be non-critical and sound like a simple reminder, or it could have a shaming quality to it that would likely convey: *You screwed up – you're bad!*

The line between shaming and verbal abuse is blurry. Both are expressed with a cutting and belittling tone. "Act your age." "How could you be so stupid?" "You ate all that?" "You're so selfish!" "Oh, stop crying! You're all right." "Won't you ever learn?" "You're not nice!" "You're a spoiled brat!" "You'll never amount to anything."

Dr. Susan Forward, in her book *Toxic Parents*, writes:

> *Most parents will occasionally say something derogatory to their children. This is not necessarily verbal abuse. But it is abusive to launch frequent attacks on a child's appearance, intelligence, competence, or value as a human being.*

68

Frequent is the vital word here. Repetition of any word or phrase chisels a pattern in our brain that's hard to eradicate. Not impossible, but hard.

Labels can be nasty. Tom, a man in his forties, heard, "You're a dumb-ass," from his father all the time.

When six-year-old Ethan kicked a cat, his father became furious. Among the nasty labels he shot at him was "cruel." Instead of coming down hard on him, he should have viewed the situation as an opportunity to provide a lesson on kindness. A non-shaming approach communicates that the action is wrong, not the child. Yes, Ethan needed to learn that it's wrong to hurt animals. But he also needed his sense of self-worth to remain intact. Ethan was just beginning to learn how to function appropriately on planet Earth. So the situation called for patient leadership, conveying, *I'm at your side, son, ready to show you the ropes.*

Yes, the labels children hear become the filters through which they view themselves. In the examples I've given so far, the parents might as well be saying: *You're a defective, heartless, moronic loser.* Whether or not parents intended to convey that message is irrelevant – that's the message the children most likely received and the one they carried forward into adulthood. Words, tone, and shaming are significant building blocks in the formation of an Inner Bully.

I want to emphasize an extremely important fact: Inner Bullies are fairly common because there's no such thing as a perfect parent or a perfect childhood. In the majority of cases parents are goodhearted, highly devoted, and well-intentioned. Most were victims of the very thing they unconsciously pass down to their kids.

Our Inner Bully
Sounds a Lot Like Our Parents

Kurt, thirty-eight, was sitting in the bleachers watching his son Dustin's baseball game when he saw something that shook him to the core. After striking out, Dustin began hitting himself over the head with the bat. "I couldn't believe my eyes!" Kurt said. "It made me wonder, what have I done to cause this overreaction to a game that's supposed to be fun?"

Kurt was witnessing Dustin's Inner Bully at work – an Inner Bully he unknowingly helped create. Although Kurt never hit Dustin with a bat or anything else, he realizes now that he *verbally* hit his son on multiple occasions. Dustin's Inner Bully was merely echoing Kurt, just in a more physical way. Dustin had internalized the messages and attitude he'd experienced from his father over and over.

That incident not only opened Kurt's eyes but it also opened his heart. Healthy guilt and love for his son drove him to become conscious of the programming he was passing down, and it drove him to make changes.

"I ride him too hard," he said, "just like my father did with me." Kurt explained that the constant message he got from his father could be summed up in a few simple words: *I'll accept you as long as you're perfect.*

"Lord knows I tried," Kurt said, "but it was never good enough. I didn't do the yard right, I didn't take out the trash right, I didn't even sit at the table right."

Now as an adult, the words, "I'm never good enough," echo in his head constantly.

"The other day I was trying to install a screen door," he said. "It wasn't cooperating. I went back and forth between cursing it and cursing myself for being such a ham-fisted moron."

Kurt wasn't solely influenced by his father. Our society tends to value accomplishment over effort – achievement over struggle. Children are praised for getting As or for making their bed perfectly. An outcome-focused mindset produces people who are driven to attain perfect results. Struggle isn't seen as praiseworthy, and appreciation for the process is largely an alien concept in our culture.

"What can I do to help Dustin?" Kurt asked.

"He needs the same thing you need to give yourself, Kurt," I said. "Loving acceptance."

I suggested he compliment Dustin on his efforts more than on winning. Even his efforts at being kind to himself when his performance is less than perfect.

"Give him plenty of high fives for that!" I said.

Just as with Kurt, we all eventually internalize the negative messages we receive from the key figures in our lives. They get encoded into the fabric of our mind, and we unconsciously accept those negative messages as fact.

Kurt's story has a happy ending. He was able to make the necessary changes to his thought patterns and interactions with Dustin. The abundant high fives must have replaced the negative messages Dustin had been telling himself because from what I hear, Dustin – who's now an adult – is leading a happy and fulfilling life. It's clear to me that he reaped the benefits of his father's changes. That's not unusual. It's called reprogramming.

Our Inner Bully tells us things like we're selfish for wanting something, cowardly for being cautious, bad for speaking up, weak for crying, and a loser for our failures. Brad's badgering Inner Bully would regularly tell him what a loser he was. It nagged him constantly about being lazy and worthless. Understandably, such messages have a way of killing all motivation.

"I hesitate to make more of myself ... to even try," he said. "Because I think, *What's the use? Why try? I'll never get it right.*"

By the time Brad was old enough to leave home, he had been fully conditioned, and his Inner Bully was firmly established. It criticized and shamed him the way his parents had. He left his critical parents behind when he grew up and left home, but his Inner Bully, who did an uncanny imitation of them, came with him.

It's important to note that Brad's parents didn't see the light (as Kurt did), so they didn't change their manner of interacting with him. Instead, Brad learned how to improve the way he interacts with himself. You'll learn about that in a later chapter.

Natalie, like Brad, was another client who illustrated how the shaming that one receives as a child can follow us right into our adult years. I recall her saying in our first session: "I gossip about myself." I soon learned that what she really meant was: *I have a problem with critical self-talk.* We explored where this mental habit of judging herself came from.

"Well, my mother criticized me all the time," she said. "In her eyes, I wasn't even capable of brushing my hair." She described an especially traumatic incident in which her mother angrily slapped her hand and said – while grabbing for the hairbrush – "Here, give me that brush! I'll do it. You'll never learn!"

After telling me that story she asked, "What's wrong with me? Why is my mother so nasty to me?"

I answered her question with a question of my own: "What's wrong with your mother? Why can't she see your value?"

Natalie couldn't answer that. She was too busy wiping away the tears.

Brad and Natalie couldn't control how their parents treated them in the past or even how their parents view them now. But they can control what they accept as fact and what they tell themselves. You'll learn how that's done in later chapters.

As I indicated earlier, children are easily molded and therefore fertile soil for the formation of an Inner Bully that judges and reprimands unmercifully. Natalie no longer needs to be near her mother to receive harsh criticisms. They now originate inside her head. She's internalized her mother's negative attitude and treatment of her. The problem Natalie must face isn't what her mother did to her, but what she continues to do to herself.

The critic's programs are not only burned deeply into
our psyches by our parents, but we also unknowingly
emblazon them into our mind by mimicking our parents.
We are now the key reinforcing agents of their toxic legacy.
With little mindfulness of it, we injure ourselves with
countless angry, self-disgusted repetitions of their judgments.

—PETE WALKER,

COMPLEX PTSD: FROM SURVIVING TO THRIVING

Remember Meg, who was stranded on the freeway in Chicago? Meg was fully capable of tackling Chicago traffic, but she surrendered her power to her mother-in-law. Meg didn't abandon the wheel, but she did abandon herself. The culprit? Guilt, and not at all the good kind.

Now, in order to *abandon* her habit of self-sabotage, Meg had to figure out why she did it in the first place. What was it about Meg's past that was still motivating her actions in the present?

I started out by asking Meg for a detailed description of the Chicago incident. She recalled how her mother-in-law "began her typical backseat driving routine" as they neared Chicago and merged onto a busy expressway. It wasn't long before her mother-in-law started getting worried that they might be lost. Although Meg was certain they were *not* lost, she suggested that her mother-in-law look at a map. "I was hoping it would keep her busy doing something else," Meg explained.

But the suggestion backfired. It sent the message: *Yes, indeed, we're lost!*

Soon Meg's husband joined his mom in providing "helpful" suggestions.

In a short span of time, Meg relinquished the confidence she originally had in her own expertise. She kowtowed and meekly turned the reins of control over to her husband and his mother. Following their suggestion, she switched to a slower lane. Soon, they weren't moving at all. And there they sat, stuck, for a very long stretch of time.

"What prevented you from honoring yourself?" I asked.

"I was afraid of hurting her feelings," Meg said.

"Why don't *your* feelings matter?" I asked.

She said nothing, as a wave of sadness spread across her face. "When did you start deserting yourself?" I asked.

After a long silence, Meg brought up her childhood. Children, in her household, were expected to be seen and not heard. Her parents didn't welcome or encourage conversation in which their children could freely and comfortably express their thoughts and feelings. Instead, Meg learned that "the way to please them was to be quiet and not be an interference."

Passivity was considered a good thing in her family. Not only was speaking up frowned upon but being sure of yourself and standing tall were seen in the same light as arrogance and, were therefore bad. Meg learned at an early age that squelching herself was the acceptable way to be and that "honesty, although the Christian thing to do, wasn't always welcomed."

Change, for Meg, involved overriding that self-defeating programming and challenging her Inner Bully – that menace within that kept echoing the programming. She did it! Here are a few things she changed about her thinking:

- Passivity is a bad thing – not a good thing
- Standing tall is not the same as arrogance
- The concern over hurting someone's feelings is never a just cause for abandoning oneself

Chapter Seven

How to Debunk, Defy, and Disempower Your Inner Bully

A free bird leaps
on the back of the wind
and floats downstream
till the current ends
and dips his wing
in the orange sun rays
and dares to claim the sky

—MAYA ANGELOU

Let my spirit be free – wherever I be!

—SALEE

Once you have learned how to spot your Inner Bully in action, discovered where it came from, and identified exactly how it's wreaking havoc in your life, you're ready to take that next step to freedom. In the chapters that follow, you'll discover the many tools at your disposal for deactivating and gaining control over your Inner Bully. You'll also read stories about how others (including myself) have successfully used these tools in their own lives.

Love Yourself ...Yes, You Must!

Your Inner Bully can't survive in a climate of self-love.

—SALEE

Meg would have been incapable of making the shifts she did without that vital component we refer to as self-love. While in therapy, she learned what it means to love herself. One of the things she came to realize is that self-love is at the root of honoring ourselves. When we're honoring ourselves, we're loving ourselves. In contrast, when we yield to bullies – including the one in our head – we're not loving ourselves. Pure and simple.

Remember when I talked about how a general sense of well-being is a default for we humans? Good feelings are natural and bad feelings are not. Well, the same is true of self-love. It's built in. Once again, we can look to small children as our role models. They naturally love themselves. It's evident in an assortment of ways. One clear sign is how they express sympathy for themselves. They cry when sad, when disappointed, or when they're hurt. And *what* do they do when the tears start to flow? They usually seek comfort. They know what they need and unhesitatingly go after it. That's self-compassion in action. And it's big!

Small children are also expressing self-love when they stand up for themselves, seek attention, go after the things they're passionate about, or even protect themselves against unfairness. But while self-love is an integral part of their nature, it must be nurtured. Children are similar to plants that need watering on a regular basis. That is, they need a supportive relationship in order to thrive. This is true of plants and humans alike, and both start to wilt without it.

The need for a supportive relationship begins very early in life. From the moment we show up on this planet, we need to feel that our mother's heart lights up – uncontrollably – each and every time she sets eyes on us. That joy is communicated to us through the happy rhythm of her voice, the tenderness of her touch, and her steady, affectionate gaze. How could that experience possibly get even better? If we also have a father who is equally starstruck and giddy about our existence.

There's a term for that experience: It's called feeling *cherished*. We need to feel that our parents are insanely in love with us from the get-go. It establishes a psychological foundation that operates much like a healthy immune system, protecting us from the stresses and psychological pathogens that permeate daily life. That sense of being cherished also strengthens us, preparing us for life's inevitable difficulties.

When we feel cherished, we find it easy to love ourselves. As a result, we naturally avoid things that would prove detrimental to our well-being. Children who feel cherished grow into adults who are confident, competent, and optimistic. They trust those who love them, and they trust themselves. When they're old enough to leave the nest, they trust their own ability to make smart decisions and manage their lives independently.

If you lacked that sort of upbringing, all's not lost. You can make up for that lack by learning how to love yourself and by removing all the things that contaminate and obstruct self-warmth and self-acceptance. That includes eliminating the head of the department – your Inner Bully. He needs to be fired.

Sean came to see me because he was struggling to quit smoking. Together we discovered that the degrading effect of self-shame undermined his capacity to take charge of himself and finally quit. As we all know, shaming ourselves when trying to give something up doesn't work. It only worsens the problem. Why? Because self-shaming fuels self-loathing … and self-loathing is the *opposite* of self-love.

After a few weeks of therapy, I knew Sean was making progress when he came to this powerful epiphany: "Torturing myself is so ludicrous because it isn't making me stop. The basis of my problem is beating myself up."

I'm happy for Sean. He gave up two habits that day.

Memorize this please: *My Inner Bully cannot survive in a climate of self-love.*

Adopt that powerful statement as your mantra. Your Inner Bully actually obstructs self-love, and I'll be showing you how to deal with that dude extensively as you read on.

Realize Your Bully's a Liar

The bully residing in your head loses its stronghold
when you no longer believe it. So just know, the fear
of you becoming enlightened keeps it up at night.

—Salee

Freedom from any obsessive critic – including the one hanging out in your head – entails questioning whether it is aligned with truth. We need to be asking ourselves: Do the criticisms and judgments waged against me square with reality? And if not, why do I continue my allegiance to such a deluded falsifier? Let's face it, continuing to do so merely exalts the absurd.

What's the alternative? you may ask. The answer is *clear-minded self-appraisal.* We rescue ourselves by questioning adopted assumptions about ourselves.

Think about it. Your Inner Bully has been conning you for years about how perfect you should be. It's running a scam. *Be sure to let this truth settle over you.*

Realize It's Delusional

Here's the bold and naked truth: Your Inner Bully
is mentally imbalanced. It doesn't see you correctly.
Not only that, but it also distorts facts and suffers from
delusions. One client summed it up perfectly: My Inner Bully
is exceptional at promoting its own version of the truth.

—Salee

I have to ask: What if a ten-year-old boy got in your face and accused you of spitting on his pet turtle? Unless you had actually spat on his turtle, you would be thinking something like this: *Well now, that's sheer ridiculousness. I've never been near his pet turtle. I didn't even know he had one! And I don't spit!*

Instead of taking it personally and then frantically trying to defend yourself, you would remain composed. You might even be amused. That's because taking offense would be difficult. Why? Because you don't have a shred of doubt that the accusation is groundless. It's an outlandish distortion on his part.

No matter where a distortion hails from, whether it comes from outside yourself or from the voice in your head, it's important to see it as sheer ridiculousness, and chill.

How about seeing your Inner Bully as a ten-year-old with an oversupply of goofy allegations about you?

My advice: Get some healthy doubt going. Stop thinking your Inner Bully is right.

Stop. Believing. It.

Just Know You're the Smarter One

Your Inner Bully is the dummy in your head that does a lame job of giving you advice. It isn't the wise one up there!

—SALEE

Hostages of Inner Bullies say "yes" too much, endure too much, give too much, give in too much, do too much, and they ignore themselves way too much. Ironically, they are imprisoned by something that doesn't think. Get wise to the fact that your Inner Bully lacks intelligence, and things go wrong when it runs the show. It simply cannot do a good job of steering you.

Reason gets sacrificed whenever we blindly follow the lead of any bully – the internal ones and those walking around on two legs. And reason is the last thing we should lose sight of. Inner Bullies are relentless and don't simply go away unless an entire arsenal is deployed against them. Logic is a phenomenal weapon because your Inner Bully doesn't know how to use it. It can't. So *you* can, and you must.

Toni, the devoted businesswoman I mentioned earlier, was convinced that people would think less of her if they knew she wasn't perfect. When we started working together, she realized perfectionism was a source of constant stress for her. That's entirely understandable. Trying to be perfect in an imperfect world is enormously stressful!

I asked her for an example. She recalled driving to work one day and feeling anxious about making it to an important meeting. All was well until she spotted road construction up ahead and traffic slowed to an exasperating crawl. "I knew instantly where the morning was headed," she said. "I was going to be late for my 9 o'clock meeting." Within a matter of milliseconds, her stress level skyrocketed and ohhhh, did the obscenities fly. Road rage was in full swing. The culprit? Not the roadwork and not the other people creeping along at glacial speed. It was her browbeating Inner Bully, shaming her for something she had no control over. But Inner Bullies don't care about logic or whether shaming is called for. Why? Because they're kind of empty-headed!

It doesn't even matter what her Inner Bully was railing on about. All that really mattered was that she had no control over the situation and that getting enraged solved nothing. It obliterated any possibility of surrendering to the only reasonable option she had: an opportunity to sit back and smell the roses. The situation just didn't warrant a sledgehammer. No one in that scenario was deserving of that kind of hostility – not the construction planners, the workers, the other drivers, and certainly not Toni. The situation called for logic and self-compassion, not a whipping.

So how do perfectionism, anger, and guilt come together to create such drama? How to best explain Toni's reaction? Psychologist Lynn D. Johnson in his book, *Get on the Peace Train: A Journey from Anger to Harmony*, supplies us with an answer:

> *Perfectionism is a habit that comes in two flavors: self-focused and other-focused. The self-focused people are angry at themselves. They just aren't doing enough, being enough, and pleasing enough. Their anger at themselves is a type of depression. "How could I have been so stupid?" they ask. "What is wrong with me? Why didn't I do better?" But something turned against the self can turn against others, too. Criticizing others, pointing out their faults and flaws, showing others how they should have done something different are all forms of other-directed perfectionism. It is anger based on a kind of insecurity. The fear is that if things are not just so then it will be awful! Some authority figure (parents, neighbors, God) will be angry if things*

aren't perfect. The perfectionist's own anger is a disguised way of staying out of trouble themselves!

In these instances, rather than swallowing the blame and shame from the voice in our head, or from an actual person, we direct the blame outward. In Toni's mind, the other drivers were at fault. It's a common defense mechanism we all use and, for the most part, we aren't even conscious of doing it. We'll employ anything to get the Inner Bully off our backs! Twisted, unhealthy guilt does that to people. That particular defense mechanism shows up in our relationships, creating a stir on a regular basis. And no, as you might guess, anger at others is not the right way to conquer our Inner Bully. There is a better way, and I hope you're learning that new way as you read this book.

What Toni needed to do – what we all need to do when we get swept up in our emotions – was to put on the brakes, do some serious introspection, and question exactly why she got triggered.

If you really think about it, much of our time is spent on autopilot. We're largely oblivious to what's occurring just beneath the surface at any given moment. This leads us to the discovery of an indispensable tool.

Use Mindfulness Compulsively

*You need to use mindfulness so compulsively,
in fact, that you end up overworking it.
Wear it out like your favorite pair of jeans!*

—Salee

85

When it comes to gaining mastery over your Inner Bully, the practice of mindfulness has few rivals. It's an unparalleled force that positions you firmly at the helm. How? By directly placing you in the observer role, which brings your unconsciousness into full awareness. You might say mindfulness turns the lights on in your head. With this tool at your disposal, you get good at noticing how your thoughts are impacting your emotions and actions at any given moment and in any given situation. Said another way, it allows you to spy on your Inner Bully. With mindfulness, you get to have the advantage.

Think of mindfulness as your personal jetpack, a cloud cruiser propelling you upward and transporting you to higher ground. When you get thrown, like Toni, it's time to strap on that trusty jetpack of mindfulness and transport yourself to where the air is clear – to that elevated zone of wisdom and higher thinking. From that vantage point, you automatically possess a crisp and logical mind that is capable of seeing more deeply and objectively.

That's what mindfulness does for you. It's innately calming, allowing you to separate and rise above all internal drama. It sets the stage for objective, factual, and logical thinking. That powerful state of consciousness makes it possible for you to contrast the bully's brand of truth against your own and to poke holes in its many judgments and baseless claims about you.

Without question, Toni's plight would have played out differently had she employed mindfulness. It could have started with a simple, inwardly directed question: *Whoa! What just rocked my boat?* Or, more accurately, *What just threw me out of my boat!?*

Likewise, when our feelings get stirred up, we need to be asking, what's happening *in here* instead of what's happening *out there*. We must become familiar with the internal dialogue and the programming that trips us up. Mindfulness is being conscious: *What's igniting my emotions right now?* We have little – if any – control when it comes to external circumstances. But we can definitely control how we *react* to those situations once we learn to recognize our reactions. Mindfulness is the perfect tool for that.

Imagine relaxing in your favorite chair, and a light bulb suddenly flickers out. What happens to your internal state? Perhaps you worry a little about whether there are any spare light bulbs in the house. Or perhaps you're annoyed because now you have to get out of your comfortable chair to change it. Maybe you decide you'll change it later but find you can't relax with that chore hanging over your head.

In the midst of all that, your phone rings and it's your mom. What's happening internally? How do your feelings shift? Is it a happy interruption or are you annoyed? And while all of this is going on, what has your Inner Bully been whispering in your ear? How has it been judging you? Did it sneakily tack the lazy label on you? If you really didn't want to chat with your mom, what accusation did it slap on you? Mindfulness is your superpower for noticing Inner Bully attacks.

Awareness of what's occurring internally empowers you to decide how you really want to look at something and interpret your circumstances accordingly. That leads you directly to whatever you need to do about it, if anything. *That's* freedom.

Jon Kabat-Zinn, the author of the powerful book *The Healing Power of Mindfulness: A New Way of Being,* defines mindfulness as "paying attention, on purpose, in the present moment, non-judgmentally." It amounts to deliberately paying attention to what's going on inside us and doing so without self-judgment or condemnation.

The next step is to deliberately choose our responses to particular stimuli. My husband Don has put a lot of time and effort into creating and maintaining a beautiful flower garden next to our house. One day we were admiring it, and he said, "Right now, I can feel one of two things. I can either feel peacefulness or stress. Do I see the beauty, or do I see the work? Do I experience the calm, or do I feel driven by what needs to be done? It's a choice."

Toni eventually became adept at thwarting her automatic reactions. She learned to shift gears, step back, and take a look. But before she could do that independently, she required a little assistance, so together we looked for the root cause behind her angry panic. She began to see some things.

"My parents always got on my case whenever I was late," she said. "I couldn't even be one minute late without them getting furious with me!"

That all started when she was very young. Over time, she adopted the idea that being late was both shameful and unpardonable. Call it her programming. So now, as an adult, her Inner Bully echoes the scolding condemnation she received as a child. What was her initial thought when it dawned on her that she might be late for work? "I imagined people glaring at me as I walked in," she said.

Toni's thought process highlights a major problem in regard to programming. It contaminates reason and results in generalizations that leave gaping holes in logic. Assumptions are formed that simply may not be true. Her co-workers might not even be aware that she's late. Her Inner Bully had created a theater in her own mind and used it to make her feel bad.

By learning where her Inner Bully was getting its material, Toni took a giant step in getting the upper hand. Her insights allowed her to scrutinize it, out-think it, and then utilize logic to dispel it.

With mindfulness, we're able to use rational thinking to dispel antiquated or inaccurate beliefs that have been silently operating under the surface for years.

It's good to know that the false notions we learned about ourselves can be unlearned. Eventually we will be able to control our automatic reactions, but reaching that goal takes time. It also takes self-compassion in the form of patience. (That's a goal in and of itself!) We certainly don't want to be setting ourselves up for more self-disapproval if we fail. After all, if self-examination doesn't result in self-acceptance, then it's missing the point.

If you're interested in learning more about mindfulness, including detailed instruction on how to use it, I highly recommend the workbook entitled *Get Out of Your Mind and Into Your Life* by Steven Hayes, PhD, and Spencer Smith. With its thorough, step-by-step guidance, I'm confident it will enhance your journey of finding freedom from negative thinking and self-judgment.

Meditation

Awareness is like the sun.

When it shines on things, they are transformed.

—THICH NHAT HANH

Meditation is an equally effective tool that quiets the chaos swirling endlessly in our heads. You know, the mental chatter that takes up so much of our brain space – uninvited.

Meditation cuts through all that and helps us develop the awareness that we're much more than our physical and programmed selves. Through the practice of meditation, we transcend opinions about ourselves, including our own faulty array of opinions about who we are.

The Buddha is rumored to have been asked what he gained from meditation. He replied, "Nothing!" But then he added, "Let me tell you what I lost: anger, anxiety, depression, insecurity, fear of old age, and death."

Whether or not this quote can be accurately attributed to Buddha is arguable, but I still love the truth of it. And I would go one step further and add guilt to that list, specifically the oppressive, toxic brand.

Mindfulness and meditation are close cousins. Mindfulness is something you can engage in on the fly, and meditation involves sitting for a few minutes in a quiet place that's relatively free of distractions. Meditation is a technique that involves focusing on something intently (like one's breath, a word, or an object). The point is to rein in the incessant brain jabber that dominates most of our waking lives.

Meditation transports us to a space of peace and calm, both ideal conditions for some robust mindfulness. The two practices combined (referred to as mindfulness meditation) strengthen our capacity to function as detached observers of ourselves. Through mindfulness meditation, we learn to get good at being aware of our thoughts as they drift in and out of our minds. It establishes a platform for keeping an eye on our Inner Bully from a neutral position. I read somewhere that meditation is the practice, and mindfulness is the result. I like that.

The practice of meditation is relatively easy. Seek out meditation classes available in your area or explore meditation sites online, including apps such as Headspace and Insight Timer. An author who I find particularly effective in educating readers on the how-tos of meditation is Jack Kornfield. His book *Meditation for Beginners* has gained a lot of attention over the years. I also recommend the works of Jon Kabat-Zinn and Steven Levine. I would encourage you to delve more deeply into both of these subjects, and these authors are a great place to start.

Studies have shown that both mindfulness and meditation are powerful forces in rewiring the brain. This means that both practices can be used in tandem to ultimately disable self-defeating mental patterns.

Our programming *can* undergo change. That's positive news.

Baffle Your Inner Bully
by Setting Boundaries

We must get good at setting boundaries against all the toxic players in our life, and that includes that one bossy, demeaning internal tormentor we put up with every day, the Inner Bully. For now, I'll be focusing on that guy. Later on we'll talk about boundaries and external bullies.

Here's a personal example. One day it dawned on me that if someone decides to follow their passion – like writing a book! – they must get really good at saying no, and then be prepared to tackle their Inner Bully to the ground. Writing a book is a stressful, all-consuming, time-drain. Not a surprise to anyone.

Drum roll, please. To remain shy about saying "no" is to court disaster.

That modest, two-letter word is the most potent boundary-setting device known to man (and woman). Why? Because it involves making ourselves a priority – something frowned upon by most Inner Bullies. And mine is no exception, by the way.

My book-writing project forced me to defy my Inner Bully because I had to ask my husband, Don, for help doing tasks that I like to handle myself. Don's a sweetheart about it, but not my inner you-know-who! (There's one thing for sure. We'll never have to worry about wasting that "sweetheart" label on our Inner Bully. That label will not apply, not at any time and not on any world. Nope. It won't happen.)

I'm among the many who resist setting boundaries. That resistance is just another example of bad guilt controlling our lives. Our Inner Bully will likely accuse us of not being loving or fair to the other person. One client described her resistance in very graphic terms: "I'd rather gnaw my arm off than set boundaries." That may sound a bit extreme, but it does speak to the level of internal struggle we endure over the whole idea.

I suggest you fight your resistance and instead tirelessly practice saying "no." Think of it this way: learning new habits is not much different than working out at the gym. The more you exercise that "no" muscle, the stronger you'll become at facing down your Inner Bully. Such tenacity and stamina will escort you naturally to the seat of authority, which is precisely where you need to be.

Just so you know, your relationship with your Inner Bully will start to change. Applaud that miniature, two-letter powerhouse of a word!

Eyeball It

In case you haven't noticed, you have a mental dialogue going on inside your head that never stops. It just keeps going and going. . . . If you're smart, you'll take the time to step back, examine this voice, and get to know it better.

—MICHAEL SINGER, *THE UNTETHERED SOUL*

When it comes to sizing us up, Inner Bullies are wretched authorities. They don't even vaguely measure up to the task. Face it. Anything or anyone who's predominately condemning is ill-suited for assessing anyone objectively! Their critical bias automatically disqualifies them.

The only course of action is to rise above the brainwashing long enough to take an objective look – a necessary step for combating your Inner Bully's patently false allegations. So once again, strap on that trusty jetpack, and propel yourself to a higher perspective. You'll be able to take in this revelation: *You are not at the mercy of your programming.* As a child, you couldn't avoid being programmed, but as an adult you have the advantage of wisdom. You can now out-think erroneous allegations, both internal and external, instead of absorbing them. Because you are wiser, you can conquer the Inner Bully by distinguishing fact from fiction.

A Tool for Sizing up Your Inner Bully

To assist you in this process, I've included the Self-Evaluation Exercise (SEE), a tool I devised for my clients. You'll find it in Appendix One at the end of this book.

Here's what you do: use two pens with different color inks. For example, one red and one black. Circle the traits that best describe you with one pen, and circle the traits that best describe your Inner Bully with the other. Upon completing the exercise, make a list of your traits and place them alongside your bully's traits. Compare the two.

As you might have guessed, after completing the exercise, many people have a hard time thinking of themselves in positive terms. It felt odd to them, even unnatural. Some have told me that the very act of circling positive traits riled their Inner Bully, who had been silently watching with a menacing sneer on its face. The exercise activated their shame.

Believe it or not, I consider this kind of awareness a sign of progress for my clients. Why? Because they are becoming conscious of the inner workings of their mind. And since logic tells us that we can't control what we're not conscious of, getting free of our Inner Bully requires an opened-eyed awareness of it. Then and only then do we have a chance of being empowered to examine, question, and ultimately dispel it. From there, we can discard ingrained beliefs about ourselves and identify with our True Self.

I suggest that any time you're feeling shame, ask yourself, "What part of me is feeling shame?" Is it the wiser, truer me, or the me who was molded by the key people in my growing-up years? That will immediately put you in an observer role, separate from the shame. You will realize at that very moment that the real you is completely separate from the shame. You're the observer. The part that feels the shame is a fabrication that stems from your programming.

Keep in mind that to attain freedom from your Inner Bully – your shamer – you must be able to objectively watch it in action and observe how that shamed part of you reacts to it. Michael Singer describes it well: "If you're hearing it talk, it's obviously not you. You are the one who hears the voice. You are the one who notices that it's talking."

Turn the Tables on Your Bully – Criticize It

Once you get good at observing your Inner Bully babbling on about your failings and countless flaws, you'll learn how to turn the tables on it – critiquing it and ultimately overthrowing it.

—SALEE

The SEE exercise is useful not only for viewing your bully through an objective lens, but also for illuminating material you can use for calling it out. You can turn the tables on that thorny monster.

Do you recall Holly? Shining made her feel guilty. Holly's Inner Bully had been working tirelessly for years to convince her that she should dim her True Self in order to please the significant people in her life. All that self-squelching made her unhappy and depressed. Once Holly's Inner Bully was fully exposed, I encouraged her to talk back to it. "Turn the tables on it," I said. "Don't allow it to bully you with things like *Who do you think you are, young lady.*"

"Okay ... but how?" she asked.

"When it talks to you like that, what do you really want to say?" I asked.

She thought for just a moment, and then, with a refreshing air of cockiness, said, "Wait a minute, who do you think *you* are!" Without any further prompting, she proceeded to unleash a stockpile of stored-up anger, resentment, and criticism onto the beast. By the end of that session, she looked a thousand pounds lighter, and a big smile lit up her whole being.

Like all habitual patterns, her bully didn't just abruptly fold up shop and leave the premises. It continued to hang around. Consequently, she was forced to handle the intruder in the same way she would have to handle an actual person exhibiting bullying behaviors: by being bold and remaining muscular. Standing up to it once was not enough. She had to get good at exerting her power over it – repeatedly.

The magic is in that word *repeatedly*. As you know, the more repetitions you do, regardless of what you're trying to change about yourself, the more likely you are to succeed. Change requires practicing a new pattern. Again, it's similar to going to the gym; results come from repetition.

Let's say you chew gum on the right side of your mouth, but one day you decide that chewing it on the left side would improve your life somehow. With enough practice and time, you'll achieve that goal, and your success will become evident when you catch yourself automatically chewing on the left side. Done without forethought! On that fateful day, left-side chewing became your new normal. Congratulations!

The same principle holds true with moving into a power position over your Inner Bully. The more you stand up to it, the weaker it grows and the stronger you become. Practice makes permanent.

Realize You're a Lot Nicer

The bully lacks compassion,
but that's not true of you.
So who's better?

—SALEE

Upon completing the Self-Evaluation Exercise, the first thing you'll probably notice is the striking differences between you and your bully. When it comes to admirable traits and being an overall decent human being, I'm certain you are light years ahead of your Inner Bully.

Author and psychologist George Simon would diagnose your bully as having a character disorder. In his book, *Character Disturbance: The Phenomenon of Our Age,* he points out that people who have a character disorder fail miserably at treating others with respect and kindness. He describes them as conscience-deficient and empathy-deficient. You could say they lack a caring heart.

Okay, so your Inner Bully is uncaring, insensitive, empathy-deficient, condemning, and harsh. Briefly said, it's emotionally abusive. It lies, and it's irrational to a staggering degree. It distorts reality, and yet you give this thing the authority to poison your existence!? You give it the power to influence how you feel about yourself and to define who you are. Yessiree! You've been surrendering your control to a hostile intruder who doesn't care a hoot about you!

What's up with that? Does this mean you're crazy?

No! It means you're stuck in your thinking. That can change. You are being intimidated by a mirage. One could say you're running from a dog that barks loudly but in reality has no teeth.

I'll be less flippant about it. As awareness of your Inner Bully increases, it's normal to be asking yourself the question, "Why do I let this revolting and abominable thing rule my life?" If that thought ever crosses your mind, be gentle with yourself. Realize it's a habit, a habit formed when you were very young. Also realize that *habits can be broken*.

You also need to be celebrating. I can't emphasize enough how significant it is that you're having such thoughts. It means you're in the midst of awakening. Not only that but you're also starting to perceive yourself in a positive light and deserving of respectful treatment. It means you're tapping into self-love. That's pretty remarkable!

Chapter Eight

The Glittering Truth About You

*You have the same force running through you
that allows the planets to move, the earth to turn,
the seeds to sprout, and the flowers to open...
There is one universal intelligence
flowing through all of us.*

—WAYNE DYER

Daryl, a sweet soul I counseled a few years back, recalled an incident that epitomizes what growing up with his father was like. "I asked my dad if he would play a game of badminton with me," Daryl said. "He agreed, and I remember how excited I was."

But things quickly went downhill. On the very first serve, Daryl hit the birdie out of bounds. His father, looking disgusted, dropped his racket and walked away, saying: "Well, if you can't hit it right, I'm done."

That episode, along with thousands like it, fueled Daryl's disdain for himself. "I came to believe that I was a problem for people, that I can't get things right, and that it's my fault others don't want to spend time with me."

The voice in his head – his Inner Bully – mirrors his father in that it reiterates those very messages over and over again.

If you relate to Daryl, here's something you need to know: The only thing tainted is your self-impression. Your essence is pure. And how on Earth is it possible to despise purity?

Remember Vanessa, the young mother in Chapter Two? Her mentally abusive childhood crippled her perception of herself. She didn't believe she was lovable, but Carson, her baby, didn't seem to agree. His loving gaze clashed with her tainted view of herself.

In therapy, Vanessa dug into the origins of her self-loathing and became keenly aware of her unconscious and habitually undermining thought patterns. She came face to face with her Inner Bully and proceeded to dismantle falsehoods about herself that she had blindly bought into. In the process, her True Self was unearthed. Yes, initially, Vanessa had bought into a lie. But eventually, she came to see that Carson's perception of her was the simple, beautiful truth!

Love of oneself is empowering. In fact, it's the strongest power we have for overthrowing our Inner Bully. Bullies of all shapes and sizes simply cannot exist in a climate of self-love.

Beverly Engel, in her book *Healing Your Emotional Self*, echoed that thought when she cited Byron Brown, the author of *Soul without Shame:* "Compassion is the greatest antidote to the poison of your pathological inner critic."

Engel continues with her own thoughts:

> *When you are being compassionate toward yourself, you essentially gag your pathological inner critic, who cannot tolerate compassion because it renders him powerless. Compassion is the essence of self-esteem. When you have compassion for yourself, you understand and accept yourself the way you are. You tend to see yourself as basically good. If you make a mistake, you forgive yourself. You have reasonable expectations of yourself.*

Your True Self:
The Place Untouched by the Inner Bully

Your True Self is the core of your being – your pure and unchanging essence. It surfaces when you're out in nature, being creative, when you laugh and run, when you sing without restraint, when you pause and look up at the stars, or when you think your own thoughts, choose your own color, play your own music, know what you want, and say what you think. To be exact, it's your free spirit expressing itself – your actual Self.

Your True Self didn't go anywhere. It just got a tad bit buried. At a very young age, you started getting bombarded with a constant shower of opinions about who and what you were. Those opinions formed your self-conception – how you saw yourself. They redefined and overshadowed your true essence.

Your True Self merely got submerged beneath layers and layers of opinions – opinions that you in turn elevated to the status of Truth. Every significant person in your childhood, including siblings, had a hand in shaping your self-concept. If your sister viewed you as a bothersome brat, that might have become one of the many labels you assigned to yourself. If your parents perceived you as a talented soloist – constantly praising you for your wonderful singing voice – it would be just a matter of time before "soloist" would be instrumental in forming your self-image. The same would hold true if you were told repeatedly that you were smart, pretty, a great hockey player, or well-mannered. But those rosy *opinions* don't define your actual Self any more than the derogatory ones. Your True Self exists above and beyond all opinions – it is completely immune to outside influences.

Your impression of yourself – your self-concept – extends beyond family influence. Socioeconomic and peer status and cultural and racial biases also play a significant role in sculpting how we see ourselves. Others' behaviors toward us and around us – for example, growing up in a home with an alcoholic parent, or in a rough neighborhood – are instrumental in forming any ill-conception we may have of ourselves. All of this "noise" is called programming. Your True Self, though, is different and grander than mere labels and opinions. It has nothing to do with your talents, your brains, your physical body, your skills, your social standing, or your environment. And it's impossible to discover it in a book on personality traits.

Your True Self has to be experienced to be fully understood. I'll be saying more about that shortly.

You Were Birthed by the Universe

It appears as though a large chunk of our lives
is spent acquiring faulty notions about who we are
while the remaining portion is spent freeing
ourselves from that sticky mess.

—SALEE

French philosopher Pierre Teilhard de Chardin once said, "We are not human beings having a spiritual experience; we are spiritual beings having a human experience." Or, as Deepak Chopra so wisely put it, "You are spirit carrying a body around with you."

If that's true, and I personally believe it is, then every single one of us is a unique expression of the universe: a fundamental self that can't be polluted. Our True Self is more massive than the opinions we've absorbed about ourselves and brighter than the camouflage of the daily existence that dominates our attention during our waking hours. And because it transcends day-to-day consciousness, it mostly escapes our notice.

That wasn't always the case.

Our True Self was more apparent – more out in the open – in our younger years, way before labels, rules, and reprimands stifled it. Yes, we need to learn constraints, limits, and discipline in order to function in a society, but there's often an unfortunate price: the True Self begins to fade from our awareness, and a more "acceptable" version emerges to take its place.

At a very early phase in our life, we're put through a process that's similar to the shaping of bonsai trees. Branches on the young bonsai are wired down for as long as necessary to assure they remain fixed in a particular position even after the wires are removed.

But there's a stark difference between our process and that of bonsai trees. The trees lack *free will* and they lack *choice*. Once we humans become adults, we have the option to remain fixed – styled permanently by our shapers – or we can return to our original form. We can transcend our programming, instead of remaining helplessly tethered to it.

The challenge includes becoming conscious of that programming with the goal of reclaiming our True Selves – the original shape of our "tree." It's a shedding process we generally approach with mixed feelings, however. No question, we yearn for our freedom, but at the same time we resist letting go of what feels familiar to us. Although the status quo has its drawbacks, it has a way of bathing us in the security it offers. We feel safe. We feel grounded. When we dare to step outside that comfort zone, our fears and doubts gang up on us. We ask ourselves: *Does anything actually exist beneath the layers of programming? If I let go of it, then who am I? And how do I operate without all these layers of definition that I've acquired?*

The only time we get serious about dismantling the illusion is when the level of our pain or discomfort mandates it – when the price of maintaining that illusion becomes greater than our fears.

Responding to the summons to unravel is a scary move. I congratulate my clients and anyone for taking that on. It's a courageous step.

Brad, the man you met earlier who suffered from severe depression, took that step. When I first started counseling him, he defined himself as worthless and a loser. His negative self-image was based on erroneous conclusions, and those beliefs about himself played a significant role in his depression and life dissatisfaction. His pathway out of that murky quagmire of self-degradation and into the fresh air of clarity involved disbelieving those conclusions.

Discovering the Real You

Your Inner Bully will be rendered powerless as you
reconnect with the truth of who you really are.
You'll automatically dismiss its lies, rants, and insults.

—SALEE

Only from the space of our True Self are we able to cease believing in the self we aren't. We realize we've been identifying with a programmed self: a fictitious self that is nothing more than a mere fantasy. Compared to the True Self, it's just an empty shell, an illusion or dream that we erroneously imagine as real. This is key: Any tainted view you have of yourself isn't the real you. It's an illusion originating from your programmed brain. It's a dream and you're the dreamer. Beverly Engel summarizes the problem and its solution in this brief statement:

> *The negative messages you received from your parents (spoken and unspoken) became an overlay on top of your essence, often hiding it from your awareness. In order to reconnect with your essence, you may need to go beneath the negative parental messages you received, beneath the inner critic, and beneath your own self-judgment.*

That basically describes where I go with my clients. I aim to awaken them from their dream-state by illuminating their habitual, self-defeating, and self-destructive thought patterns. Once that's achieved, they often do a marvelous job of healing and freeing themselves.

In our sessions, whenever Brad uttered something negative about himself, I challenged it – demanding evidence supporting his allegations. I got ruthless at times! Finally, after enough exposure to this, he began questioning his negative self-talk on his own. That was the plan.

"Those internalized messages obscure your True Self," I said bluntly.

"My True Self is foreign to me," he insisted, "so I don't feel it's attainable."

Like so many of us, he had fallen into a habit of giving his Inner Bully and his programmed self more reality than his True Self.

"How do I figure out what my True Self is?" he asked.

"We don't figure out who we are," I said, "we experience it, Brad."

I had him close his eyes as I guided him to go within and connect with his stillness deep below the surface. Then I instructed him to imagine a time when he felt free from guilt. Without the slightest hesitation he said, "Being out in nature." Then his voice began to crack as he described what it was like spending time in the woods near his house while growing up. He hung out near a creek, climbed on logs, and built forts. He was alone out there but far from lonely. No one was around to disturb his peace. His siblings weren't there to pick on him, and his parents weren't there to shame or judge him. He felt peaceful and self-assured. He didn't need his father's acceptance out there. He was experiencing *self-acceptance.*

Deepak Chopra says that acceptance, security, peacefulness, and confidence are the elements we experience when we're in touch with our True Self. That perfectly matches Brad's experience in that woods. I urged him to tuck that memory away and pull it out whenever he sensed a guilt-attack coming on. "It'll guide you back to the truth of who you are," I said.

He liked that idea.

We did some more exploring, and suddenly he had a life-altering realization.

"You know what," he said leaning forward, "my Inner Bully's a liar!"

We high-fived that one! That single moment of clarity, by the way, came straight from his True Self.

I left him with some specific instructions: "Be sure to share that lovely piece of awareness with your Inner Bully. After all, it has badgered you senselessly for years. It's high time you got even!" He laughed ... a freeing laugh.

Another client, Aria, experiences her True Self while playing piano – when she gets to a space where the music is "effortlessly flowing through my fingers and the whole world shrinks to nothing," she said. "When that happens, there is only that moment."

That ties in with something else Byron Brown had to say: "The soul's true nature exists most fundamentally as a nowness; it is a nature that does not depend on the past or the future..."

Those words make me think of small children. They exist solely in the here and now. They aren't hampered by schedules or thoughts of what went wrong a few days ago, or even a few hours ago. And they aren't focused on what's happening next, either. Not only that, but they're also wonderfully connected to their natural feelings. And they're unapologetically spontaneous with every single feeling on the emotional spectrum. They laugh when they're moved to laugh, they squeal when they get excited, they cry when they're moved to cry, they get angry when anger wells up, and they scream and hide when they get scared. It never occurs to them to question whether their feelings are right or wrong.

If you offer them something they don't like, they simply refuse it, and they don't worry about it ruining your day or making you mad. They chase down their passions with tireless enthusiasm, and if they get bored with something, they simply move on to something else.

No question, small children do a perfect job of modeling the concepts of nowness and True Self.

One of my own earliest memories of my True Self was blissfully experiencing the "now." I was three years old, on my awesome tricycle, and had the outdoors all to myself. Not a soul in sight. It was one of those sunny, deep-blue-sky days. I loved how such days felt – still do. Adding to the visual enchantment, I could hear the distinctive cooing sounds of a mourning dove in the background. But back then I didn't know about mourning doves. I just assumed that such blue-sky days sounded that way. Still do.

When do you experience your True Self, even for brief moments? I suggest you indulge in the luxury of contemplating that question and jotting down your thoughts.

Perhaps Brad's, Aria's, or even my experience resonates with you. Or maybe for you it happens when you're absorbed in a sunset, listening to ocean waves or beautiful music, walking trails, gardening, creating art, dancing, or lying on your back gazing up at the stars. I don't know what it is for you, but I do know this: A magically serene door opens up, and we leave behind the thoughts of what's "wrong" with us as we enter a warm realm of being present with ourselves in a tender way.

This is where mindfulness becomes useful again. It gives you access to your True Self. As I stated earlier, your Inner Bully will be rendered powerless as you reconnect with the truth of who you really are. You'll dismiss its lies, rants, and insults because mindfulness makes it possible to control your mental activity. Mindfulness, as you recall, is the method used for bringing the unconscious into full awareness.

You Have a Giant-Sized Heart

Your capacity to feel guilt is something to be admired.
It means you have a warm heart.

—SALEE

Here's a bit of a surprise for everyone who feels guilty about feeling guilty. You may have overlooked something very important about yourself: the enormity of your heart. Although we've never met, I know beyond any shadow of a doubt that you're innately kind and considerate. How do I know that? Because guilt – including the over-the-top type – can only arise in people who *care deeply*.

As I said before, a healthy conscience is a good thing. (Personally, I prefer to avoid people who don't seem to have one.) Brad felt guilty because his depression crippled his ability to be a better dad. That guilt was rooted in love. The same is true of the others you've read about so far: those who struggle with setting boundaries, saying no, or letting people down. Each one possesses a giant heart. They care about other people. And they, along with many others (that includes you) are the giants among us.

Heather, a former client, was one of those giants. Like many, she had a harassing Inner Bully and generally felt bad about herself. In one particular session, I simply asked: "When do you feel really good about yourself?"

Suddenly her whole face lit up as she started talking about helping Angela, a coworker with a disability. "She works alone and doesn't seem to have any friends," Heather explained, "so I make it a point to strike up conversations with her."

The change in Heather's demeanor was dramatic as she went on and on about all the ways she makes it a point to bolster Angela's self-worth. I made sure Heather realized that what she was doing for Angela was both rare and hugely significant. I topped it all off by declaring: "What a gift you are to that woman!"

Heather looked away, suddenly shy, uncomfortable with the compliment.

I focused on how empathetic she was being with Angela. "Look, you have something invaluable to offer others," I said. "You can make people feel good about themselves. This world needs people like you! And if you don't think so, I'm sure Angela would strongly disagree."

Chapter Nine

Life in the Command Module: Making Change Stick

Once you have understood the basic principle of being present as the watcher of what happens inside you — and you "understand" it by experiencing it — you have at your disposal the most potent transformational tool.

—ECKHART TOLLE, *THE POWER OF NOW*

Remember, I promised earlier to share with you how I learned to silence my Inner Bully when it scolded me for wasting food and insisted that I clean my plate? I was gradually putting on the pounds and needed to get the thing to shut up. So here we go.

As you know, one way of tackling the Inner Bully to the ground is by out-thinking it: attack it with logic. That's exactly what I did. I remember asking myself: *Okay, why am I gaining weight?* The answer was clear: I felt guilty if I didn't clean my plate, and I traced that guilt back to Dad and how he had programmed me.

My next step was to examine the logic of such programming. I looked this whole food-wasting issue squarely in the face. I asked myself if there was something innately or morally wrong about wasting food. I came up with a profound answer: not really. It's more of a practical matter. For instance, it's just not wise or responsible to waste food if it's in short supply, or to eat my sugary desert and skip the meal sitting in front of me. Most importantly, I realized the food was still going to waste when I ate it, if my body didn't really need it.

Operating wisely and responsibly is the key, not stuffing myself due to being bullied by a misinformed conscience. Such mindless obedience was glaringly counterproductive. Why? Because it led to another form of wastefulness. An oversupply of food in the digestive system gets transported to fat storage. That is, my body will utilize the food it needs for energy and nutritional purposes while stockpiling the rest. To put it simply, unneeded food gets stored as fat, which is as much of a waste as tossing it in the trash.

My dad meant well. His intention wasn't to saddle me with an internal bully that would harass me to the point of gaining weight. Nevertheless, I would have been spared the guilt and the overeating had Dad altered his message a wee bit: *I want you to try to clean your plate, but most of all, I want you to listen to your body. Be sure to stop when you feel full.* Had he taken that route, he would have conveyed that fullness should dictate how much I eat, not guilt.

I can't change the past. I can't miraculously turn back the clock and have Dad do a better job with his parental guidance. But when my Inner Bully heckles me about wasting food, I can reprogram myself by replacing his original message with the wiser one. Does that voice still heckle me? Occasionally, but with far less intensity and frequency. The volume has grown weaker.

Basically, in the process of out-thinking it, my Inner Bully lost its authority. I don't believe it anymore. I don't even believe it's real. So when the heckling begins, I immediately dismiss it because I recognize it for what it is. I tell myself: *That's just my programmed brain.* When I do that, any messages that come from my Inner Bully immediately lose their punch. Like a dog being denied any leftover scraps, it crawls back into the corner and sulks.

Here's the plain and simple truth: your Inner Bully and its messages will begin to fade automatically when you refuse to give it power. No, it won't fizzle out completely, but it will stop running your life.

I hope you're beginning to understand how vital it is to be in the driver's seat versus being chauffeured around to undesirable destinations by your Inner Bully.

117

It's exciting to watch a client suddenly realize that their programming is the problem – not them! A noticeable identity shift occurs: a vibrant and confident self emerges. Yep, it's exciting!

In a therapy session with Brad, I had planned to explain something by using a whiteboard. That idea necessitated setting it up, and of course it was tucked behind a sofa. The whole process was cumbersome and took a whole lot longer than I anticipated. I remember growing impatient with myself and telling him that my bully was badgering me about taking so long and making him wait.

"I too have an Inner Bully," I said, "and there was a time when I'd get seriously captured by it."

"How did you get free?" he asked.

"By identifying with my True Self," I answered. "I came to realize that my guilt-self isn't me."

I went on to explain that my guilt-self is a product of my early childhood programming. It's based on an inaccurate belief about who I am – a self-image that isn't real. "And Brad, the image you have of yourself isn't you either." He looked a bit confused. "I'll show you what I mean," I said.

By this time I had the whiteboard up and ready to go. I drew three stick figures. Two were facing each other, and the third one was situated in the foreground. Pointing at that one I said, "He's the Observer. It's you, your True Self."

I then pointed to the two figures facing each other and explained that the one on the left was his Inner Bully and the one on the right was his image of himself. "The one on the right represents your unreal and tainted view of yourself," I said. "He's also the recipient of all your bully's nastiness. Let's call him the Target." I explained that Observers are never the Target. That's because bullies are incapable of even seeing our True Selves.

"You're invisible to him," I added. "So you're not the one your Inner Bully is picking on. The real you is the detached Observer, the one who's always standing back watching the drama going on between your Inner Bully and your programmed self: the Target."

The Observer is detached, objective, and free.

Brad was listening intently. I noticed an uncharacteristic exuberance about him. He was ramping up to say something.

"Got some thoughts?" I asked.

"Inner Bullies are the byproduct of programming," he said. "They're not real! They operate automatically just like breathing, and most of the time we're not even aware of it."

It was clear he was on a roll, so I wasn't about to stop him. I just sat back and grinned. He was *getting it*, and it was exciting to watch.

"My brain just keeps playing the same tape over and over," he said, and then he went into greater detail about how his brain unconsciously operates on autopilot on a regular basis. He concluded with this: "It's clear what I must do now – I have to reprogram myself."

Brad also made it clear just how he was going to achieve that: "It's what you've been telling me all along. Since we get programmed through repetition, we can also get *reprogrammed* through repetition."

So instead of telling himself over and over again how worthless he was, his plan was to start telling himself the truth about himself over and over again. In effect, he'd be arguing with his Inner Bully – and winning!

Like Brad, your job is to commandeer your brain's automatic operating system. In other words, get good at interrupting it and heading it off at the pass.

Unfortunately, Inner Bullies don't just go *poof* and disappear merely because we get wise to them. It takes time to reprogram our brains. Yes, Brad had successfully transcended his programming on that particular day in my office. He saw things with clarity. Nothing had changed externally. All of the changes took place internally. He merely took control of his automatic thoughts

Now in order for *real*, lasting change to take place, he would have to dedicate himself to repeatedly replicating that mental shift. We're habituated creatures, so if we're to change patterns, we must choose our actions deliberately until a new pattern takes hold. I'll say it again: change requires practicing a new pattern. Inner Bullies are nothing more than habitual mental patterns, and like any habit, they are notoriously difficult to break. Reprogramming entails continually pushing against the gravitational forces of a fixed pattern, then consciously replacing it with a new one until it sticks. It's not easy. In fact, the process can be immensely irritating!

Here's an everyday example. Have you ever moved a wall clock to another spot in the room? Well, I have, and I don't know about you, but I find myself automatically and unconsciously glancing at a blank space on the wall many times over. It's maddening! My rational mind knows better. But my rational mind doesn't have control over the situation, my programmed brain does – at least for the time being. And it will continue to happen until my brain finally adapts to the new status quo.

Whenever you change a behavior, learn something new, or change how you think, you're actually altering the neurochemistry and structure of your brain; you're creating new pathways. So each time I catch myself looking at the blank space on the wall, and then deliberately shift my gaze to the clock's new location, I'm actively reprogramming my brain. Eventually, the action will occur automatically. I won't even have to think about it.

Toothpaste is another common example. How many of us squeeze the tube in the middle versus squeezing it from the bottom? I don't know of any actual studies done on tube-squeezing habits, but I'm certain we tend to adhere to a certain pattern. Now, let's say someone challenges us to change our automatic style. It won't be easy, but we can do it. What does it take? A combination of focus and determination. Every time we go to brush our teeth, we have to wake up to what's really important here. Is it brushing our teeth or changing an ingrained pattern? I advocate for the latter, and with enough practice, it's just a matter of time before we get used to a different squeezing method.

The process of gaining control of our Inner Bully works the same way. We must consciously and deliberately take control of the thoughts that pollute our well-being. They're just as automatic as checking on the time in a familiar location or the act of squeezing a tube of toothpaste.

As for Inner Bullies, they're merely the voice for those polluted thoughts. Brad is right: "Inner Bullies are the byproduct of programming. They're not real."

By consistently replacing repetitive thoughts that don't serve us with thoughts that do, our Inner Bully will start to fade and will finally become powerless over time. Keep in mind, however, that it's unrealistic to expect it to disappear completely. As life tosses some curve balls our way or when we get tripped up or hit a low point, it can and probably *will* resurface.

I told Brad to expect setbacks but to view them as temporary. Serious backsliding is impossible at this point because he's too aware – too awake to stay lost. Breakthroughs such as his – clear-eyed perception – cannot be reversed.

Overthrowing or toppling your Inner Bully requires practicing a new habit: taking the controls, if you will, while stationed in the command module. That's what I mean when I tell clients to "commandeer your brain's automatic operating system."

Let's dissect how I internally dealt with the whiteboard scenario. First came the triggering incident: the difficulty I had setting up the whiteboard. My Inner Bully reprimanded me for making Brad wait. I immediately felt the sting of shame, but in that fleeting second, I dismissed it because I knew that shame in this situation was a pile of nonsense. (There's a more descriptive word. Feel free to use it.) I recognized it as an archaic relic stemming from my early programming.

By catching my Inner Bully in the act, disbelieving it, understanding what was happening internally, and utilizing logic, I dismantled the shame and reduced my Inner Bully to the size of a pea. Within seconds it was transformed into something manageable and, therefore, rendered powerless to the point that I could casually talk about it with Brad. Yes, that voice will surface again, but each time I successfully derail it, it'll grow weaker and weaker. You, too, will experience the emergence of your True Self while simultaneously witnessing the diminishing power of your Inner Bully.

A book I frequently recommend to my clients is *You Are Not Your Brain* by Jeffrey Schwartz, M.D., and Rebecca Gladding, M.D. It adeptly shows readers how to rewire their brains and offers steps for ending those pesky, deceptive brain messages.

The Skinny on Brains

The circus we refer to as the brain
isn't what we should be identifying with.

—SALEE

I was walking – no, sleepwalking – in the gym one day when I became aware that I was doing a whole lot of judging. I judged people on how they looked, how they walked ... the list seemed infinite.

In the past, I would have been critical with myself for that sort of thing. Ironically, self-criticism is an act of judgment, too, so how is that okay? For the duration of that walk, I would have become guilt's hostage – or hostage to my Inner Bully, so to speak. Not anymore. I've come to understand that judging is a natural function of the brain. The judging function of our brains is connected to our survival instinct. Without it, we would be handicapped in our ability to navigate the world we live in.

In truth, it wasn't me doing the judging, it was my brain. As long as we have a brain, we'll be inclined to judge. Why?

Our brains are wired to compare, evaluate, and critique. So the tendency to judge is hardwired – innate. It's an activity our brains do constantly and automatically. We compare yesterday's weather with today's, we decide if it's a good idea to cross an intersection. We determine whether it's safe to approach a stranger standing on the corner, or a barking dog. *Should I eat that purplish food or not?*

So with all that said, the goal isn't to stop judging. We can't. Believing we can stop such an automatic process merely sets us up for lots of self-punishment. The realistic goal is to commandeer it. Take over. It's akin to tending to a small child. We monitor where she is going and what she is doing. When she's headed in the wrong direction we say, "Hold on. We're not going that way." She doesn't need to be punished, only redirected.

The truth is we need to disidentify with our brain. Remember, our True Self is the one observing the mental voice. In his book *The Power of Now*, Eckhart Tolle had this to say: "The beginning of freedom is the realization that you are not your mind – the thinker. The moment you start watching the thinker, a higher level of consciousness becomes activated."

So let's recap, shall we?

I was walking in the gym one day when I noticed that my brain was doing a whole lot of judging. It commented on how people looked, how they walked, the style of their shoes, you name it. I chalked it up to a brain operating in default mode. This objective observation allowed me to redirect my brain. A higher level of consciousness was activated, and those judgments toward others *and* myself were immediately replaced with acceptance and compassion. Nice, huh?

Before I understood how our brains work, I would notice the judging and then judge myself for judging. Knowledge about the brain has saved me from getting swept up in guilt and shame because I now understand that *I am not my brain!* The core me (my True Self) is separate from my brain.

From Bully to Cheerleader

Your will is stronger than
the habit of listening to that voice.

—MICHAEL SINGER

You're learning that negative self-talk is a habit, and habits are something we can break and replace with something better. It just takes practice.

When shopping for a new inner voice, keep in mind that it should be helpful, supportive, uplifting, positive, and nonjudgmental – without even the slightest hint of self-condemnation. If the voice is lacking those qualities, it isn't right.

For starters, I suggest you intentionally talk to yourself the same way you talk to those you care about and respect. Get into the practice of doing that. Deliberately converse with yourself – out loud if you like.

And remember: Practice makes permanent. When you make mistakes, use them as opportunities for being supportive and understanding toward yourself. Be comforting when you experience disappointment. Self-soothing when you experience anxiety or distress.

In his book *Chatter*, psychologist and neuroscientist Ethan Kross has some useful strategies for managing a negative inner voice. He has done extensive research on how we talk to ourselves. His findings show that having a nonstop inner voice is not only normal but can also be beneficial. His book provides help with shifting that voice from tormentor to ally/coach, and how to change the conversations we have with ourselves.

When Toni got caught in traffic and it dawned on her that she would be late, her self-talk could and should have been helpful, supportive, uplifting, positive, and nonjudgmental. A better internal dialogue would have gone like this: *You're okay. You did nothing wrong. This could happen to anyone and, remember, kind, heart-centered people get that. When you arrive at work, focus solely on those people. Ignore the rest. Just keep in mind, the negative people are not looking at things right. See them as visually impaired.*

My second suggestion is to use your favorite people as models. The ones who produce good feelings in you. This includes those from your past and those who are currently in your life. Borrow ideas from how they have talked to you and how they have talked to others.

You could also choose public figures or celebrities. Maya Angelou or Mr. Rogers would make excellent models. For example, when it comes to pursuing your dreams, your Inner Bully continuously discourages you from even trying. In contrast, your new Mr. Rogers voice will be warmly encouraging while declaring: "Never give up on your dreams."

Your Inner Bully also badgers you with humiliating criticisms, whereas your new Maya Angelou voice is warmly caring and understanding.

At the end of the day, your Inner Bully reminds you what a bad person you are, but your Mr. Rogers voice will have this to say: "You've made this day a special day, by just your being you. There's no person in the whole world like you, and I like you just the way you are."

Here's a sampling of how my inner voice has changed. Instead of calling myself 'stupid' or 'clueless,' I might say, "Salee, that was staggeringly mindless! What were you thinking!?" The difference? Rather than being self-condemning or tinged with shame, I've added a dollop of humor! By the way, humor vaporizes shame.

Wired for Guilt

Repeat this over and over:
guilt is part of my brain, but I'm not my brain.

~ SALEE

I posed the following question to a colleague: "What type of person do you think is more prone to have a problem with guilt?"

"Kind people," she replied. "People who care about others or if they were raised Catholic like me."

We had to laugh at that one.

Among the hundreds of clients I've seen over the years, those who were likely to have guilt-related issues also possess a warm heart. They seem to be innately caring. In fact, I don't know a single uncaring person who has ever suffered a case of the guilts. They don't seem to be hounded with self-condemning messages like: "That wasn't very nice," "You hurt her feelings," and "You let him down."

Perhaps there are people who are just naturally and biologically more guilt-prone than others. Is that possible? Could be. Just as there are people with an overactive thyroid gland, there could be something equivalent when it comes to guilt. Let's call it an overactive guilt gland.

I'm reasonably certain that guilt glands don't exist, although neuroscience *has* discovered a region in the brain showing increased activity when we feel guilt. That region is called the precuneus. The size of the precuneus varies among people. Findings suggest that the more guilt-prone you are, the larger the size. The opposite seems to be true, as well: those who lack a sense of guilt – as in psychopaths – possess a very small precuneus.

I'll leave it to the scientists to figure out what that all means. In the meantime, it remains clear to me that some people tend to have a punishing monopoly on guilt and shame. Am I a charter member of that club? Absolutely. Heck, I can struggle with guilt at the grocery store checkout when challenged with the question, "Paper or plastic?" I feel guilty about my stack of unread books, yet I'd feel guilty for taking the time to read them all.

What to do about such absurd bouts of guilt? Just laugh. Realize your brain is acting wacky, whatever size precuneus you may have. So celebrate your softness and sensitivity. But most importantly, accept your guilt as an outgrowth of your tender nature.

Chapter Ten

Ditch Perfection: Go Easy on Yourself

Let's repeat our mantra:
My Inner Bully cannot survive in a climate of self-love.

—SALEE

Imagine a roomful of babies all trying to perfect the skill of walking. There's a lot of falling down. But we don't have unrealistic expectations of babies. We don't scold them for failing in their attempts. Instead, we're warmly amused by the sight. That's how we should be with ourselves: warmly amused.

And if it weren't for our Inner Bullies we probably would be. They're notorious for making us feel bad about being imperfect and making mistakes. It's time we took a hard look at the facts. Don Miguel Ruiz, in his book *The Four Agreements*, suggests we borrow the perspective of the animal kingdom:

> *How many times do we pay for one mistake? The answer is thousands of times. The human is the only animal on Earth that pays a thousand times for the same mistake. The rest of the animals pay once for every mistake they make. But not us. We have a powerful memory. We make a mistake, we judge ourselves, we find ourselves guilty, and we punish ourselves. If justice exists, then that was enough; we don't need to do it again. But every time we remember, we judge ourselves again, we are guilty again, and we punish ourselves again, and again, and again. If we have a wife or husband, he or she also reminds us of the mistake, so we can judge ourselves again, punish ourselves again, and find ourselves guilty again. Is this fair?*

Of course not! Ask a child. They haven't yet been contaminated with the concept of "perfection." I remember hearing about an eight-year-old girl who painted a picture of a fabulous elephant. What made her elephant earn the distinction of being fabulous? All the colors! She used a generous assortment of unconventional colors!

Unfortunately, her teacher was saddled with an adult brain and was therefore incapable of seeing the fabulousness of that elephant. Instead of enjoying the unique creation, she felt it her duty to inform the little girl that elephants are not multi-colored.

Undaunted, the little girl had an immediate comeback: "You don't know elephants very well."

No, we adults don't know elephants very well. We don't know a lot of things very well because our perceptual filter is so narrow. Children, on the other hand, are not confined to a rigid idea of reality. They think outside the box. Not by choice, mind you. They simply do not see the box. In a child's mind, the box doesn't exist.

Perfection Is Pure Fiction

Adults, like the teacher, are expert box-builders. For some people the box is having a perfectly clean house, being an "A" student, or having a stellar career with an envious upward trajectory. Maybe the box is orderliness, having a perfect body, or accomplishing certain tasks perfectly. Perhaps the box is expecting a perfect performance from ourselves every time. This could apply to sports, the arts, cooking, or nailing a presentation at work.

One of the most common boxes we construct for ourselves is being the perfect parent.

Yes, the pressure on parents is great. Moms, especially, are guilt magnets. They're easy targets for nearly all the psychological ailments that may afflict their children – and our world, for that matter. Under the weight of such immense responsibility, why don't mothers just hide out in a cave somewhere? Who could fault them?

Hiding out in a cave – symbolically, anyway – is exactly what Denise did once her six children got out on their own. She shied away from family gatherings as much as possible because "I just can't bear hearing their stories about what I did wrong while they were growing up," as she explained. "I look forward to seeing everyone, but the next day I'm literally tortured by all the guilt!"

Denise said she knew her children didn't intend to make her feel bad because their stories were always expressed in a lighthearted manner. So the problem was Denise's harping Inner Bully. We spent a few sessions exploring that bully and where it originated, but one thing stood out. Our explorations revealed what many, many parents feel deep inside.

"I have this picture of what a perfect mother is supposed to be and do," she said with a sigh, "and I always fell short. Still do."

Denise's standards were horrendously unrealistic. And, as I pointed out, she was overlooking the fact that children have a marvelous capacity for bouncing back or rising above negative circumstances. It's called resiliency – a quality that is innately cultivated in an environment saturated with love.

After talking at length with Denise, I had become convinced that her children always sensed they were loved despite her imperfections. There were other clues as well. For example, when they got together as a family, the atmosphere was always jovial. They seemed to *want* to get together, and they seemed to *want* to be around their mom.

The presence of a guilty conscience is also a clear sign that a parent has a caring heart, even if the guilt is overblown. At the end of the day, Denise's kids always knew they mattered.

"Yes, I'm certain you made some mistakes as a parent," I said. "We all do. But it sounds to me like you parented primarily from a place of love."

I then shared a little theory of mine.

"Denise, if Mother Nature wanted perfection, we women would be having babies much later in life when we're wiser and more mature. Say at fifty-five, sixty, or even seventy."

She laughed.

Denise walked away from that session hundreds of pounds lighter. Later she wrote to tell me of her progress:

> I was able to invite my children to my home and actually enjoyed the experience! It was Mother's Day, and I felt such love for them, from them, and for myself. I realize that being a mother is a very difficult job for which we have no instruction manual. Wise people over the ages have said that pain is the path to spiritual strength. Today, I am feeling much less guilt, knowing they're strong and they've survived my less-than-perfect parenting skills ... and maybe even benefited from any pain I may have caused.

We can all find relief by realizing a single, startling fact: Perfection is unobtainable. Being driven by a pursuit of flawlessness is a futile and wasted effort. Think about it. Things are always falling apart, getting dirty, disappearing, dissolving, and running amok. We can't get everything right even if we try – at least not for long. We *will* have burnt toast, traffic delays, a losing score, botched recipes ... and of course, kids presenting unexpected challenges.

So here's some food for thought: Since imperfection seems to be built into the design, isn't it possible that it might even have a purpose?

To highlight that cosmic question, I'd like to quote the famed American author, Joseph Campbell: "Out of perfection nothing can be made."

We must train ourselves to ignore all these boxes. Our well-being and sense of self-worth *must* transcend the boxes.

What box are you building around your reality? Do you see the box you have created for yourself?

Ralph Waldo Emerson had some wise advice for his daughter, which I'll paraphrase here:

> *Finish every day and be done with it. You have done what you could. Some blunders and absurdities crept in; forget them as soon as you can. Tomorrow is a new day. You shall begin it serenely and with too high a spirit to be encumbered with your old nonsense.*

Chapter Eleven

Heed the Call to Self-Protect: It's How We love Ourselves

Our upbringing played a major role in compromising our self-loyalty; therefore it's imperative we revive it through the act of setting boundaries.

—Salee

Construct Some
Impressive Boundaries

It's pitiful that our Inner Bully's voice is often louder and more powerful than our natural instinct to look out for ourselves. And this seems to be especially true of women. "It's still somehow unacceptable in society to be a woman with boundaries, who says no as much as she says yes, who advocates for her own well-being and sets her own rules," says author Laura Jane Williams. She goes on to say that women remain uncomfortable "putting their needs first, or even suggesting they have needs in the first place." She's so right. And the end result is always, always some type of self-sabotage.

I'm thinking of Janelle. A friend of hers had been going through some trying times lately. "She needs someone to talk to," Janelle explained, "and I've been told I'm a good listener. So I've made myself available to her any time she needs me."

That's a nice, altruistic gesture, but there was a problem. Janelle was starting to feel weighed down by it all. She was experiencing burnout. That was understandable because at any time of the day, she could be interrupted by a phone call that might last up to forty-five minutes. For the most part, Janelle merely listened while her friend chatted on and on about, well, lots of things. "I'm becoming resentful," Janelle declared with a sigh, "and it's causing me to want to distance myself from her. What can I do?"

Janelle had reason to be concerned. If resentment is ignored, pushed down, and allowed to fester and build up, damage to the relationship is almost a certainty. Janelle was likely to start viewing her friend as *the enemy* and feel justified in unloading her stored-up anger.

Janelle's resentment stemmed from blaming her friend for what she felt powerless to do for herself: to make herself a priority by setting a boundary. Janelle's problem had very little to do with her friend. And it had everything to do with her own Inner Bully, who was busy peddling guilt while preying on Janelle's innate compassion. Janelle felt pushed to do what her Inner Bully told her was the morally "right" thing to do – even when it meant sacrificing her own well-being.

I helped Janelle see that she was projecting her Inner Bully onto her friend. "You believe that your friend is taking up your time or pressuring you when, in reality, the culprit is what?" I asked.

She responded with a single word: "Guilt."

I asked her another important question. "You've been told you're a good listener. Are you a good listener to *you*?"

That took her by surprise. "Probably not," she said with a sigh.

I went on to explain that resentment is a valuable signal rooted in self-preservation. "It's alerting you to set boundaries."

When Janelle reflected on what was driving her and questioned the logic behind it, she realized something. "Wait, my time is important to me, too!"

She was on to something. Time is one of the most valuable gifts we can give to ourselves. Janelle's need for time was just as precious as her friend's need to talk.

Janelle's next step entailed asking herself: *When do I want to be available to talk and for how long?* After brainstorming that for a while, she decided to give her friend small pieces of her time. So when her friend called, Janelle would inform her at the onset just how much time she had to spend on the phone. Guarding her boundary was the next challenge. So if the conversation started to run over, Janelle would say something like: "Oh, I just noticed the time ... it's time for me to go." She would then say her goodbyes and wish her friend well.

This strategy was a way of showing respect to her friend and to herself. It was the recipe for keeping a relationship intact and creating a win-win situation.

Resentment is only one of the discomforts that sounds an alarm and warns us that we're overextending or forsaking ourselves in some way. Our body also alerts us. Sometimes it manifests as a certain sick feeling in the pit of our stomach. Remember Lori? She was the nurse who habitually sacrificed her own needs and wants in nearly every arena of her life, not just in her role as a nurse. Her warning signs were exhaustion and grumpiness. But those symptoms were overridden by a tyrannical Inner Bully who accused her of being lazy and uncaring while relentlessly pushing her to give more of herself.

What should Lori have done? For starters, she needed to learn the wisdom behind grumpiness and exhaustion. The human body is an unparalleled tool for communicating what we need.

Young children, once again, are a model here. They don't seem to have a problem with asking for and giving themselves what they need. When they're tired, they take a nap. When they need to play, they play. When they need time by themselves, they take it.

And interestingly, when they're grumpy, they don't judge themselves for it. That comes later, after the programming phase of their life kicks in. When they're trained on how they "should" be and what they "should" feel guilty about.

Successful boundary-building necessitates listening to the truth of our feelings instead of listening to the programming that tells us how we should feel. It's important to note that there's nothing inherently wrong with being responsive to the needs of others. And there are times when real sacrifice is called for. But wisdom should be the driving force – not guilt.

With wisdom at the helm, we take into account the whole picture, including what's best for *our* well-being. Balance is the key. Compassion not only for the other person but for ourselves as well.

My own crankiness is a signal telling me I should feed Salee and put her to bed. I've learned over the years that fatigue and an empty stomach bring out my worst. The same happens if I surrender my power to "shoulds" and spread myself too thin. The result is a mixed brew of crankiness, resentment, and impatience. I suffer and so do those around me.

What this amounts to is that I'm no good for others or myself if I ignore what's right for me. Feeling bad about it and punishing myself with the guilts is wasted energy and remedies nothing. It's a whole lot smarter to just eat some nice cheese and go to bed.

Buddha put it perfectly when he said: "If your compassion does not include yourself, it is incomplete."

When we establish good personal boundaries we consistently and comfortably balance our needs with the needs of others. Yes, we continue to be there for others, but not to the point of compromising our well-being. The needs and desires of others simply should not overshadow our own. When someone requests something of us, we should always remain self-loyal.

Protection from External Bullies

Our soul recoils when exposed to something toxic.
It sounds a distress call that reverberates throughout
our very being and won't stop until we wake up.

—Salee

For the duration of your lifetime, you're assigned one person to fully watch over, to love unconditionally, and to envelop with constant caring and protection. That person you're commissioned to take care of is none other than you. So when someone crosses a line or poses a threat to your physical or psychological safety, your instincts sound an alarm. Listening to and honoring those instincts is an act of self-love.

Out for a walk one day, I was struck by how natural it is for animals to protect themselves from harm. Their survival instincts aren't cluttered with emotional logjams such as second-guessing, guilt, or denial. At the first sign of danger and without the slightest hesitation, birds take flight. Land critters like rabbits dash for safety. Birds and rabbits don't question – even for a second – their right to self-preservation. And the predators of the world have learned just how difficult it is to lay a paw on them. Why should we, more complex thinking creatures, be easier prey?

Clearly, birds and rabbits have something to teach us about boundaries.

The movie *As Good as It Gets*, starring Jack Nicholson as Melvin and Helen Hunt as Carol, is a good illustration of the importance of boundaries. One of Melvin's least desirable traits was verbal harshness. Without batting an eye, he would make a demeaning remark to anybody and at any time. Carol, the woman he was dating, was no exception. She endured insult after insult until she just couldn't take it anymore. One day she boldly confronted him with the truth of how she felt. "I don't think I want to know you anymore. You make me feel bad about myself."

How admirable! Her statement was a ballsy refusal to continue to let herself be a target of his verbal abuse. He had to change, or she was out of there.

Carol demonstrated how we must begin the journey of freeing ourselves from any toxic voice – inside or out. Her words bear repeating: "I don't think I want to know you anymore. You make me feel bad about myself." Essentially, she was saying: "You're a carrier of negative energy for me, and I don't want it polluting my joy anymore. So long."

Cassandra, a distressed client, once asked me, "Is it okay to skip being nice to people who mistreat you?"

"It's more than okay, Cassandra!"

I gave her the lowdown on birds and the rabbits while highlighting that we're supposed to be resolute – obsessed, even – about protecting ourselves.

Cassandra possessed weak boundaries because they were discouraged when she was a young child. Her older brother was often mean to her but her parents did nothing. In fact, they excused it, saying something along the lines of "boys will be boys." In contrast, she was taught that girls should always be nice. This meant she wasn't allowed to object loudly or react spontaneously with anger. She didn't feel free to yell, "Stop it!" She had to stay nice.

Consequently, she learned to doubt the accuracy of her own feelings.

Because we're drawn to what seems familiar and natural to us, we tend to surround ourselves with people who psychologically resemble those from our past. So, not surprisingly, Cassandra was married to a man who treated her like her brother did. And instead of objecting to his hurtful behavior, she took it. The result was a dampened spirit and constant knots in her stomach. There were times when she entertained thoughts of leaving him, but those thoughts soon died out. "I'd feel guilty leaving him," she said in a somber tone. "I can't hurt him. He doesn't have any friends."

"Of course he doesn't have any friends," I countered. "Making and keeping friends requires being kind!"

It would have been more appropriate for Cassandra to feel insulted rather than guilty.

Before getting married, Cassandra always seemed to date men who were similar.

"How do I end up with this type of guy?" she asked. "Am I some kind of magnet for users and abusers?"

"No, you're not a magnet," I assured her. "It's just that you force yourself to endure too much. If you were an enlightened butterfly, you wouldn't hang around after the third or fourth uncaring comment." *Huh??* was written all over her face, so I gave her the scoop on butterflies.

I explained that an enlightened butterfly is incredibly smart. She may land – accidentally – on some inhospitable spot, but soon after seeing how toxic it is, she takes off. On the other hand, an unenlightened butterfly hangs around far too long. The negative energy of the place has a poisoning effect on her spirit, and before long her existence is one of despair and joylessness.

The moral: A smart butterfly doesn't force herself tolerate the intolerable. On the other hand, a not-so-smart butterfly settles for inhospitable conditions.

Cassandra sustained a blank facial expression for a few more seconds, but I could tell her wheels were spinning. Suddenly, something sparked new life into that girl! She flashed me a knowing smile, signaling that she got the connection. "Okay! I get it," she announced boldly. "Now, how do I become one of those smart butterflies?"

Cassandra was ready to dump her unenlightened butterfly status. "You need to begin listening to yourself," I replied. "When you feel emotionally assaulted, own that feeling," I continued. "Don't ignore or explain it away. Don't make excuses for him, and especially don't feel sorry for him. Feel sorry for you!"

In the weeks ahead, Cassandra and I worked on boundary-building. As we proceeded, the words of the acclaimed poet, Walt Whitman, served as a fitting backdrop:

Re-examine all that you have been told . . .
dismiss that which insults your soul

As for reading material, I recommended a book I would love to hand out on street corners. It's called *The Nice Girl Syndrome* by Beverly Engel. Cassandra befriended that book. In fact, she couldn't put it down.

Listen to Your Gut, Not Your Guilt

The pain you feel is a message. Listen to it.

—RUMI

Casandra's first step in boundary-building began by tuning in to her gut. Just as our nose tells us when we encounter a foul odor, our gut does something similar. Some consider it a reliable source of factual information, over and above the intellect. Here's Deepak Chopra's take on why that's the case: "You can trust your gut more because gut cells haven't yet learned how to doubt their own thinking."

Hmmm. I'm wondering if our gut is more attuned to our soul than our brain is.

It's important to be in touch with our feelings as they are occurring. Keeping the switch on, not off, allows us to be aware of any psychological distress we might be experiencing – a necessity if we're to erect effective guardrails (boundaries) for protection.

I explained to Cassandra that setting boundaries is essential to self-care. They're like the locks on our doors. We're careful who we let in. For example, we wouldn't hesitate to ban an alligator from entering our home. It would be insanely dangerous to do otherwise. The same logic holds true when it comes to unfriendly human beings.

I urged her to never let put-downs, name-calling, insults, and nasty accusations go unchecked. Instead, nip them in the bud. To allow even one zinger past your threshold sends a message that the offender is welcome to dish out more. I suggested she stand tall and say, "Each time you treat me like that, it drives me further away."

The really important question isn't why she attracts men who are unkind and inconsiderate. The more important question is, *Why does she stay once they reveal their true colors?*

We should reject those who deflate our spirit. We owe it to ourselves. Author Laura Jane Williams has some worthy advice along those lines: "If a friendship makes you feel unmotivated, smaller than you are, or downright crappy about yourself, then nobody said it had to be forever."

Remember Carol, Melvin's girlfriend in the movie *As Good as It Gets?* She demonstrated something worth noting. When we tune in to our feelings instead of sweeping them under the rug, we set in motion a revolution of sorts. We stop being compliant and start caring and advocating for ourselves. We become our own ally.

You Need Your Anger ... Go Hug It

*People pleasing has probably
made you a stranger to your anger.*
—HARRIET BRAIKER, *THE DISEASE TO PLEASE*

Your anger tells you what you're *really* feeling and what you're *really* thinking. Your anger brings you home to you. You need it. It releases you from the grip of self-compromise, and it reveals what lies beneath the socially conditioned roles – the "acceptable" veneers and behaviors you've mistakenly grown to identify with.

145

And it's absolutely vital for creating barriers against the things that harm, undermine, and limit you.

As I alluded to before, being aware of every single one of our emotions is a prerequisite for setting boundaries. Just as a conductor of an orchestra needs every instrument in the ensemble, we need every emotion in order to be whole and fully expressive. It's impossible to take down an Inner Bully – or any bully, for that matter – by being only half a person.

Your two-year-old self is playing *all* the instruments. That's good, but two-year-olds also throw tantrums and fail to exercise constraint when it comes to their angry impulses. That's not admirable. It's important to discern the difference between being in touch with our feelings of anger and acting on that anger. The person who is solidly in control channels their anger in ways that align with their principles and higher values. They know there's nothing courageous about uncontrolled and unchecked anger just as they know there's nothing courageous about playing small.

Typically, anger is viewed as a negative and dark emotion. Certainly it's a far cry from warm and fuzzy. Yep, anger's not welcoming, not like happiness and love are. So is anger innately negative and destructive? No. It all depends on what we do with it. The same is true of fire. If we're not careful someone may get burned, but otherwise it can be immensely beneficial. Is fire innately bad? Far from it. And neither is anger. Just like fire, anger can light the way. And that's what we need it for. It can assist us as we move through life.

Karla McLaren, in her book *The Language of Emotions*, states it wonderfully:

If I were to personify anger, I would describe it as a mix between a stalwart castle sentry and an ancient sage. Anger sets your boundaries by walking the perimeter of your soul and keeping an eye on you, the people around you, and your environment. If your boundaries are broken (through the insensitivity of others, or in any other way), anger comes forward to restore your sense of strength and separateness.

A sentry is a soldier standing guard, on the lookout for anything that may pose a threat. You need your sentry for strength and protection. So when you squelch your anger, you simultaneously squelch that sentry of yours. That makes you vulnerable and defenseless against the bullies – those on the outside and that one big one on the inside.

Your ability to sense your anger may have been stifled early in life. Like many children, you may have developed deep shame for feeling angry and concluded that it's best to sever ties with that emotion. You learned to stuff it deep inside.

Such attempts fail miserably. There are studies on bottled-up anger and how it impacts our mental and physical health.

The shame associated with anger is created because grownups typically view an angry child as misbehaving. They say the child is trying to be difficult. Instead of approaching the child's anger with curiosity and compassion, the caregivers may scold or spank the angry child.

Interestingly, the Buddhists believe that suffering is at the root of anger. Therefore, a more appropriate response to anger, including our own, is tenderness.

Sadly, many adults don't understand that children lack the capacity to explain what they're feeling. If their child is upset about something, that child simply does not know how to talk about it. Anger is often their only means of expressing complex emotions like a sense of injustice or feeling misunderstood or disconnected. Anger is a normal response to loss for all of us when things aren't the way we want them to be.

One client expressed a prevalent problem: "When I get angry, I'm unable to identify why." How can we control and direct what we don't understand? That's why it's vital that young children begin the process of learning how to identify, understand, manage, channel, and ultimately talk about their anger. But they need a listening ear for that to happen. They can't learn it if the adults around them are shaming, rejecting, and reacting angrily themselves. When that happens, their growth in that area gets stunted.

Parents deserve a break here. In most cases, they're merely passing down a pattern they experienced and observed while growing up. They may not know how to respond appropriately to their child's anger. That makes sense because, more often than not, tenderness toward *themselves* – especially when it comes to their anger – is totally foreign to them. A great resource for teaching kids how to identify their feelings and express them appropriately can be found at verywellfamily.com.

Embrace Your Fierce Side

The essence of fierceness is empowerment and resoluteness – the exact opposite of succumbing, surrendering, and diminishing. It's your spark and your will in full throttle mode.

—SALEE

Controlling the destructive elements of your anger is a worthy objective, but you should never ever give up your capacity to be fierce. I think that's what Maya Angelou was alluding to when she said, "I've learned that you shouldn't go through life with a catcher's mitt on both hands; you need to be able to throw something back." Your fierce side is you being a little bit prickly and a little bit feisty when necessary. It's important to know how and when to get pissed off. With that said, see yourself walking arm in arm with your sentry. I call that fiercely showing up for yourself.

Kari, as you recall from Chapter Four, had been raised to be "a nice girl." Her fierce side had been stifled eons ago. She was agreeable and compliant with just about everybody. And although pleasing people was draining and robbed her of the things she wanted to do with her time, she just couldn't bring herself to say no. To her, "no" was a four-letter word, and using it would trigger a severe Inner Bully attack – way too much for her to endure. That bully of hers wouldn't hesitate to tell her how selfish she was and then proceed to fling a few more choice labels her way. Ironically, her Inner Bully was scarier than the mistreatment she endured from the people around her.

Her boyfriend took full advantage of her tendency to invalidate herself. Month after month, he neglected to pay his portion of the rent. It infuriated Kari, even affecting her sleep, but she couldn't bring herself to confront him about it.

The problem remained stuck in a holding pattern for months. Meanwhile, her irritation was mounting, and at some point she came out swinging. Guess what? Kari discovered that the world wouldn't end if she got pissed off. On that day, Kari embraced her fierce side. Kari was able to reunite with her two-year-old self on the spot. That fierce part inside of all of us – before getting submerged by our upbringing – knows full well how to say no.

Months later Kari gave me a progress report. "I'm still with the same person, but I'm not in the same relationship." She explained that she had greater respect for herself, which spawned greater respect from Paul. He held up his end by paying his share of the rent each month.

"I'm no longer a pushover," she explained. "I stand my ground, and I can easily say no and confront him when I need to, without instantly thinking I'm being mean."

Wonderful. Kari is no longer a pushover, and she's no longer half a person, either. That's huge.

But there's more. Kari's ability to fiercely show up for herself had very little to do with her relationship with her boyfriend and everything to do with her relationship with her Inner Bully. In fact, that entire no-longer-a-pushover statement could and *did* apply directly to her Inner Bully. She would not have been capable of standing up to her boyfriend had she not first stood up to her Inner Bully. She had to conquer her susceptibility to that one menacing oppressor hanging out in her head first.

What changed? She quit viewing her bully as an objective authority on what she should or shouldn't do – or even on how to think. Consequently, she stopped listening and deferring to it. She told me that she taps into another authority figure. "It's higher, kinder, and wiser," she said, and it renders her Inner Bully null and void.

"It's my higher power," she explained. "I've come to see that my first impulse – my default – is to feel guilty." Instead of being controlled by that automatic impulse, she developed a new habit. "I pause, take a minute to step away, and I simply pray. I use that calmer space – that spiritual space – as my new compass."

For more information about boundaries, check out Vicki Tidwell Palmer's podcast titled *Beyond Bitchy Podcast: Mastering the Art of Boundaries*. In addition to explaining just what boundaries are and how they look, she emphasizes that setting them is not a hostile act waged against another person. Not at all. In fact, it's not even about another person. It's what you're doing for you. It's about self-care.

Even if it *is* related to how you're being treated by another person, boundaries are not inherently offensive and aggressive in nature.

Your boundary need not be an angry electric fence
that shocks those who touch it. It can be a consistent light
around you that announces: I will be treated sacredly.

—JAIYA JOHN

Your Body Knows Some Things

You met Rae earlier. Her family had planned her birthday celebration at a restaurant that didn't have the kind of food that was right for her. Rather than speak up, she merely went along. Not only was her birthday a big letdown, but she also suffered physically because the food she ate didn't agree with her.

Fast forward a year. Her birthday looked entirely different because she made her wishes known. What changed? Rae didn't let unhealthy guilt block her from being true to herself.

"My problem had always been feeling guilty for saying no," she said. "But I'm now realizing that such a mind-space doesn't have to be my normal. In fact, I've come to see that saying no is saying yes to my truth."

Feeling guilty – about anything – was familiar territory for Rae. Her mother's ongoing criticisms and shaming messages had taken their toll. Instead of feeling cherished by her mother, "I felt like an object," she said, "unseen and worthless. I wasn't supposed to have emotional needs. It was all about my mom and her feelings and *her* needs."

How did Rae cope? "I would do anything to shove down those painful feelings," she said. "I would overeat and a slew of other things that I would later regret, like people-pleasing, being overly nice, or pushing myself to be perfect. But now I know when I do those things that I'm disowning myself and sacrificing my power."

When I first started working with Rae, she was incapable of that much self-awareness. Her True Self was overshadowed by a horde of adapting and appeasing behaviors. To a large extent, she was estranged from herself. She wasn't even sure what *she* really felt, or what *she* really thought or what *she* really wanted in any given situation. Bottom line, she wasn't home!

The journey that finally led to honoring herself and choosing a restaurant of her own liking began with unearthing her True Self.

Along with the work she and I had done together, she also received help from a somatic therapist*, who focused on how emotions felt in Rae's body. Through body awareness work, that therapist helped her reconnect with her toddler self – that part of her that was fully aware of what she really felt, what she really thought, and what she really wanted. She not only learned how to tune into her body's signals but she also learned how to interpret them.

"When I feel obligated to do something," she said, "I'm aware of my body tensing up. I feel a resistance, a kind of dread – even revulsion. There's wisdom in our bodies if only we learn to tap into it."

Other physiological cues that we can learn to recognize and respond to include accelerated or shallow breathing, increased heart rate, knotty feelings, a lump in the throat, and sweaty palms. Any of these physical sensations can point to internal distress. And mindfulness, as an enhanced state of awareness within, allows you to detect all physiological cues.

Rae had more to say. "When we feel pushed, we naturally feel irritated, whether we're aware of it or not. It's important to tune in to that irritation. It's telling us something. A year ago, I was irritated with the idea of going to a restaurant that didn't appeal to me. But I wasn't aware of that irritation at the time."

We hinder our ability to access an invaluable internal compass when we're disconnected from our body or our emotions. I compare it to flying a plane in the dark … while blind!

It brings to mind something my husband once said: "If I'm feeling discomfort or irritated, something is trying to reveal itself." The same is true of guilt feelings. Rae expressed it perfectly not long ago. "I'm learning that I need to lean into my guilt instead of run from it. It's a red flag that tells me I'm not loving myself."

I like that. The use of guilt as a sensory device, a gauge for measuring the degree of love we have for ourselves.

For more information on somatic therapy, see inner-healing. com/somatic.htm, *hosted by F. Michael Montgomery, LCSW, LMFT*

Chapter Twelve

Roadblocks:
Why We Stay and Endure

*Daring to set boundaries is about
having the courage to love ourselves,
even when we risk disappointing others.*

—BRENÉ BROWN

We are hardwired to sense toxins both physically and psychologically, and this means we have instincts we should honor. Those instincts protect us from eating spoiled food, stepping out in front of traffic, and getting close to a raging dog. It's how we stay safe. But there's a problem. While avoiding spoiled food, highway traffic, and raging dogs doesn't produce much guilt, if any, avoiding people who have a toxic effect on us is another matter. Especially if a heavy-handed Inner Bully is standing in the wings ready to lay a huge guilt-trip on us.

Merely describing someone as "toxic" – even if it's well-deserved – can result in a hefty case of self-recrimination. That internal bully of ours wastes no time in accusing us of being unkind, unfair, unloving, and judgmental. Once the Inner Bully weighs in, choosing to distance ourselves from such people doesn't feel like a precautionary measure rooted in self-care. Instead it feels like cruelty. Sadly, our guilt over that causes us to question the very instincts that were designed to serve us.

The problem is magnified when we're dealing with relatives, friends, or a person we are married to or in a relationship with. That's because we also have another emotion to contend with: grief. Backing away from someone we love or care about can be extremely painful. Fears and self-doubt also make it hard. So we stay and endure. Enduring, however, is never a good plan because an unhealthy pattern never improves on its own.

Even if we get good at speaking up and advocating for ourselves, change is not guaranteed. The sobering truth is that no matter how hard we try, we can't convert another person into a more positive version of themselves. Deep down we know this to be true, but we tend to forget. We simply cannot make someone become less toxic. They have to want to change.

Our Inner Bully would have us believe otherwise. It tells us that it's our fault they're not nicer, and that we're ultimately responsible for bringing out the best or the worst in that other person. So what do we do? We bend over backward to make things right. We subdue, suppress, and succumb. And if we fail at that, we feel compelled to alter ourselves and appease even more.

It never works. In fact, continuing to go along to get along with a person who has a toxic effect on us merely gives that person the green light. It reminds us – again – just how inept guilt is at directing our thoughts and actions. Guilt is simply an inferior mechanism for dealing with life.

Placating another person is a form of self-desertion, and it carries with it a colossal price. We lose ourselves, which can only result in our feeling unhappy and empty inside. For some, this may tip over into depression. It's miserable, but it's often the very thing that forces us to stop and look truth squarely in the face.

Dr. Alan Godwin, the psychologist I mentioned earlier, would probably shout this from the rooftops: "Stop all your appeasing, pleasing, and self-blaming." He would then proceed to explain that there are people who are just plain difficult to deal with.

In a seminar of Dr. Godwin's I attended, he pointed out that the world is populated by two groups of people: those who can be reasoned with and those who can't ... or won't.

Ever been around someone who makes you question your sanity because there's no working things out? Any attempt to reason with them fails miserably. Nothing works. Presenting facts doesn't work. Even staying composed doesn't work. Those hair-pulling moments can reduce an otherwise stable person to a pitiful pile of frustration and self-doubt in a flash.

On the other hand, those who *can* be reasoned with, he says, possess three psychologically healthy traits. They self-observe, self-monitor, and self-correct. That means they're willing to take an honest look at themselves. They *want* to know their flaws, and they *want* to monitor them. They admit to being wrong, and readily take responsibility for their actions and shortcomings. Then they go that next step – they make things right. Godwin says that when such people see their wrongness, they *cringe*. Call it a healthy dose of feeling ashamed of oneself. It's a response rooted in a fully developed conscience and demonstrates the presence of a strong moral core. They cringe when they violate their own personal standards and principles.

The opposite of cringing, Godwin says, is shrugging. Shrugging is an indicator of a poorly developed or missing conscience. You can spot a shrugger by their "so what?" attitude and general lack of empathy.

Godwin states loud and clear: "If personal wrongness doesn't bother us, we'll do nothing to correct it." So true. In fact, we may deny its existence, gloss it over with elaborate excuses, or simply shrug it off. It's more than apparent that shruggers don't care about the quality of the footprint they leave on the landscape of humanity.

So here we are, finding ourselves living among cringers and shruggers – reasonable and unreasonable people. It's good to know the difference, especially for those of us who believe we will be understood if we just try hard enough. We can delude ourselves into thinking that logic and common sense will inevitably transform any feud or misunderstanding into a harmonious state of connection, compromise, and appreciation.

That's all true – if you're dealing with a reasonable person. But, as Godwin says, "You can't reason with unreasonable people."

It's also helpful to know that unreasonable people are chronologically older than their developmental age. That is, you may be trying to communicate with a twelve-year-old who's walking around in a forty-year-old's body. Your attempts to reason can only go so far. With that in mind, it's advisable to have realistic expectations.

How to know if you're in the presence of a reasonable versus an unreasonable person? You'll know the reasonable ones by their willingness to hear contrary opinions. They welcome feedback and are open to changing how they see and do things. When wrong, they show remorse and apologize.

Reasonable people embrace truth. They don't deny or distort it. Godwin says, "It may be painful to acknowledge wrongness, but they'll do so because being truthful has a higher value to them than being right."

In contrast, if you try to talk to an unreasonable person, they're likely to distort the meaning of your words and not allow you to correct any misinterpretation. They make a habit of interrupting or hearing only what they want to hear. Being right and winning is all they care about. Enhancing a climate of mutual cooperation, problem-solving, and goodwill isn't even on their radar.

Blaming is a characteristic of unreasonable people. When they argue, Godwin says, "they play the 'blame game,' absolving themselves of responsibility and attributing exclusive blame to the other side."

What to do about these people? Godwin suggests we avoid them when we can, and if that's not possible, establish firm boundaries. This entails distancing ourselves emotionally and accepting the fact that our relationship with them will be limited – lacking depth and a level of intimacy that accompanies open and honest sharing between two people.

"I Don't Like to Cause Pain!"

When we protect people from experiencing pain,
we're really not acting in their best interest.

—SALEE

When I asked Kim why she stayed with a man who put her down, lied, and was one hundred percent self-absorbed, her answer was simply: "I don't like to cause people pain."

"What's the good side of pain?" I asked. "How is it a good thing?" That made zero sense to her, so I asked: "Have you ever had a pebble in your shoe?"

She nodded and recalled a day when she wore a pair of sneakers without socks and how uncomfortable it was. "I'll never do that again!" she said.

"Okay, so the pain you felt taught you something, right?"

"Definitely! It taught me to always wear socks," Kim said laughing. But suddenly her levity came to an abrupt halt as her eyes narrowed in speculation. "Ah, I see where you're going with this."

I continued. "Would you say you've been preventing him from learning a valuable lesson?"

She gave an exasperated sigh. "I'm preventing him from learning that he can't treat people badly and still expect them to stay around."

"Very true," I said. "You could say you're in the way of his soul growth, right?"

"Absolutely!" she said. "I'm not holding him accountable. I'm letting him get away with things."

"Let him feel the pain," I advised. "It's fodder for his growth. How else is he going to grow a heart?"

Not long after that particular session, Kim told me she had made the decision to end the relationship. This is what she told him: "I'm distancing myself not because I want to hurt you, but because my own peace and sense of joy demand it."

The Jenny and Joey Story

When we deny people our honesty,
we deny them the opportunity to grow.

—TAVIS SCHLUNDT, CLINICAL SOCIAL WORKER

Several years ago, I made up a story about boundaries. Imagine a classroom of small children, crayons in hand, each thoroughly absorbed in their own drawings. Jenny is sitting beside Joey, and at some point, he reaches over with his crayon and marks on her paper. Jenny objects, "No Joey!"

while pushing his hand away. He stops, briefly, then repeats the offense. Again Jenny protests but this time she grabs her paper and briskly moves to another spot in the room.

This scenario would have played out quite differently had Jenny been instilled with the directive to always "be nice." In this case, she would have wilted when Joey marked on her paper and let him have free rein. Believing that objecting is hurtful, she would be ruled by restraint. Striving to be nice is a worthy ethic to teach children, but it should be a two-way ethic.

Niceness should run both ways. Jenny should be nice to others, but she should also hold the belief that the very same virtue applies to everyone else as well. Joey wasn't being nice, and that shouldn't be overlooked.

Jenny's actions preserved her well-being and dignity, but she also did Joey a favor. She gave him the opportunity to learn an important lesson: "If I mistreat people, I'll alienate them. They won't want to be around me."

Had Jenny folded and submitted to Joey's will and disrespect, she would have sent the opposite message. It's an almost inescapable fact: we humans don't grow when others are placating or pretending to go along with us. We have no reason to.

The best mirrors we have available are the authentic responses given by other people. It's not always easy to look at ourselves through the eyes of others. It can be painful, but some deeper, truer part of ourselves finds it gratifying to be shown the truth.

Confronting isn't hurtful if done correctly. Being enlightened by truth is quite different from being punctured by it.

When Jenny expressed her annoyance, she wasn't being hurtful. If Joey was hurt, he was hurt by the truth, not by Jenny.

Divorce Guilt

Beth and her husband inhabited a tomb called their marriage. It was as cold and lifeless as a mausoleum's marble walls. Although they coexisted in physical proximity of each other, they rarely uttered a word. Their relationship was characterized by detachment and indifference. Long ago they had given up occupying the same bed – even the same bedroom.

Was it a marriage? Legally, yes. Emotionally, no. One could say they'd been psychologically divorced for a very long time.

Beth came to see me because she could no longer endure the life she was living. She wanted a divorce. "I'm lonely in my own house," she said, fighting back the tears.

The gap between them became painfully apparent to Beth after their children left home. At that point, she realized something. "We're not companions," she said with a heavy sigh. "We live separate lives." They continued to do things as a couple, but Beth described it as window dressing. "There's no life in what we do together."

As we talked more, Beth revealed that she hasn't felt love for her husband for some time. It was hard for her to admit that. She sat quietly for a long time, just staring down at the floor with a pained expression. When she spoke again, she made a profound point: "How empty it is to stay with someone just because you feel sorry for them."

Why didn't she cut the cord and seek a more enriching life? "I can't bear the thought of hurting him," she said.

Here's the strange irony: Beth *was* hurting him by living dishonestly. Maintaining the illusion that all is well – merely going through the motions – is a form of deceit.

"If he knew how you truly felt, would he want to stay married?" I asked.

"That's a really good question," she said. "I've never thought of it that way."

"If the relationship is no longer rewarding for you," I continued, "it can't be rewarding for him either."

It was important for Beth to view things through a broader lens. I pointed out that since she couldn't be what she wasn't and couldn't feel what she didn't, she should love him enough to release him to pursue more gratifying connections with other people. It is, perhaps, a higher form of love.

I emphasized that we hold our partner hostage when we stay in the relationship because we feel we should. Yes, it would be painful for him, but better to experience the pain of truth than to go on living a make-believe existence. Fantasy doesn't nourish – it leaves us empty and unfulfilled.

I explained that life resembles a flowing stream in which change is an inevitable fact of life. Nothing stays put, even if we would like it to.

"You're blameless ... and so is he," I assured her. "You two have grown apart, a natural byproduct of change."

"What do I tell him?" Beth asked, her voice cracking.

I suggested that she warmly convey her truth along with her heart's regret. "You didn't anticipate or plan for this to happen," I said. "Something in you shifted. You're not the same person you were twenty or so years ago. It's something you hadn't counted on. Tell him that."

Ideally, Beth and her husband would not only have a long-overdue heart-to-heart about their marriage but they'd also join hands and grieve together. It isn't easy saying goodbye to a person you've been sharing your life with for several years. You've built things together, and typically this includes forming a family. You've had experiences that have become a part of you. There have been frustrating and painful moments, but there have been endearing moments as well.

Nope, divorce isn't easy – it's damned hard. The divorce experience has been likened to experiencing a death, and rightfully so. I understand that. I've been there.

Along with the heavy grief and distress associated with divorce, your Inner Bully hounds you about being self-centered, hurtful, and cruel. It also accuses you of giving up, even if you've exhausted all efforts to revive a lifeless marriage.

Some people struggle because they think that divorce is synonymous with failure. When I hear that from a client, I counter it with this: A failed marriage is one in which you cannot detect the many gifts it has brought you – the ways it has enriched your life and your soul.

Chapter Thirteen

Perceive Your Parents Through Fresh Eyes

*Oh, how humorous it is to be affected
most of our lives by people who were
afflicted with a bad case of tunnel vision.*

—Salee

You grow up and grow free the day you realize your parents had problems with their vision. They weren't seeing you when they labeled, discounted, or distorted you. They were submerged in the fog of their own programming, childhood experiences, and assorted woundedness. And perhaps they still are.

Emily loved her father but had to limit the amount of time she spent with him because she found it toxic to be in his presence for long periods of time.

"My light gets put out," she said. "I get drawn into his darkness."

Her father hibernated in a cocoon of good versus evil, shame, judgment, and condemnation. He believed that in order to appease a condemning God, people must be punished with shame – starting at a very early age. That's what happened to Emily.

"I can't be around that," she said. "It's crippling emotionally."

Emily had given up the idea of opening his eyes. "I don't think he can see outside his reality. He can't see me," she said. "He's lost in his darkness, pinched off from his light. It's sad."

Emily's father was *pinched off* from his *True Self*. Like all of us, his early training and life experiences influenced and colored his ideas and perceptions. Even years later they continue to poison his mind, push people away, and deny him an interior experience of joy. That *is* sad.

This brings to light a fundamental truth: A particular person may have a toxic impact on us, but inherently, they're not toxic. Like Emily's father, their interaction style is a product of their upbringing. Most people are innocent and oblivious, lacking any ill intent.

Viewing her father through this broader lens, and the sadness she felt for him, was a significant step in Emily's healing journey. It meant she was able to rise above his effect on her. Guilt was less and less a magnetic force keeping her connected to him – instead, love was.

This doesn't suggest that she could or should have endured his toxicity. She needed a boundary. One aspect of that boundary, she realized, was reducing her exposure to him. She had also been speaking up more and saying what was on her mind, including objecting when he related to her in a rude or insensitive manner.

She offered an example, then shared her new insight. "He was shaming me the same way he would when I was ten." Instead of wilting or just sitting and taking it, she called him out. "I told him that shaming me wasn't okay thirty years ago and it isn't okay today."

Wow! You could say she had just earned her black belt in assertiveness. Not only that, standing her ground was a clear sign that she was making some headway in freeing herself from her Inner Bully. Being bold and brave with all outer bullies translates to being bold and brave with your Inner Bully.

How did he respond? He excused it away, saying he was "coming out of love."

Emily's powerful response: "Dad, being loving is building someone up, not tearing them down." He had no words.

The wonderful news: she was seeing progress. He seemed to be catching himself when he was about to make a caustic remark, and he was being more respectful toward her.

That's what happens when we set boundaries. It tells the other person: *I'm not playing by the same old rules. I'm changing my dance step. Such a stance invariably disrupts* the status quo. It breaks a pattern, and that causes the other person to stop and take notice. Remember the old expression: It takes two to tango. Oftentimes, if there's any hope that our loved one might begin a metamorphosis, it lies in us making the first move. We must change up the dance.

In considering a course of action, we may believe we're being selfish if we lean in the direction of what feels right for us. But nothing could be further from the truth. In reality, we simultaneously honor the higher self and path of the other person when we honor our own.

For exact guidelines and an abundance of examples on being assertive, standing firm, and staying true to yourself – and in a non-attacking or rude way! – I highly recommend the book *Recovering from Emotionally Immature Parents* by Lindsay Gibson.

Question Your Parents' Objectivity

We must move beyond the need
to have imperfect beings perceive us perfectly!
—SALEE

Thirty-two-year-old Tricia felt like one of life's mistakes. "I'm not what my mother wanted," she said. "She wanted me to be a powerful, independent, millionaire woman." Tricia's voice was quivering. "Instead, I'm nothing but a screwup and a loser!"

Unfortunately, at an earlier point in her life, she decided that her mother was right. "I'm a worthless drifter," she said.

Tricia had always wanted to become an interior decorator, but she lacked the confidence. Like countless others, she bought into an opinion and made it the truth.

"Tricia," I said, "don't let your mom's blindness define who you are."

Tricia wasn't alone. Hers is a universal problem.

. . .

When I first started seeing Trent, twenty-eight, suicide was on his mind. He had just experienced a string of losses that included a lost job, a loss of income, and the end of a relationship. Trent was gay, and the man he was dating had just broken up with him.

Trent didn't see much point in going on. To him, his life was over. He described himself as a "shameful failure in every way."

"When did *that* seed first get planted?" I asked.

"I'm fairly certain my dad hated me all my life," he said. "I could never measure up. I was one disgusting disappointment to him."

Being gay didn't help matters. Trent was in grade school when his father noticed that Trent wasn't like *other* boys. Homosexuality was something he just wasn't going to tolerate.

When describing his father, Trent used terms like judgmental, rejecting, ridiculing, and physically abusive. His siblings endured the same treatment to some extent, but not to the same degree as Trent. Any sense of being loved unconditionally came from his mom. He felt the shelter of her love on many occasions.

After college, Trent was determined to make his dad proud, so he worked hard to become successful – but on his dad's terms. "That meant earning a lot of money," Trent explained.

He *was* "successful" – briefly. Then the bottom fell out, along with the dream of making his dad "proud."

As is often the case, I felt that the best way to help Trent was to tackle his distorted thinking. Namely, about himself.

"Are you really the way your father sees you?" I asked. "Does he really know you?"

Lowering his head he said: "I – I couldn't say that he does."

"Then quit living as if what he says is true," I said. "You're the authority on you, he's not."

Since Trent was suicidal and at risk, I had to get straight to the heart of the matter in our first session. This is what I conveyed to him in so many words: Your father is actually good for you in developing stamina and a sense of dignity about yourself. You can't leave us yet. You have something to show your dad. He needs to see that you're bigger than his narrow opinion of you, and that you've overcome his spirit-crushing treatment. Your soul needs that and so does his.

Trent was challenged to love and accept himself despite his father's narrowness. That is to say, he needed to do something I recommend for anyone who doubts their value: Question your parents' objectivity.

"Your opinion of you should far outweigh his opinion of you," I said. "And someday, when you're old and gray, lying on your deathbed, you can look back and celebrate what you have overcome and say – with peace and utter conviction – I won!"

Trent got there! In the months after that, he successfully shifted from self-loathing to self-acceptance. The last I heard, he was running his own business and his relationship with his dad had improved significantly. Not because Trent was enjoying business success but because he got open and honest with his dad.

Here's the letter he sent his dad that kick-started a much overdue dialogue between them:

> *Dad: treat your children with respect and get to know the people they are. Show some interest in the people your kids have become and be proud of them, no matter what they do or how they behave, even if that is different from what you would do. Don't be afraid to tell them they are loved and that you are proud of them. They need to hear that.*

To me, being successful is the ability to take life's problems and struggles and use them to escort yourself to some better place. Trent did just that by coming to realize that his father's rejection and nonacceptance had nothing to do with him. It was about his father's limitations.

To Forgive or Not Forgive

You may ask, should I forgive my parents? First of all, exercise caution when it comes to that word "should." If you feel you "should" do anything, it can easily mean that a shaming Inner Bully is lurking in the shadows somewhere. What's more, we can't force forgiveness by shaming ourselves. It simply doesn't work because forgiveness can't be forced. Period.

Think of forgiveness as a space. Something we feel, not something we do. We can tell somebody that we forgive them, but if we don't *feel* it, that act alone will be hollow and flat. No one benefits from hollow and flat – not us and not the other person. Forgiveness as a space is a natural outcome of the healing process. So it's futile to try to make it happen before its time.

Your healing journey will organically usher you to a space within yourself where you no longer view your parents through the myopic lens of your wounds. That lens will be replaced with a wide-angle lens, allowing you to attain greater understanding of yourself, your parents, and your circumstances. At that point, it's possible that compassion will take center stage – not your wounds. As for forgiveness? As I said before, it's a space and a natural outgrowth of understanding and compassion.

Transport yourself back in time and imagine that you're in a high place looking down on your parents struggling to fulfill a role that they're vastly unprepared for. You may see them behaving a bit like robots: programmed and powered by mindless traditional patterns. Or maybe they're bent or wounded in some way. Or even broken.

Let's face it, we're all trying
to remain upright in a lopsided world.

~ SALEE

Few parents intend to cause harm. Some have big hearts; some have buried hearts. Some relate well; some don't. Most never learned how to communicate well, which includes listening and showing empathy. They missed out on those skills along with many, many other skills. No question, parenting is a haphazard and sloppy enterprise.

The forgiveness I'm talking about is not a matter of sanitizing what they did or what they neglected to do as parents. There's a vast difference between forgiving and approving. When we forgive our parents – or anyone for that matter – we're forgiving them for being imperfect. We forgive them for their humanness and for being unfinished. For being asleep. It's all based on recognizing that *they are products of imperfect parenting themselves.*

From that higher space, I look down warmly on my parents. I even see things that were endearing and cute about them. Compassion sprouts because I understand that it's hard to be a human. I forgive my dad for his drinking and his detachment. And I forgive my mother for her angry lashings and emotional remoteness. No, she wasn't the cookie-baking, stereotypical nurturing type, but she *did* nurture, in her own way. I came to see that. She nurtured my mind by sharing her knowledge, cutting out articles for me to read, and exposing me to stimulating authors. My mother's love wasn't expressed outwardly, but it was something I felt nonetheless. My interests, natural talents, and aspirations didn't go unnoticed. She was always a supportive and unwavering presence in the background. I felt her devotion to my growth, allowing me to find my own way, follow my own path, and blossom into the woman I wanted to be. My parents never imposed their belief systems on me. So, unintentionally, they nurtured me to be a free thinker. And, unbeknownst to either of them, they nurtured my spirit. Mom fed my mind, and Dad fed my belly, and both of them fed my spirit. They were perfectly suited for my development. Namely, their imperfections provided the very challenges that helped me grow into the person I am today. David Hawkins, psychiatrist and author, sums it up when he says: "The world is perfect just as it is. To believe that you must understand that the world's purpose is to evolve us."

Let's just call planet Earth a cosmic kindergarten, and your parents – in all their imperfection – were ideal for helping you grow. If you doubt that, just ask yourself what you would be lacking in terms of understanding and wisdom if you'd had different parents. In a perfect world, troublesome people who cause us strife simply would not exist. But then there would be no chance for growth! I'm also convinced that such people are in our life so we can learn to love ourselves better.

Do you not see how necessary a world
of pains and troubles is to school
an intelligence and make it a soul?

—JOHN KEATS

Chapter Fourteen

When Inner Bullies Pop Up in Relationships

Count on your Inner Bully issues spilling over into your relationships.

—SALEE

We unconsciously project our Inner Bully onto the key figures in our lives. And if we're not aware and mindful about it happening, things can get muddied up in a hurry.

Joe's a good example. In our session, he described himself as a failure, a label that took root when he was very young. "My dad found fault in everything I did," he said. "I could never get anything right. No matter what, it was never perfect enough."

Interestingly, he described his marriage in much the same way. "She's always putting me down!" he said. "It would be nice if once in a while she were actually supportive of something I did or said, instead of automatically putting it down!"

Obviously, her derogatory remarks struck a sensitive chord in Joe. His split-second defensive reaction reveals that. "I know my anger gets way out of hand," he added, "but she can be mean! I'm at my wits' end. I don't know where to go with this."

She wasn't innocent by any stretch, but the real problem ran much deeper.

"You know, Joe," I said, "the enemy's within you. Your wife couldn't affect you if she didn't echo the voice in your own head."

I explained that the appropriate battleground for him was in his mind, and that the perfect classroom for his growth was his marriage. As he learned to deal differently with his wife's put-downs, he would gain strength in handling his Inner Bully. His ultimate goal? To remain confident and unflappable when either one berates or criticizes him.

"What do you do for a living?" I asked.

"I'm an auto mechanic," he said confidently.

"Are you good at it?"

"Damn good," he said with noticeable pride.

"Would it set you off if I criticized your work?"

"No."

"Why not?"

"Because I would know you were full of it."

"Exactly!" I said.

I pointed out that he needs to start thinking of his Inner Bully as full of it. "And anyone else, for that matter, when they're wrong," I said. "That's how you'll eventually free yourself, Joe."

• • •

Monica is another example. In one of our sessions, she pointed out that her mother's favorite strategy for getting her way was through pouting. When her mother planned a family gathering, she expected everyone to show up. And they did.

If Monica has made other plans, she obligingly broke them. Obviously, her mother's pouting had an iron grip on both her will and her freedom.

"How does your mother have so much power?" I asked.

"She has a way of making a person feel *really* guilty," she said.

It would be easy to say that Monica was afraid of her mother, but it's far more accurate to say she was afraid of guilt. Giving in to her mother kept her guilt appeased. It silenced her Inner Bully.

"I'm guilt-free if I give in to guilt," she said.

This exact same pattern of appeasing – giving into guilt – described her relationship with other people, including her husband. That's no surprise because we tend to play out the same interaction patterns we acquired as children.

Monica toyed with the idea of leaving him, but that wasn't a solution. Instead, she was challenged to attain mastery over her learned patterns, mainly seizing power over her Inner Bully. If she didn't, she'd merely play out the same unhealthy dynamic with another person.

Monica saw the common sense of taking that route. In due course, her pattern of interacting and responding would change dramatically. One day, she would be a different person in the relationship. In other words, she wouldn't be dancing the same dance. Consequently, her husband would be challenged to change. If he chose to remain locked into the old pattern, their relationship would simply not work. He'd be dancing one dance, and she'd be dancing another. Their marriage would simply stagnate while mired in lots of conflict and dissatisfaction.

In summary, for their relationship to work at all – for it to be positive and satisfying for both – she had to cease being susceptible to her husband's guilt ploys, and he had to be willing to give them up.

Examples from My Marriage

If you want to know where
your shortcomings are, get married.

—ALAN GODWIN

The Unpacking Incident

I like taking vacations, but what I don't like is facing the chore of unpacking upon returning. My husband, Don, is innately faster at it. This is a fact. It takes him a mere couple of hours to put his things away, while it takes me a couple of days. For those couple of days, I used to imagine that he was wondering, "What is her problem?!"

On one occasion, I just had to say something. "You expected me to have more things put away by this time, right?" It came off a teeny-bit accusatory.

He seemed confused. "No," he said, "I have no expectations about that. Nothing."

That didn't silence my Inner Bully. Instead, I felt guilty for accusing him of such a thing.

The Chocolate Sin

One day, while running errands, I honored a temptation and walked into a wonderfully lovely chocolate shop. I bought two pieces – one for me and one for Don. The clerk placed them neatly in a tiny, cute bag. Soon I was on my way home. I ate mine right away, but I had trouble putting Don's piece out of my mind. It kept tugging away at me, and it wasn't long before I found myself reaching in for it. Yep, you guessed it. I ate it. None for Don, and boy oh boy, my Inner Bully had a heyday! It berated me brutally. It accused me of being selfish and tore into me: *You say you love Don, but what you did, Salee, was not an act of love!*

That Inner Bully of mine can be an inner abuser! I was supposed to suffer – and I did. I even thought I should confess to Don so he could make me suffer more. So I confessed. Did he join forces with my Inner Bully? No. He laughed. In fact, his amused, caring heart awakened me to my ridiculousness, and I ended up laughing with him.

Reflecting back on that event a few hours later, I asked myself if I would condemn anyone else for that same "crime." The answer was no. Just like Don, I would laugh warmly. It's all so funny.

The Generator Story

You've been learning that awareness of your automatic thoughts is the doorway to freedom. By freedom, I'm not implying that your Inner Bully will be gone for good. Freedom is achieved by gaining power over it, and that requires being awake to it.

Your Inner Bully will begin to fade as you attain mastery over it, but it won't cease to exist. That's because negative self-talk, aka your Inner Bully, is an automatic, habitual pattern of the brain. Stressful, unpredictable challenges, the usual stuff of everyday life, can throw us out of our command module at the snap of a finger. This means that your Inner Bully may re-emerge larger than life. But rest assured, only temporarily.

I'll give you a personal example, an experience similar to one you might have had yourself. One day our generator broke down, so Don arranged for a repairman to show up at 8:30 in the morning. While leaving for coffee at 7:30, Don assured me that he would be back before the repairman arrived. Well, that didn't happen. At 8:10 the doorbell rang, and we all know who that was. Yep: the repairman.

I opened the door. Despite the frigid temperature and blowing snow, I was greeted with a friendly smile. "Where's the generator?" he asked. I explained that it was out back next to the garage. I also told him Don would be home shortly. He seemed satisfied with those two pieces of information, and off he went to meet up with the generator.

Although the repairman may have been fine, I was far from it. The thoughts swirling around in my brain went like this: *Oh no, he has to go all the way around to the other side of the house in this snow, and I don't know when Don's coming home in case he needs his help in any way. Maybe I should invite him in until Don gets back? What to do? Wait a minute. Why am I suddenly responsible for this guy anyway? Why did Don leave in the first place? Was it worth the few piddly minutes of coffee with the guys?"*

The moment I closed the door, I wasted no time in calling Don and letting him know who had arrived. Early. I managed to communicate all that minus an ugly attitude on my part. "Okay," he said casually, "be there in a bit."

Be there in a bit? I remember thinking. *What in the h*** does that mean? And where's his damn sense of urgency? He sounded way too relaxed on the phone. Brother!*

He got back home within five minutes, but I still had an urge to shame him. I wanted to say, *What were you thinking?* And proceed to tell him how unrealistic his time frame was.

But I didn't do that. Why? Because some remnant of self-awareness kept me decent. I knew the problem was within me – not out there. Such strong emotions and reactions are a clear signal telling me it's time to get contemplative (become mindful). So I went inside myself and looked around. I came to see that the root of my distress was none other than an overblown – and unwarranted – sense of responsibility and guilt.

What did I do with that guilt? Transferred it onto Don. I shifted it away from me to him, making him the target of my Inner Bully instead of me. After all someone had to pay for such a severe act of wrongness. If my Inner Bully is not shaming me, it's got to shame somebody. That's what it does: shame and criticize.

When it comes to projecting guilt, relationships are extremely handy. It's a bonus you don't even consider when you enter a relationship. It's comparable to buying a home and then finding out the seller's brand-new washer and dryer stays with the house! Bonus.

Where was my logical brain when all that was taking place? Asleep. For some unknown reason I believed the repairman should be spared dealing with a snowstorm. Now how clown-shit crazy is that? After all, when he elected to be a generator repairman, didn't he sign up for such unpleasantries?

I was also solidly convinced he needed Don to be there. In retrospect, I realized I could have – should have – saved myself a whole lot of distress by getting my facts straight. Directing the right questions to either Don or the repairman would have taken care of that. Or I just could have read the signs. They were there. Specifically, the peaceful demeanor of both men should have been a loud clue, telling me something like, *Duh, there doesn't seem to be an emergency here. Hello!*

What this illuminates is that it merely takes one unpredict-able, minuscule event or upheaval to reactivate old, outdated patterns. On that particular day, up to that point, my Inner Bully had been well-managed and relatively silent. I was merely blindsided.

No question, the unforeseen and the unexpected have a way of throwing us off kilter. Actually, any number of things can do that, including high stress, fatigue, physical aches and pains, fears, and insecurities. The foods we eat and the beverages we drink also affect our sense of stability and groundedness.

In a nutshell, a stressed and overwrought brain reverts back to old patterns, causing us to fall out of our command module. It leaves us momentarily distracted and disoriented. We can't prevent this from happening, but we can prevent ourselves from staying lost in our sleep state.

This little scenario not only demonstrates the power of guilt – how it can sabotage rational thinking – but it also illuminates how Inner Bullies can trigger unnecessary drama and discord in relationships. It can trigger all the unhealthy relationship habits that are baked into our brains.

Don and I didn't go there, but it's easy to see how we could have. What prevented us from venturing down that rabbit hole? Simple. I saw where that parade was headed and chose a different route. I climbed back into my command module and – for the millionth time! – took control of my automatic reactions.

Without a doubt, mindfulness saved the day. That is, paying attention, on purpose, to what was occurring in the present moment within me. The outer circumstances were irrelevant. They usually are.

Did I share all this with Don? Absolutely. But I expressed it in the spirit of adding just one more story to our library of laughable moments of temporary insanity. Especially our Inner Bully stories. We both have them.

To reiterate: We're able to avoid getting tangled up in a blame-slinging fest because we both take ownership of how we feel and how we react internally and externally. We're not inclined to blame or feel victimized by the other. If we do, it's fleeting, and in a matter of seconds we self-correct and switch back into self-examination mode. We become introspective, asking ourselves, "What just got triggered in me?" versus "What was done to me?" We follow that up by together processing our insights into what we discovered about ourselves.

Don sums it up perfectly in a matter of few words: "I'm working on being a better me, so we can be a better we."

How did we get good at this? Lots of sweat, knowledge about ourselves, self-discipline, and an abundance of trial and error. And, oh yes, and we mustn't forget about the importance of a sense of humor. When it comes to being in a relationship, one must be able to laugh, mainly at oneself. It helps.

What to do when you have a legitimate gripe? What if Don really *had* been in the wrong? Here's my shorthand advice: Operate from your command module. Present your complaint without attacking, shaming, or blaming. That approach increases your likelihood of being heard since you won't be triggering negative feelings in the other person. Realize that when people feel attacked, they automatically switch into survival mode. They become focused on protecting and defending themselves. It's human nature to react in self-defense whenever we feel threatened.

Growth from an Earlier Marriage

Far from being a raging alcoholic, my dad was a depressed and *withdrawn* alcoholic. His sadness stirred within me both sympathy and a sense of helplessness. I yearned to make things better for him, but no matter how hard I tried, I just couldn't. His somberness drove me to seek solace in activities outside the home. I felt guilty for wanting to get away.

Fast forward ten years.

When I married Dave, I didn't realize I was marrying someone like my father. He wasn't an alcoholic, but he did suffer from depression. As with Dad, I tried ever so hard to make him happy. Predictably, it never worked.

There was yet another reason living with Dave was really difficult: he was a master at pushing my guilt buttons – at activating my Inner Bully. He used guilt as a tool to manipulate.

He played the role of victim very well, subtly blaming me for his unhappiness. Later, I came to understand that he learned that unhealthy pattern due to unmet emotional needs and insecurities from his childhood. But at the time, while we were married, I continually felt it was my role to rescue him, and I felt horrendous guilt if I couldn't. Over time, a combination of powerlessness, exhaustion, and psychological distress started taking a toll on my well-being. I was growing depressed myself!

We were like two pieces of a very unhealthy puzzle.

That particular low point in my life forced me to make a grim decision. I knew I'd have to leave Dave. Since I couldn't rescue him, I had to rescue me. That decision didn't come easy. It came with immense mental torment, including super-sized guilt.

Did we seek therapeutic help? The answer is no. I wish we had. It would have been a wise move.

Initially, I viewed Dave's guilt-inducing, manipulative tactics as the crux of my problem. Getting away from Dave seemed like the logical solution. Not true. My problem was me, and it was my Inner Bully. I was blindly imprisoned by a script I acquired as a child. I felt I had to make my dad feel better. Dave represented my dad psychologically, so it was no surprise that my life revolved around his emotional well-being.

The divorce triggered some serious introspection on my part, launching a journey inward. I didn't know it at the time, but I needed to understand and ultimately overcome my codependent and unhealthy guilt tendencies. I had to acquire self-understanding, which included becoming aware of my Inner Bully. Ultimately, I came to realize that Dave didn't make me feel guilty, my Inner Bully did.

In essence, I didn't divorce Dave, I divorced an unhealthy life pattern.

When I left my marriage, I went back to school in order to get a master's degree in clinical social work. But I put pursuing my career temporarily on hold. Dave required medical assistance.

Roughly a year before I graduated, Dave contracted ALS (Amyotrophic Lateral Sclerosis), commonly known as Lou Gehrig's disease. ALS is a rapidly progressive neurological disorder that attacks the nerve cells responsible for controlling involuntary muscles (motor neurons).

Dave was able to operate independently for that first year, but by year two, it was apparent that he was severely declining and needed someone to care for him. Bottom line: he needed me. I had to step in and help. It was either me or our son, who was in college at the time, and there was no way I was letting him take this on.

But the very thought of going back into that situation terrified me. I likened it to a recovering alcoholic accepting a job offer at a bar. I wasn't terrified of Dave. I was terrified of my weakness. You see, my addiction wasn't alcohol, it was feeling ultra-responsible for another person's emotional well-being. My weakness was being susceptible to guilt ploys and being totally unpracticed at setting boundaries.

And so we began a new dance. We quickly got into our new routine. I spent every day with Dave, morning until night. It wasn't too long before he slipped into an old pattern. He tried to guilt me about something. But this time, I was ready. To my amazement, I wasn't triggered as I had been in the past. In fact, I was amused. I looked him straight in the eye and simply said: "Dave, if you try to make me feel guilty, this just isn't going to work."

Dave responded by looking at me with a sheepish smile, as if to say, "Shucks, ya caught me." And that's all it took. Poof! The bully was declawed. I felt free.

From that point on, he never attempted to push my guilt buttons. We spent the remaining months of his life enjoying our soul-deep connection – a connection that had brought us together in the first place. Those days were laced with numerous priceless moments that cause me to smile yet today.

Dave's health, though, continued to decline, and it soon became apparent that he needed more extensive care – more than I alone could offer. So I pulled together a team of helpers

– friends and family – to provide round-the-clock care. And for a while we all functioned like a well-oiled machine. It ran smoothly and without a hitch! But the task became too great, and the helpers started experiencing burnout. At some point, a social worker approached me, saying that home care for Dave was not enough and that he would be better served in a nursing home. That news devastated me. Up until then, I had been assuring Dave that I would fight tooth and nail to keep him at home.

I dreaded breaking the news to Dave. As I sat on the edge of his bed, I tried my darnedest to keep it together, but to no avail. As I talked, I just couldn't fight back the tears. I cried after each sentence! What happened next gave me a memory I cherish to this day: with his weakened hand, Dave struggled to reach for a tissue. He somehow managed to pick up the tissue, reach over, and dab my tears away while mouthing the words, "It's okay." We had come full circle. He was caring for me.

Chapter Fifteen

Going Forward:
What to Expect

We drag that programmed younger self of ours around wherever we go. Looking as far back as yesterday, I see that I should always be sending loving understanding to that tangled-up part of me.

—SALEE

Patterns that were formed in your childhood are hard to shake. Tenderness and unwavering patience are called for. You must watch that you don't set the bar too high for yourself. Unwittingly, you could be inviting an avalanche of self-disapproval. It's far smarter and less stressful to regard progress as a gradual process characterized by two steps forward and one step back. So when you notice that you're snagged by an old pattern, such as taking on more than you should (failing to utilize that "no" muscle of yours) or if you find yourself dismissing compliments, dole out some compassion to yourself.

As I mentioned before, compare it to babies learning to walk. At some point in their crawling career, every baby decides to abandon crawling and give walking a try. Predictably, their attempts are never smoothly executed. There will be those inevitable moments when they fall flat on their cute little faces. We're no different. But each time we fall, as with babies, we get a little bit stronger and a little bit wiser about how to do it right.

And to prove I'm not just blowing smoke, enjoy hearing about some of the adults who are learning to "walk" a little better every day:

Kate

As you recall from Chapter Five, Kate was a special education teacher who became overwhelmed by the increasing demands and her ever-expanding class size. Her soul was expressing itself through the dread and panic attacks she experienced on the way to work, seemingly out-of-the-blue crying spells, sleepless nights, stomach pain, and constant headaches. It was all rooted in the distress she was feeling on a soul level.

Kate's problem at the root level was an overblown sense of responsibility, fueled by guilt. She was forcing herself to endure something that was deflating her spirit.

"How has your life improved?" I asked recently.

"What has changed most is that my responsibility is to myself first," she said. "If I'm not responsible for my own peace and well-being, I cannot help anyone else. It's just not possible." Every morning, Kate now spends several minutes making a deep connection with herself through meditation and yoga. "I've found that making myself a priority is an act of loving myself," she added.

Kate left her position in the school system and is now working for an organization that supports parents who have children who are receiving special education services in public schools. She's also a yoga and meditation instructor and volunteers for an organization that supports pregnant teens and teen mothers.

Kate maintains that society really hasn't changed much since she was a pregnant teenager. "Pregnant teens and teen mothers are still ostracized and shamed," she said. "They get judged and portrayed solely by their circumstances. They're viewed as a label, not as individuals possessing a personality and having value. I want to change that. They deserve greater respect and support."

Kate experienced a significant loss of income when she left her teaching position. "I lost hundreds of thousands of dollars by leaving that job," she said. "But staying there wasn't worth my physical and mental health. It's strange, but I'm making less and I'm doing okay. I'm amazed!"

That's not surprising. Financial security seems to be a common outcome for people who align themselves with their soul and follow where it wants to take them.

Meg

Meg was our Chicago freeway driver who took a back seat to her imposing mother-in-law. Meg felt powerless and deflated. Not long ago, I had an opportunity to ask Meg how her life looked years later.

"I honor myself now," she said. "I can honestly say that it's so much easier to be confrontational and communicate my feelings right away. I refrained from doing that before because I never wanted the other person to feel the pain that I felt early in my life. I grew up not feeling loved, and I did not want anybody else to ever feel that way. Especially from me. I used to think it was easier to just blow it off rather than be confrontational, but I came to see that it really isn't easier because feelings fester until they become a much larger problem. So much of my life was spent being angry because I would stifle my feelings instead of expressing them."

"What about your Inner Bully?" I asked. "When you consider being assertive with someone, does it harass you about hurting their feelings?"

"The voice is there for a split second, but *only* for a second," she said. "I've learned to take a look at myself and do what I call 'a check.'" She went on to explain that she steps back and takes a look at what's going on inside, and also what might be going on inside that other person. From there, she decides what to say and how to say it.

In short, Meg now takes the reins and operates as her own decision-maker instead of listening to her Inner Bully.

"How else has your life improved?" I asked.

"I feel stronger and happier, and I'm certain it's because I'm more self-empowered."

Brooke

Brooke, the woman you met in Chapter One, had an Inner Bully who mirrored her father. It rode her constantly about being perfect. The pressure was so great, in fact, it kept her from living her life to the fullest.

"How are you doing with that Inner Bully of yours?" I asked.

She explained that it can still give her fits for failing to be perfect. But it doesn't capture her for long because she has fully embraced a crucial truth. "It's impossible to be perfect," she said. "Perfection is non-attainable." That logical conclusion has made it possible for her to venture out from her comfort zone and dare to try new things, meet new people – and, yes, make mistakes!

Brooke used to define progress as achieving perfection. Now she defines it as being aware of her Inner Bully pressuring her to *achieve* perfection. "I'm getting really good at that," she said, "and that feels so wonderful!"

Chapter Sixteen

Wallow in Freedom!

*Once we experience a new way of being,
our old life is no longer available to us.*

—SALEE

Perhaps this scenario will sound familiar to you:

I answered the phone. It was a request for a donation. I refused, but that didn't satisfy the caller – she persisted. Finally, I interrupted her, saying firmly: "I'm going to hang up now. Goodbye!"

And I did.

My Inner Bully, looking bored over in the corner until that very moment, suddenly lit up like a dog being tempted with a bone. In the past, my mind would have been flooded with self-berating comments: "You weren't very nice to her! That was so rude of you! You should have donated. You're so selfish."

But it didn't work. Not this time. My bully just went back to being ... bored.

There comes a time when we must stare down our Inner Bully instead of cowering – or grin at the silly thing. After all, it's no smarter than a bored dog salivating over a bone.

The Inner Bully thrives because we feed it. Take away its food supply, and it skulks into the corner. I've shown you how to send that Inner Bully of yours back to the corner. Bored and starving.

Something amazing happens when you assert your will against your Inner Bully. You automatically switch from a capitulating stance to one of empowerment. Instead of bowing to your internal captor, you reject enslavement and conclude that what it has to say is baseless baloney. You get good at questioning its reality. In time, you come to see that you are more real and accurate than it is.

Once you see your Inner Bully for what it is – a product of your conditioned brain – you 're able to realize that the bully within is all bluster and its bark is all show. Its power is nothing more than what you give it. That's why defeating your Inner Bully amounts to retraining (and rewiring) your brain.

This process is no different than overcoming any other bad habit. It requires learning a new way of thinking, acquiring new skills, and then practicing those skills consistently. This means you operate with the same dedication and deliberateness as if you'd decided to commit to walking twenty minutes each day. You make it a part of your daily routine.

Before you started this journey, you were largely in the dark, overpowered and intimidated by that voice. But now, when it makes its presence known, you're increasingly capable of calling it out. Instead of being bullied, you merely pat it on the head and say, "There, there ... now go sit in the corner." You're stepping into the power position.

Something else wonderful happens. You find yourself not just able to overcome your Inner Bully but also all bullies – those who reside on the outside as well as within. None deserve your allegiance. You will live out the African proverb that says, "If there is no enemy within, the enemies outside cannot hurt you." You have sovereignty and peace.

When you're not spending so much energy battling your Inner Bully, you'll have the brain space for experiencing your True Self. Better yet, you'll be able to give yourself the love and compassion your Inner Bully is incapable of. You'll do the things that bring you joy. You'll eliminate things that dampen your happiness and cause you distress. You'll distance yourself from people who dampen your spirit. You will shine.

A caveat: your Inner Bully represents a longstanding, habitual mental pattern. It won't go away completely. You'll still feel it hanging around and hear it piping up from time to time. But that's okay. Why? Because you'll no longer get taken in by it. You'll recognize it as just another habitual clump of bothersome and irrelevant mental debris, like the lyrics to the theme from *Gilligan's Island.*

So that bully of yours will still be lurking in the back of your mind. And it will remain persistent. Bullies don't like to be ignored, so it will eagerly look for opportunities to lunge back into action. It's up to you to avoid giving it your attention and your energy, thus granting it power. Don't let your guard down. It's sneaky, so continued vigilance must become an established norm for you.

That won't be as hard as it might sound because you will be enjoying the dramatic changes in yourself that come with stifling your Inner Bully:

- You'll start to feel lighter and freer. You won't be weighed down by guilt or shame.
- You'll come to question your guilty feelings instead of assuming they're accurate. You'll realize that such feelings can be activated merely because you have a habit of blaming yourself for everything.
- You'll notice a new spring in your step and that you're taking time out to smell the roses.
- You'll start to experience what it means to love yourself.
- You'll be able to look at your flaws and mistakes from a space of self-compassion. From that space, you'll be patient and understanding with yourself instead of self-condemning. The mistakes you made yesterday will seem trivial. But above all, you'll regard them as forgivable.

- You'll be immune to the insidious effects of regret.
- You'll increasingly find it natural to speak up and say what you really think and do so without feeling bad about it and without apologizing.
- You'll be able to accept a compliment.
- You'll be aligned with your instincts, your body, your emotions, and your inner wisdom.
- You'll appropriately prioritize your own needs and self-care.
- You'll feel okay saying no and setting boundaries, and you'll know when that's called for.

Just as your inner world will change, so too will your outer world, including your relationships with others. You'll likely find yourself unconsciously gravitating toward people who are the polar opposite of your Inner Bully. You'll feel worthy of people who will love you and treat you right. This can shift all kinds of relationships, from the people you follow online to your life partner. You will know that you deserve someone who will cherish and respect you.

You've been living small, bowed under the weight of your Inner Bully's withering judgment and nonstop nitpicking. But now that you've seen that critical inner dialogue for the nonsense it is, you'll realize that your list of "flaws" is distorted, even meaningless, compared to all the marvelous things that make you, you.

You will no longer be interested in – or willing to – shrink in order to make others, including your Inner Bully, more comfortable. In fact, that kind of self-sacrifice will feel all wrong and leave you with a bad taste in your mouth. You'll see it for the self-abandonment it is, and it will be something you simply won't tolerate anymore.

This is your birthright: to step fully into the power of your True Self, unfettered by anyone's judgment, criticism, or cautions. After all, you were born free of self-doubt and self-condemnation. It's time to reclaim that freedom – for good.

Something amazing happens when you assert
your will against your Inner Bully:
your spirit grows wings.

—SALEE

Self-Evaluation Exercise (SEE)

Supportive/Helpful	Inflexible/Rigid	Humble
Understanding	Team Player	Willing to Listen
Kind	Considerate/Tactful	Reassuring
Cold & Uncaring	Encouraging	Self-centered
Insensitive	Tyrannical	Judgmental
Mean-spirited	Discourteous	Belittling
Caring	Discouraging	Unselfish
Comforting	Open-Minded	Fair & Unbiased
Respectful	Friendly	Empowering
Heartless	Know-it-all	Oppressive
Flexible	Arrogant	Forgiving
Disrespectful	Opinionated	Protective
Empathetic	Sarcastic	Humane

The Inner Bully
and Addiction

To further address the role the Inner Bully plays in sustaining addiction, I invited the thoughts of my son Tavis Schlundt, a mental health and substance abuse therapist.

When asked how their use of drugs or alcohol served them at first, before their lives became an unimaginable mess, many in drug and alcohol recovery will speak of its numbing effects. "To numb what?" I ask. It is a logical next question asked by any drug and alcohol counselor, which I am today; a question forever close to the heart and mind of anyone in long-term drug and alcohol recovery, which I also am today, and will always be.

While the answers I receive as a practitioner vary, the central theme given is often close to this: for a period of time early on, fondly remembered by many as a consequence-free, "honeymoon stage" of using, drug or alcohol use is described as having numbed, or otherwise dealt with, some unaddressed emotional pain.

For those willing to do the hard work to stay clean and sober, this is sometimes the first recognition of emotional suffering underlying their deadly affliction. For those who benefit the most, uncovering it often ushers in the return of much needed self-compassion, through reminding them of the rational, self-protective reasons why they resorted to self-medicating with their substance of choice in the first place.

Almost universally, as I accompany clients on this important leg of their journey, there is a rediscovering of an earlier time in which, out of great pain and desperation, they turned to drinking or using drugs to address some significant emotional trauma or unmet emotional need. This new narrative, rediscovered through honest self-examination, invariably runs counter to the negative self-talk they have grown accustomed to. Little do they know they have begun the life-long process of not only liberating themselves from drug and alcohol use, but also liberating themselves from the belligerent Inner Bully who's played such a big role in sustaining their self-abuse.

In whatever form it is conceptualized, good recovery work next involves helping someone keep the spotlight on this shady, untrustworthy character in their head. We are, basically, helping someone learn how to recognize their Inner Bully's handiwork and keep tabs on it, while learning how to live with it and control it in every way possible. In the spirit of a good detective drama, the demands of drug and alcohol recovery require that one's Inner Bully be contained and interrogated, kept on watch, "one day at a time," for the rest of one's life.

Those who have never experienced the disease of addiction to drugs and/or alcohol, or who have never experienced a sustained and healing period of recovery, may wonder, "Why the shakedown?" What exactly is to be accomplished by the analogous, heavy-handed tactics of isolating, interrogating, and challenging the Inner Bully? How does this help establish a strong sustainable recovery, and why must it continually be done?

For someone in active drug and/or alcohol addiction as well as early recovery, self-shaming and negative messaging about oneself, including unexamined low self-appraisals, often receives no fact-checking. They are received and emotionally experienced as true. During active addiction, such negative thoughts help to keep one locked into a cycle of addiction, causing them to experience negative emotions that motivate them to self-medicate, leading to more shame and guilt that motivates them to use again. It is the peak opportunity for a power-grab by the Inner Bully, who is the purveyor of so many of the negative self-directed messages that merely keep the addict locked in their addiction.

It's a maddening paradox. What the addicted person needs most at that very moment – self-compassion and a muzzled Inner Bully – is denied them. Instead, that wretched voice in their head is amplified and more vicious than ever.

For someone in long-term drug and alcohol recovery, this voice of one's Inner Bully is recognized as an eternal, existential threat. Drug and alcohol addiction are deadly. Words matter, and we must be especially tuned in to the ones we use against ourselves. We come to realize that although our Inner Bully is a life-long tenant in our head, our power over it grows with our capacity to recognize its voice among the inner chatter. The more we keep tabs on it, surveil it alongside the support and guidance of others in recovery, the less control it will have over us.

Drug and alcohol addiction recovery work would tell us that when the Inner Bully has been quiet, we best not deceive ourselves into thinking it will stay that way for long. We must choose instead to stay, as often as possible, mindful and vigilant, accepting and aware of our Inner Bully's existence while exerting control over it where we can. Recognizing that the better we understand it, the less we are afraid of it, and the more we recognize it as the sad character in our life that it is, the more insights and power we will enjoy.

Acknowledgments

This book has been a long time in coming. Starting out as a mere sprout of an idea, it began taking shape as I gained a greater understanding of the human psyche—including my own. Personal experiences, classes, workshops, books on the topic of self-loathing, guilt, shame, and the inner critic all contributed to my knowledge.

Yet another contributing factor shines even brighter: my clients. As I heard each story—their struggle with their own personal bully—I became convinced that this book needed to be written. The truth is, it would not have happened without the willingness of several of those clients to share their stories so that others could be helped. It is from their lives that the examples in this book were drawn. To protect their anonymity, their names and other identifying information have been altered. I am immensely grateful to those wonderful people as well as countless other clients over a span of three decades who entrusted me with their vulnerability and pain. All deserve to be congratulated for their courage, persistence, and commitment to growth. I thank them for their trust, their time, and their connection.

To write this book, I've had to rely on countless people for support, knowledge, and skill. Special thanks go to Patti

Quintano. Over the years, I've described her as "my techie," but she has provided far more than mere technical support. Not only did she graciously devote countless hours of her valuable time to see this project through but also her editing prowess, her intelligence, her tenacity, and her attention to detail were invaluable. Those qualities of hers kept me amazed! I have immense gratitude for her patience as I struggled to understand grammar rules and her willingness to support me as I willfully broke them.

Patti's the one who took the entire journey with me. She had an uncanny knack for knowing exactly what I was trying to say. This phenomenal ability became evident whenever I struggled with finding just the right word or constructing just the right sentence. I found myself saying, "That's it!" on multiple occasions. We laughed and cursed together, and at times squabbled like ten-year-old siblings. Sometimes we would clash over certain nonsensical things like colons or commas and at other times, we would clash over my choice of an adjective. (I usually got my way!) In the final analysis, the ride was fun. It was play. Again, special thanks to Patti!

I am deeply grateful for the emotional support of and enlightening discussions with my two sons Rod Pasko and Tavis Schlundt. They, along with their wives Robyn and Terri, provided useful advice. Above all, they were there. All four would allow me to randomly interrupt their lives at any time just to get their take on a title or to share my excitement over something I just wrote!

I thank my family of origin. I'm grateful to my parents for encouraging me to follow my dreams and to believe I am capable of anything I set my mind to. Above all, I thank them for their imperfections. We need people, in part, because they complicate our lives and challenge us. That's how we grow into our fullness. The insights gleaned from my bumpy childhood provided rich fodder. Without it, the intimacy and empathy would be missing from the pages of this book. It would lack heart. So I thank my parents and my two siblings Susan and Nancy. Those sisters of mine taught me how to squabble and stand up for myself.

My deep thanks go to Virginia Nixon, who in our long friendship has taught me a great deal about dedication to dreams and determination. From the bottom of my heart, I thank her for believing in my book and in me. She, along with her husband Dan Servos, offered encouragement and suggestions at the very start of this journey. Other friends along the way have been equally supportive: Karen McFarren, Tina Eisenhart, Kelly Shepherd, Casey Chrzan, Andy Wilson, Patti Hays, Becky Yager, Jennifer Hunter, Leslie Gamble, Myra Tovey, and David Tovey.

I'm grateful to my colleagues Wayne Gerard, Susan Tielker-Sharpe, Jeanette Boerger, Lili Carroll, Rachel Taykowski, and Chris Potter, whose encouragement and feedback were important and valuable.

I even feel like I should include the whole crew at the 6002 Hair Salon in Fort Wayne, Indiana, for jumping in with their ideas and enthusiasm. They cheered me on as I blabbered endlessly about the book.

I will always owe a great personal as well as intellectual debt to the various mentors who coached me on how to write: Ray Moscowitz, Ann Wintrode, and Les Edgerton.

I want to thank an artist friend, Hannah Burnsworth, who encouraged me to trust my own artistic abilities in illustrating the cover.

Numerous authors have served as inspiration. Their names are sprinkled throughout the pages of this book. They include Michael Singer, Dr. Lynn Johnson, and Beverly Engel. Special thanks to Kristina Hallett, clinical psychologist and author.

Fortunately, I was able to work with Maggie McReynolds—my editor. She has been everything one could wish for in an editor: intuitive, intelligent, witty, and unrelenting in her determination to make the book a more complete and better one. She helped give structure to this book and guided it home.

I reserve my most special thanks for my husband Don Armstrong, for his undying devotion to my dream. He may not know this, but his unwavering confidence in me, his warmth, and his enveloping love sustained me on this all-encompassing journey. I thank him for willingly weathering my long, tedious hours of writing. He was always patient with the task, even when I wasn't, and demonstrated nothing but loving acceptance when my mood was ... er, let's say, less than pleasant. As I encountered roadblocks, he helped with his advice and clarity. Whenever I felt overwhelmed or discouraged, he was there with wise words of encouragement—just the boost I needed at just the right time.

This book wouldn't be the same without his influence in my life. The warmth and brightness of his spirit permeates every aspect of my being, and that includes the creation of this book. Thank you, Don. My love and gratitude are immense!

About the Author

Salee Reese, LCSW, has been a psychotherapist in Fort Wayne, Indiana, for 35 years. She provides therapeutic services to people struggling with a broad assortment of life challenges, such as depression, relationship difficulties, parenting or family issues. Some are in the wake of losing a loved one, while others are poised at a crossroads and faced with a tough decision.

No matter what the issue, her approach includes cognitive-behavioral, solution-focused, and mindfulness-based therapies.

After earning a bachelor's degree in social work at the University of Saint Francis in Fort Wayne, Indiana, she received a master's degree in clinical social work from the University of Louisville, Louisville, Kentucky.

In 2007 she wrote and illustrated *When the Cage Dies, the Bird Lives,* a book aimed at giving solace to those dealing with the grief and fears associated with life endings.

Between 2007 and 2011, Salee wrote a weekly column, *Life Changes,* for *The Journal Gazette* of Fort Wayne, Indiana. Her column then transitioned online, where she offers the same insight and guidance for dealing with life's many challenges ... and cages. Her work can be found at www.saleereese.com.

Salee believes we're born as free spirits. Yet, as she's seen in her own life and in those of countless clients, free spirits often become shackled and even obscured. One of the most common cages she has encountered throughout her career has been unwarranted, toxic guilt that's continuously rein-forced by a critical, demeaning inner voice, which she calls an Inner Bully. Helping her clients defeat their Inner Bully and rediscover their True Selves quickly became her passion.

Personal evolution and freedom are at the heart of her work, which involves liberating people from their psycho-logical cages. This is true whether she's running workshops, working with groups, or with individuals. As one client attests: "Salee sees that their soul is held captive. So no matter what they come to her for, she sees that their soul isn't free. What Salee does is reach in with her hand and say with a compassion-filled voice, 'Come out.'"

Made in the USA
Middletown, DE
30 October 2023

PRÓLOGO POR D. A. CARSON

TEXTOS FUERA DE CONTEXTO

JAIRO NAMNÚN & STEVEN MORALES

EDITORES GENERALES

ESPAÑOL

NASHVILLE, TENNESSEE

Textos fuera de contexto

Copyright © 2016 por Coalición por el Evangelio
Todos los derechos reservados.
Derechos internacionales registrados.

B&H Publishing Group
Nashville, TN 37234

Clasificación Decimal Dewey: 220.6
Clasifíquese: BIBLIA-estudio y enseñanza
/ BIBLIA-crítica / Vida cristiana
Tipografía: 2K/DENMARK

A menos que se indique otra cosa, las citas bíblicas se han tomado de la Nueva
Biblia Latinoamericana de Hoy®, © 2005 The Lockman Foundation. Derechos
Reservados. Usadas con permiso.

ISBN: 978-1-4336-9239-0

Impreso en EE.UU.
1 2 3 4 5 * 19 18 17 16

Contenido

Prólogo por D. A. Carson. v

Una palabra de los editores por Jairo Namnún & Steven Morales. ix

Capítulo 1 La oración de fe sanará al enfermo 1
por Miguel Núñez

Capítulo 2 No juzguen para que no sean juzgados 11
por Andrés Birch

Capítulo 3 Yo sé los planes que tengo para ti 17
por Steven Morales

Capítulo 4 Todo lo puedo en Cristo que me fortalece 23
por Otto Sánchez

Capítulo 5 Pide en el nombre de Jesús 29
por Nathan Díaz

Capítulo 6 Cristo se hizo pobre para que fueras rico 33
por Carlos Contreras

Capítulo 7 Instruye al niño en su camino y no se apartará de él 39
por José Mercado

Capítulo 8 Cree en Cristo y serás salvo. 45
por Matthew Hall

Capítulo 9   Dios es amor... 51
                 por Enrique Oriolo

Capítulo 10 Ojo por ojo 55
                 por Juan Sánchez

Capítulo 11 Atar al enemigo... 59
                 por Gerson Morey

Capítulo 12 Serás salvo tú y tu casa 65
                 por Daniel Puerto

Capítulo 13 En Cristo no hay hombre ni mujer 69
                 por Patricia Namnún

Capítulo 14 Dios no te dará más de lo que puedes soportar.............. 75
                 por Justin Burkholder

Capítulo 15 Si somos infieles, Dios permanece fiel 81
                 por Sugel Michelén

Capítulo 16 El conocimiento envanece 85
                 por Jairo Namnún

Capítulo 17 Traed los diezmos al alfolí................................ 91
                 por Greg Travis

Sobre los autores.. 97

Información sobre Coalición por el Evangelio 102

Prólogo

D.A. CARSON

"Todo lo puedo en Cristo que me fortalece". ¡Eso suena maravilloso! Pero, ¿qué es "todo"? ¿Ser un campeón de fútbol? ¿O un físico nuclear? ¿O un súper modelo? ¿O un magnate rico? ¿O el próximo presidente de mi país? A fin de cuentas, el texto dice "todo", ¿no es cierto? Entonces, ¿por qué limitar a Dios?

Algo nos dice que debe haber un error en esta interpretación o, de lo contrario, habría un exceso de futbolistas, físicos nucleares, súper modelos, y magnates ricos. Pero muchos cristianos no piensan en ello con la debida atención. Escuchan estas palabras, y esperan y oran que –cualquiera que sea su significado–, se puedan reclamar para pedirle a Dios la habilidad para hacer lo que sea que *ellos* quieran hacer. Y esto trae otra pregunta. ¿Por qué la gente apela a este versículo para justificar sus oraciones pidiendo riqueza y poder? ¿Alguna vez has pensado que lo que de verdad te gustaría hacer es pasar el resto de tu vida como un pastor cristiano trabajando con los más pobres de los pobres en un barrio olvidado, sobre la base de haber orado: "Todo lo puedo en Cristo que me fortalece"? ¿Por qué no?

Si lo piensas solo unos minutos, puedes ver que hay al menos dos problemas con esta apreciación, y ambos son tratados en este pequeño pero importante volumen.

Por un lado, cuando las personas abusan de esta manera de las palabras de la Escritura, la mayoría no sabe en dónde se encuentra el texto. En otros casos, sí saben dónde se encuentra, en el sentido que pueden dar una cita (en este caso, Fil. 4:13), aunque no tienen idea de lo que dice el contexto del versículo. Pero lo que es evidente es que si no prestan atención a los contextos en los cuales se encuentran estos textos, *muchos cristianos malinterpretarán gravemente estos textos de la Palabra de Dios*. Cuando yo era un niño me enseñaron esta frase: "Un texto sin un contexto es un pretexto". Pues la realidad es que el significado de las palabras está condicionado por las oraciones en que se encuentran, el significado de las oraciones está condicionado por los párrafos o capítulos en que se encuentran, y el significado de los párrafos o capítulos está condicionado por el libro en que se encuentran.

En esta ocasión no te recordaré el contexto de Filipenses 4:13, ni te mostraré cómo el contexto condiciona la manera en que debemos entender este versículo. El primer capítulo de este libro lo hará por ti. De igual manera, el resto de los capítulos se enfoca en otros varios versículos que a menudo se citan sin considerar su contexto.

Malinterpretar un texto no es solo un problema: es una tragedia. Dios tiene la intención de que Su Palabra sea entendida. Filipenses 4:13 es un texto maravilloso que tiene un valor práctico inmenso en la vida cristiana, siempre y cuando se comprenda de la manera que Dios quiere que se haga. Y Su intención no es que se entienda como una oración aislada sin un contexto. Lo sabemos porque nos lo dio *en un contexto*, lo cual demuestra que espera que aquellos que lean el texto también piensen en su contexto.

En otras palabras, no cumplir con leer el contexto de un texto no solo significa que lo distorsionamos sino también que no recibimos el conocimiento y la bendición que recibiríamos si entendiéramos el pasaje de manera cabal. Por esta razón, este libro provee 17 ejemplos breves que ayudan a los lectores cristianos a tratar la Palabra de Dios con mayor fidelidad, a fin de que crezcan en el conocimiento de la mente de Dios y en su madurez en Cristo.

Surge un segundo problema relacionado en especial con la naturaleza de nuestras motivaciones. ¿Por qué será que cuando malinterpretamos textos bíblicos al ignorar sus contextos, la mala interpretación que imponemos sobre el texto casi siempre apoya alguna motivación egoísta, o la búsqueda de riquezas, poder, prestigio, o hasta irresponsabilidad ante el pecado? Las falsas interpretaciones que surgen por ignorar el contexto no conspiran para hacernos más autosacrificiales o piadosos; más como Jesús. Casi siempre se usan para justificar el pecado. ¡Qué despreciable! Terminamos queriendo ser magnates ricos, no cristianos que sueñan con predicar y vivir el evangelio en el barrio de los más pobres. Si prestamos atención a los capítulos de este importante libro, no solo prestaremos más atención a los contextos y mejoraremos nuestro entendimiento de la Palabra santa de Dios, sino que también honraremos a Dios al tomar en serio Su Palabra y crecer en el discipulado cristiano.

Una palabra de los editores

En una de las primeras reuniones del equipo editorial de Coalición, la conversación giró en torno a cuáles serían las características principales de los artículos que el lector encontraría en nuestra página *web*. ¿Qué tipo de contenido publicaríamos? ¿Qué "sabor" tendría ese contenido? ¿Hacia dónde apuntaría? Nuestro deseo era seguir en los pasos de otros ministerios sanos en producir material centrado en el evangelio, pero también considerar las diferencias culturales de nuestro contexto hispanohablante. Para lograrlo tendríamos que hacernos unas preguntas cruciales: ¿Qué le hace falta a la Iglesia en América Latina? ¿Cuáles son los asuntos menos entendidos y más malinterpretados de su teología? ¿Qué podemos hacer para llevar la luz del evangelio a lugares oscuros?

En esa conversación surgió un anhelo común y una idea única. Nuestro anhelo era —y continúa siendo— saturar nuestras páginas no de pixeles sino con recursos que, cimentados en la Palabra revelada de Dios, apuntaran hacia la persona y la obra de Jesús para alentar a los cristianos a correr con perseverancia la carrera que tenemos por delante.

Pensando en esta realidad, desde Coalición por el Evangelio nos esforzamos por crear este pequeño título que tienes en tus manos. Los siguientes ensayos representan el deseo de hombres y mujeres de Dios de poder extraer de las riquezas de la Palabra y encontrar esa miel que tiene dentro. En esta ocasión, elegimos algunos de los versículos de los que más abusan quienes no conocen al Dios de la Biblia, o que muchas veces son malinterpretados por aquellos que no conocen bien la Biblia de Dios.

Esta obra tiene un formato sencillo. En cada capítulo vas a encontrar a un autor diferente, que analiza un versículo en particular. Podrás ver cuál es la interpretación errónea más común, y luego, a través del análisis el contexto, encontrarás cuál es la interpretación más apegada a lo que revela la Biblia, y además podrás reconocer las dificultades de interpretación de cada pasaje. Nuestro anhelo es que esto sirva como una introducción a un estudio más profundo de cada texto, y como un incentivo para el análisis cuidadoso de la Escritura.

Queremos que las personas lean su Biblia, pero también queremos que la lean de manera correcta y con regularidad. Sabemos que han quedado fuera muchos versículos, y que mucho más podría decirse de los versículos que componen esta obra. Sin embargo, oramos para que esta sea una pequeña chispa que, animada por el soplo del Todopoderoso, continúe dando fuego y calor a un mundo perdido y una Iglesia necesitada de la Palabra.

Jairo Namnún & Steven Morales
Editores generales

1

La oración de fe sanará al enfermo

MIGUEL NÚÑEZ

Y la oración de fe restaurará (sanará) al enfermo...
(Sant. 5:15).

En nuestros días, este texto es uno de esos versículos muy conocidos por muchos, pero que solo unos pocos interpretan bien. Esto se comprende a la luz de cómo se manejan hoy las Escrituras. Al comenzar un libro sobre la interpretación de la Biblia, es esencial que, antes de ver este texto en particular, establezcamos algunos principios que nos llevarán a entender mejor no solo el versículo, sino toda la Biblia.

En primer lugar recordemos que Pablo le enseña a Timoteo la necesidad de interpretar las Escrituras con extremo cuidado: "Procura con diligencia presentarte a Dios aprobado, *como* obrero que no tiene de qué avergonzarse, que maneja con precisión la palabra de verdad," (2 Tim. 2:15). La labor del maestro de la Palabra no es solo interpretarla, sino hacerlo de la manera correcta, hasta el punto de ser preciso en lo que enseña. Lo que estamos enseñando es la Palabra de Dios, la manera en que Él piensa. ¡Qué tremenda responsabilidad!

En segundo lugar, todo texto de la Palabra puede ser malinterpretado, ya sea por entender mal lo leído, por entender menos de lo que el texto dice, o por pensar que el texto dice más de lo que dice.

En tercer lugar, suele suceder que los textos son malinterpretados conforme a las corrientes de malas enseñanzas que "están de moda" en el momento. En este sentido, el texto que estamos analizando encuentra su errada interpretación, con mayor frecuencia en el mundo de hoy, dentro del movimiento de "súper fe" o de "proclámalo y recíbelo". Este movimiento enseña con toda liberalidad que nuestras palabras tienen poder por el solo hecho de ser pronunciadas, y que podemos crear la realidad siempre y cuando tengamos suficiente fe.

Sanidad y soberanía de Dios

Un análisis de la Escritura nos muestra que tal premisa es por completo errónea. Recordemos que Jesús sanó a gente que ni siquiera sabía quién era Él, como aquel hombre que había nacido ciego, que describe el Evangelio de Juan (Juan 9:34-38). Igual sucedió con el paralítico en la piscina de Betesda, donde vemos que "el que había sido sanado no sabía quién era, porque Jesús, sin que se dieran cuenta, se había apartado de la multitud que estaba en *aquel* lugar" (Juan 5:13).

A lo dicho debe agregarse que el apóstol Pablo, el gran misionero que supo sanar a muchos, no pudo sanarse a sí mismo (2 Cor. 12:8-9). Parece claro que lo importante para la sanación es la soberanía de Dios. La sanidad depende de la voluntad de Aquel que supo sanar a gente que ni lo conocía y que, por otro lado, negó la sanación a personas que no solo lo conocían, sino que ellos mismos tenían el don de sanación, como fue el caso de Pablo. Esto es consecuente con lo que revela 1 Juan 5:14: "Esta es la confianza que tenemos delante de Él, que si pedimos cualquier cosa conforme a Su voluntad, Él nos oye". Santiago está de acuerdo con esta verdad que Juan enuncia, pues, un poco antes del texto que estamos analizando dice: "Más bien, *debieran* decir: Si el Señor quiere, viviremos y haremos esto o aquello" (Sant. 4:15).

Preguntas al texto de Santiago

Ahora estamos listos para interpretar Santiago 5:15. Para comenzar, tenemos que colocar este versículo en su contexto inmediato, para luego poder responder las preguntas que el texto mismo generará. Entonces podremos sacar conclusiones en base a todo el consejo de Dios. Dice Santiago 5:13-18:

> ¿Sufre alguien entre ustedes? Que haga oración. ¿Está alguien alegre? Que cante alabanzas. ¿Está alguien entre ustedes enfermo? Que llame a los ancianos de la iglesia y que ellos oren por él, ungiéndolo con aceite en el nombre del Señor. La oración de fe restaurará (sanará) al enfermo, y el Señor lo levantará. Si ha cometido pecados le serán perdonados. Por tanto, confiésense sus pecados unos a otros, y oren unos por otros para que sean sanados. La oración (súplica) eficaz del justo puede lograr mucho. Elías era un hombre de pasiones semejantes a las nuestras, y oró fervientemente para que no lloviera, y no llovió sobre la tierra por tres años y seis meses. Oró de nuevo, y el cielo dio lluvia y la tierra produjo su fruto.

Primera pregunta:

¿De qué está hablando el texto? De la oración. Esto lo sabemos porque la oración se menciona en cada versículo:

- v. 13b: "Que haga oración."
- v. 14b: "y que ellos oren por él…"
- v. 15: "La oración de fe…"
- v. 16: "y oren unos por otros…"
- v. 17: "y oró fervientemente para que no lloviera…"
- v. 18: "Oró de nuevo…"

Primera conclusión:

El tema es la oración y la confianza en el Señor para lidiar con diferentes situaciones en nuestras vidas, y no la sanación por fe.

Segunda pregunta:

¿Cómo sabemos que no se trata solo de la oración para sanidad? Porque el texto muestra la oración en conexión con diferentes problemas del creyentes y no solo en relación con las enfermedades:

La oración se relaciona con el sufrimiento: "¿Sufre alguien entre ustedes? Que haga oración" (v. 13a). El sufrimiento es un tema importante en la epístola de Santiago desde el inicio (1:2). La oración en medio del dolor expresa confianza en Dios.

La oración se relaciona con los buenos tiempos: "¿Está alguien alegre? Que cante alabanzas" (v. 13b). Cantar alabanzas es una especie de oración cantada, porque al cantar ponemos música al deseo de nuestros corazones. La oración en medio de los buenos tiempos expresa agradecimiento a nuestro Creador.

La oración se relaciona con las enfermedades: "¿Está alguien entre ustedes enfermo? Que llame a los ancianos de la iglesia y que ellos oren por él, ungiéndolo con aceite en el nombre del Señor" (v. 14).

La oración se relaciona con la enfermedad y la posible presencia de pecado en nuestras vidas: "y el Señor lo levantará. Si ha cometido pecados le serán perdonados. Por tanto, confiésense sus pecados unos a otros, y oren unos por otros para que sean sanados" (vv. 15-16). Sabemos que no toda enfermedad es el resultado del pecado (Juan 9:1-3). También sabemos que algunas enfermedades sí son el resultado del pecado en la vida de los creyentes (1 Cor. 11:27-30). En esos casos, ¿qué debemos hacer? Orar y confesar nuestros pecados unos a otros para sanación, nos dice este texto. Aquí vemos que la fe sola no es suficiente para estos casos; además tenemos que 1) orar, 2) tener fe en Dios y 3) confesar nuestros pecados, caminando en santidad delante de Dios. No negamos el valor de la fe, como declara Santiago en 1:6-7. Pero la fe no es una garantía de sanación.

La oración se relaciona con la intervención de Dios para resolver problemas de la disfunción de la naturaleza afectada por el pecado: "Elías era un hombre de pasiones semejantes a las nuestras, y oró fervientemente para que no lloviera, y no llovió sobre la tierra por tres años y seis meses. Oró de nuevo, y el cielo dio lluvia y la tierra produjo su fruto" (vv. 17-18).

Segunda conclusión:

En este texto, Santiago relaciona la oración no solo con las enfermedades sino también con el sufrimiento, con los buenos tiempos, el arrepentimiento y el perdón de pecados, y aún con la disfunción de la naturaleza. Este entendimiento es vital. En todos estos casos, el creyente debe tener confianza en Dios para resolver cada uno de esos problemas, pero conforme a Su voluntad.

Nos quedan todavía algunos aspectos importantes en este texto que no podemos dejar fuera.

El llamado a los ancianos a orar

"¿Está alguien entre ustedes enfermo? Que llame a los ancianos de la iglesia y que ellos oren por él..." (v. 14a).

Desde muy temprano en la historia de la Iglesia, Dios ha reconocido la importancia de los pastores en la oración por las diferentes necesidades de la congregación (comp. Hech. 6:4). Parte de la función de estos ancianos que son convocados es determinar si hay o no alguna conexión entre la enfermedad y la vida de pecado del creyente. Parte de su función también sería determinar en oración, reflexión y multiplicidad de consejo, en qué dirección los está dirigiendo Dios. ¿Está Dios guiándonos a la oración por sanación, a la oración por gracia para sobrellevar la enfermedad, a la oración por ambas cosas cuando hay una falta de claridad? Esa es una situación donde la dirección de los ancianos es fundamental. De ahí la necesidad de convocarlos. ¿No podrían orar por sanación otros creyentes? ¡Claro que sí! El texto nos manda a orar unos por otros (v. 16). El enfermo mismo debe orar. Pero los ancianos deben ayudarlo a entender o a encontrar la voluntad de Dios para saber cómo orar.

La unción con aceite

"...ungiéndolo con aceite en el nombre del Señor" (v. 14b).

Creo que es obvio que el énfasis del pasaje no está en el aceite, sino en la oración, que es el tema del pasaje completo. En la antigüedad algunos usaban el masaje con aceite creyendo que poseía propiedades medicinales. Pero no hay evidencia de que el aceite fuera usado para todo tipo de enfermedades; y si el aceite por sí solo tenía propiedades medicinales, no se requeriría de los ancianos para llevar a cabo esta función. Por otro lado, el aceite sí fue usado en muchos casos para consagrar a Dios, incluyendo a reyes y sacerdotes. Consagrar es apartar para Dios. "Concluimos por tanto, que el 'ungir' en el v. 14 se refiere a una acción física con significado simbólico... En la medida en que los ancianos oran, ellos han de ungir al enfermo para simbolizar que esa persona está siendo consagrada para atención y cuidado especial de parte de Dios".[1]

Oración del justo

"La oración (súplica) eficaz del justo puede lograr mucho" (v. 16b).

La expresión "el justo" puede aludir a todo aquel que ha sido justificado por Dios a través del sacrificio de Jesús. Ahora, como hijo de Dios, él puede interceder ante el trono y saber que será escuchado.

---

[1] Douglas J. Moo, *The Letter of James* (Grand Rapids: William B. Eerdmans Publishing Company, 2000), 242.

También puede aludir al hecho de que aquellos que caminan en integridad de corazón delante de Dios son escuchados por Él de manera especial. Esto es así porque, por un lado, el pecado nos aleja de Dios (Sal. 66:18), y por el otro, porque el hombre que camina con Dios tiene, con frecuencia, mayor facilidad para discernir la voz o la voluntad de Dios, lo cual es muy difícil para aquel que vive en pecado.

Pablo nos dice en Romanos 12:1-2 que "presenten sus cuerpos *como* sacrificio vivo y santo, aceptable (agradable) a Dios…para que verifiquen cuál es la voluntad de Dios…". Aquí hay una conexión evidente entre vivir en santidad y discernir la voluntad de Dios. Antes de discernir Su voluntad, hay en este texto una instrucción a presentar nuestros cuerpos, nuestras vidas como sacrificio vivo y santo. Y como sabemos "que si pedimos cualquier cosa conforme a Su voluntad, Él nos oye" (1 Jn. 5:14), entonces podemos ver la razón por la que Santiago también dice que la oración del justo puede lograr mucho.

Conclusión

Santiago 5:15 no es una promesa incondicional de sanación si oramos con fe. Si este fuera el caso, lo único que la Palabra diría es que si hay fe, la respuesta sería siempre "sí". Pero como hemos visto, la Palabra revela que, por encima de nuestra voluntad y aun por encima de nuestra fe, está la voluntad soberana de Dios. A la luz de todo el consejo de Dios, sabemos que la oración es importante no solo en caso de enfermedad, sino en todos los casos. Además sabemos que la fe juega un rol en las intervenciones de Dios (comp. Mat. 13:58). Para concluir, podemos afirmar que la presencia de pecados en nuestra vida puede ser la causa determinante de enfermedades en algunos casos, y que la confesión unida a la oración puede lograr la sanación.

Gracias al sacrificio de Jesús, tenemos la posibilidad de acercarnos con confianza al trono de la gracia (Heb. 4:16), con la certeza de que Él nos oye (1 Jn. 5:14). A la vez, ese mismo sacrificio nos capacita para vivir nuestra vida en santidad y justicia, y nuestro Dios se deleita en la oración de los rectos (Prov. 15:8).

2

No juzguen para que no sean juzgados

ANDRÉS BIRCH

No juzguen para que no sean juzgados. Porque con el juicio con que ustedes juzguen, serán juzgados; y con la medida con que midan, se les medirá (Mat. 7:1-2).

¿Alguna vez alguien te dijo: "¡No me juzgues!"? ¿Alguna vez te han regañado por atreverte a criticar a algún predicador famoso? ¿Alguna vez oíste decir que la disciplina hacia un miembro de iglesia es una falta de amor?

¿Qué tienen en común estos ejemplos? Todos ellos están relacionados con Mateo 7:1-2, uno de los textos más utilizados aun por los que no conocen a Dios. ¿Qué significa, realmente, este tan citado texto bíblico? Tal vez estas cinco preguntas nos sirvan de ayuda:

1. ¿Qué tenemos en este texto?

¿Qué tenemos en Mateo 7:1-2? Yo diría que lo que tenemos es, por lo pronto, una advertencia: Si juzgamos a otras personas, nosotros mismos seremos juzgados; y seremos juzgados según la misma vara de medir que nosotros hayamos usado con los demás. Así que, ¡tengamos cuidado!

Si es así, no se trata de una prohibición absoluta. El Señor no nos está diciendo "¡Nunca juzguen a nadie, de ninguna manera!", sino que nos advierte: "Antes de juzgar a alguien, piensen muy bien cómo lo hacen, sabiendo que de esa misma manera ustedes también serán juzgados".

2. ¿Qué significa la palabra "juzgar"?

El verbo griego que aquí se traduce "juzgar" es el verbo *krino*, y se encuentra ciento catorce veces en el Nuevo Testamento, en noventa y ocho versículos diferentes. Abarca una amplia gama de significados: separar, distinguir, juzgar, considerar, cuestionar, pronunciar sentenciar, condenar, vindicar, etc.

Veamos algunos ejemplos:

- "Al que quiera ponerte pleito [*krino*] y quitarte la túnica, déjale también la capa" (Mat. 5:40, la única otra referencia en el Sermón del Monte).
- "...ustedes se sentarán también sobre doce tronos para juzgar [*krino*] a las doce tribus de Israel" (Mat. 19:28, la única otra referencia en Mateo).
- "Porque Dios no envió a Su Hijo al mundo para juzgar [*krino*] al mundo, sino para que el mundo sea salvo por Él" (Juan 3:17).
- " No juzguen [*krino*] por la apariencia, sino juzguen [*krino*] con juicio justo" (Juan 7:24).
- "Ustedes mismos juzguen [*krino*] si es justo delante de Dios obedecer a ustedes en vez de *obedecer* a Dios" (Hech. 4:19).

- "...quienquiera *que seas tú* que juzgas [*krino*], pues al juzgar a otro, a ti mismo te condenas, porque tú que juzgas [*krino*] practicas las mismas cosas" (Rom. 2:1).
- "Pero tú, ¿por qué juzgas [*krino*] a tu hermano?" (Rom. 14:10).
- "¿No juzgan [*krino*] ustedes a los que están dentro *de la iglesia*?" (1 Cor. 5:12).

Según estos (y otros) textos del Nuevo Testamento, hay un juzgar divino y otro humano, y hay una forma de juzgar que es buena y necesaria y otra que es mala y censurable. Como casi siempre, "el contexto es rey": el contexto determina el significado de cada texto.

3. ¿Qué luz arroja el contexto?

El contexto de Mateo 7:1-2 es el Sermón del Monte. Aunque se hable de "la multitud", el Señor se dirigía en primer lugar a Sus discípulos: "Sus discípulos se acercaron a Él. Y abriendo Su boca, les enseñaba, diciendo..." (Mat. 5:1-2).

Es en ese contexto que el Señor dice a Sus discípulos: "No juzguen, para que no sean juzgados...". Hay una manera de juzgar que no es apropiada para los seguidores del Señor, una manera de juzgar orgullosa ("Déjame sacar la paja de tu ojo"), hipócrita ("la viga... en tu propio ojo"), y sin amor.

Y si seguimos leyendo, llegamos a Mateo 7:6: "No den lo santo a los perros, ni echen sus perlas delante de los cerdos...". ¿Cómo decidimos quiénes son "los perros" o "los cerdos", si no es ejerciendo nuestro juicio?

Y si leemos un poco más adelante, llegamos al versículo 15: "Cuídense de los falsos profetas..." ¿Cómo distinguimos entre los profetas verdaderos y los falsos si no es fijándonos en sus frutos y sacando conclusiones? El contexto mismo nos muestra que Jesús no está prohibiendo de manera absoluta todo tipo de juicio.

4. ¿Hay algún texto paralelo?

Hay un texto paralelo a Mateo 7:1-2 en Lucas 6:37: "No juzguen, y no serán juzgados; no condenen, y no serán condenados; perdonen, y serán perdonados".

Hay aquí dos detalles que pueden ayudarnos: (1) Al añadir la frase: "No condenen...", parece que está diciendo: "Y cuando digo que no juzguen, lo que quiero decir es que no juzguen en el sentido de condenar"; y: (2) Cuando añade: "Perdonen, y serán perdonados", parece que nos está diciendo que perdonar es lo contrario de juzgar y condenar. En vez de juzgar y condenar a otras personas, lo que deberíamos hacer es perdonarlas.

5. ¿Qué dice el resto de la Biblia?

Sin echar por la borda el contexto de Mateo 7:1-2, debemos comprobar nuestra interpretación a la luz de la enseñanza bíblica en general. Y si, como ya hemos visto, la Biblia habla de juzgar en diferentes sentidos –divinos y humanos, buenos y malos– lo lógico sería ver Mateo 7:1-2 como una advertencia contra una manera mala de juzgar. Esa manera orgullosa, hipócrita, que carece de amor, y no tiene en cuenta que, tarde o temprano, nosotros mismos seremos juzgados de acuerdo con la manera (buena o mala) en que hayamos juzgado a los demás.

Conclusiones

1. En Mateo 7:1-2 el Señor está predicando un sermón a Sus discípulos sobre cómo debe ser la vida de todo verdadero creyente.

2. Allí, el Señor está advirtiéndoles a Sus discípulos del peligro de juzgar a otras personas de una manera orgullosa, hipócrita y sin amor, y de las consecuencias de ello.

3. También vemos que el Señor está hablando de una manera de juzgar a los demás nada apropiada, pero en el resto del Sermón del Monte y de la Biblia se habla de otras maneras de juzgar que son buenas e incluso necesarias.

4. En Lucas 6:37, el único pasaje paralelo a Mateo 7:1-2, juzgar es lo mismo que condenar y lo contrario de perdonar.

5. Debemos tener mucho cuidado de no caer en esa forma poco cristiana de juzgar a los demás, sin embargo, no debemos dejar de usar nuestro juicio, juzgar y discernir, tal como el Señor también nos enseña a hacer en Su Palabra.

3

Yo sé los planes que tengo para ti

STEVEN MORALES

"Porque Yo sé los planes que tengo para ustedes," declara el
SEÑOR "planes de bienestar y no de calamidad, para darles
un futuro y una esperanza" (Jer. 29:11).

Cuando era adolescente me desempeñé como traductor para un ministerio de asistencia médica que recibía grupos de misioneros durante un período corto. Cada semana recibíamos un grupo nuevo y nos dirigíamos a diferentes localidades para ofrecerles cuidados médicos a personas necesitadas. Al comienzo de cada jornada, el pastor compartía un devocional con el grupo, y una y otra vez él decía que Dios le había revelado un pasaje que estaba dirigido para ese grupo en particular. El pasaje siempre era Jeremías 29:11, y la interpretación siempre era que Dios quería prosperar a cada uno en el grupo.

Jeremías 29:11 es uno de los pasajes más leídos y citados de las Escrituras. De hecho, según biblegateway.com, fue el versículo más leído en el 2011, y el número 2 durante el 2012 y 2013. Su popularidad se basa en su aparente mensaje: Dios tiene planes para prosperarnos.

Dios lo sabe todo, tiene un plan, el plan es bueno para nosotros, tenemos esperanza. ¿Cuál es el problema entonces?

El primer problema: el contexto

El libro de Jeremías fue escrito para la nación de Israel, en un momento en el que estaban camino al exilio y desesperanzados. A causa de su desobediencia e idolatría, Dios permitió que Babilonia no solo se apoderara de su tierra, sino que además los desterraran.

Esto es muy significativo, porque Dios de manera directa los había guiado hasta esa tierra, y era una bendición prometida a ellos a través de su padre Abraham. Para los israelitas, que se les arrebatara su tierra era como si Dios les estuviera quitando lo que había prometido darles. Naturalmente, puesto que la mayoría en Israel le había dado la espalda a Dios, empezaron a clamarle durante la opresión. Así que Dios hizo lo que solía hacer en estas situaciones: les envió una voz para que les hablara en Su nombre: Jeremías.

Los profetas frecuentemente hablaron en el nombre de Dios y les recordaron a los israelitas de Sus promesas y liberación. Sin embargo, el mensaje de Jeremías al principio no fue positivo; él prometió juicio y exilio:

> Toda esta tierra será desolación *y* horror, y estas naciones servirán setenta años al rey de Babilonia (Jer. 25:11).

Jeremías promete en el nombre de Dios que ellos vivirán en el exilio en Babilonia durante 70 años. Pero él no solo transmite un mensaje de ruina y juicio: además les da instrucciones sobre cómo deben vivir mientras estén en el exilio, y les da esperanza para el futuro, cuando retornen a la tierra. De esto se trata Jeremías 29. Se los instruye a los israelitas a cuidar la ciudad, ayudar a sus opresores, orar por ellos, huir del engaño y no escuchar a los falsos profetas que solo buscan su propio bienestar. Falsos profetas que hablarían mentiras en el nombre de Dios y harían promesas que Él no prometió (29:21-23).

El punto es que, si nosotros reclamamos que Jeremías 29:11 es una promesa directa de Dios para nosotros, entonces también debemos reclamar que Jeremías 25:11 es una promesa para nosotros. Nos gusta reclamar las promesas de prosperidad y bienestar, pero nadie reclama la promesa del exilio babilónico durante 70 años. ¡Y así no funciona!

El segundo problema: las consecuencias

Al pensar que la promesa es para nosotros, tendremos una idea equivocada sobre lo que Dios promete, y sufriremos las consecuencias de tal idea. Si leemos este versículo como una promesa personal de prosperidad, cada uno de nosotros llegará a su propia conclusión de lo que significa prosperidad. "Después de todo, si Dios me está prometiendo que Él tiene planes para prosperarme, entonces Su plan debe complacerme a mí". Y así con cada individuo.

El pasaje no dice eso. Tampoco para los israelitas. Dios no le estaba prometiendo a cada uno que llegaría a ser rico, o que estaría sano, o que viviría una larga vida. Más bien, al ver el contexto de este pasaje (como lo hicimos antes) nosotros sabemos realmente cuál es el plan de Dios. La Biblia de estudio ESV lo resume bien cuando dice: "el plan de Dios para los exiliados es bienestar (*Shalom* en hebreo), no mal o 'calamidad'. Habiendo buscado el *Shalom* de Babilonia, los exiliados recibirán el *Shalom* de Dios en la forma de un futuro y una esperanza en su tierra".[1] El plan de Dios de prosperarlos era traerlos de regreso a casa y ser restaurados como una nación. Era una promesa nacional, no individual.

Si no tenemos este entendimiento del pasaje, entonces quedamos expuestos a pensar que Dios comenzará a prosperarnos en cualquier aspecto de la vida que deseemos. Y cuando esto no suceda (o por lo menos no suceda de la manera que deseamos), sentiremos amargura contra Dios.

El texto en su contexto

Entonces, ¿Jeremías 29:11 no tiene nada para nosotros? ¡Por supuesto que sí! Al escuchar "*...planes de bienestar y no de calamidad...*", nuestra reacción no debe ser de rechazo. Este texto es parte de la Palabra de Dios, y fue escrito para nuestro beneficio (Rom. 15:4). Debemos leerlo y aprender del carácter de Dios y de Su plan redentor. Él es soberano, Él tiene el control, Él juzgará el pecado, Él es misericordioso, Él cumple Sus promesas, y Él da esperanza futura a aquellos que escoge, aun cuando no hayan guardado su parte del pacto.

Si vemos este acontecimiento en el gran plan de la historia redentora de Dios, entonces este pasaje puede darnos esperanza de que Dios es bueno, confiable, y poderoso para guardar Sus promesas. Más todavía, podemos regocijarnos en que hemos visto Sus promesas cumplidas en Jesús, quien es la prosperidad en Sí mismo, y que más que cualquier otra cosa que pudiera darnos, se ofreció a Sí mismo como ofrenda por nuestros pecados. Dios proveyó a Jesús y Él es suficiente.

---

[1] *ESV Study Bible* (Nashville: Crossway, 2012), traducción de la nota sobre Jer. 29:11, p. 1424.

Conclusión

Tomar algo que Dios dijo y decir que dice otra cosa es una característica de los falsos profetas, que hicieron falsas promesas en el nombre de Dios (podemos ver el caso de Hananías en el capítulo 28 de Jeremías como un ejemplo perfecto de un profeta que prometió paz durante un tiempo cuando Dios había prometido juicio). Si queremos hablar acerca de la providencia de Dios, debemos buscar aquellos versículos que son más claros en cuanto a qué y cómo Dios provee. Por ejemplo:

- Hebreos 1:3 y Colosenses 1:17 nos dicen que la providencia de Dios se ve en que Él constantemente sostiene el universo, es decir sustenta el universo para que continúe existiendo.
- Mateo 6:11 y Filipenses 4:19 nos dicen que Dios provee para suplir nuestras necesidades diarias.
- Proverbios 16:1,9; 20:24 nos dicen que Dios ordena nuestros pasos mientras nos dirige sin cesar.

La provisión más grande de todas no se encuentra en una cosa, sino en una persona. Si necesitamos ver la mano providencial de Dios, solo tenemos que mirar hacia la cruz y observar cómo Él proveyó el regalo más grande de todos. Jesús se humilló a Sí mismo y se convirtió en un siervo de los hombres, vivió una vida perfecta, murió una muerte perfecta, y venció la muerte a través de la resurrección. No hay esperanza más grande que podamos tener para nuestro futuro que Jesucristo.

4

Todo lo puedo en Cristo que me fortalece

OTTO SÁNCHEZ

Sé vivir en pobreza (vivir humildemente), y sé vivir en prosperidad. En todo y por todo he aprendido el secreto tanto de estar saciado como de tener hambre, de tener abundancia como de sufrir necesidad. Todo lo puedo en Cristo que me fortalece (Fil. 4:12–13).

"Yo sé que me irá bien en el examen, porque todo lo puedo en Cristo que me fortalece".

"Estoy decidida a bajar de peso, porque todo lo puedo en Cristo que me fortalece".

"Me declaro sano, porque todo lo puedo en Cristo que me fortalece."

Creo que todo creyente que lleve cierto tiempo en el evangelio estará de acuerdo conmigo en que Filipenses 4:13 es uno de los textos más conocidos, más amados, y más citados de toda la Biblia. De lo que no estoy seguro es de si la mayoría de los creyentes estarán de acuerdo conmigo cuando afirmo que también Filipenses 4:13 es uno de los textos bíblicos más abusados y malinterpretados. He escuchado a muchos cristianos decir que pueden afrontar con éxito todo desafío de la vida porque todo lo pueden en Cristo que los fortalece. Ven este texto como un instrumento de triunfo, motivación y fe ante cualquier circunstancia de la vida, pensando que podemos llegar a ser superhéroes de la fe.

Ante esta realidad nos preguntamos ¿es cierto que Filipenses 4:13 quiere decir que los creyentes todo lo podemos —sin importar la situación— porque Cristo nos fortalece? La respuesta está en el texto mismo.

La fuerza del Señor

Antes de proseguir, debo aclarar que la dificultad en el manejo de este texto no está en que Cristo nos fortalece. Desde el Antiguo Testamento vemos la disposición de Dios de ayudar de Su pueblo. Veamos algunos ejemplos:

> Él da fuerzas al fatigado, y al que no tiene fuerzas, aumenta el vigor (Isa. 40:29).

> No temas, porque Yo estoy contigo; no te desalientes, porque Yo soy tu Dios. Te fortaleceré, ciertamente te ayudaré (Isa. 41:10).

El Nuevo Testamento nos muestra algo similar:

> Le ruego que Él les conceda a ustedes, conforme a las riquezas de Su gloria, el ser fortalecidos con poder por Su Espíritu en el hombre interior (Ef. 3:16).

…fortalecidos con todo poder según la potencia de
Su gloria, para obtener toda perseverancia y paciencia, con gozo (Col. 1:11).

El problema en la interpretación que popularmente se le da al
texto no es que afirmemos que el Señor nos fortalece. Esto es algo evidente y obvio por lo que nos dice Su Palabra, y también en las distintas
experiencias particulares de los cristianos. ¿Qué sería de nosotros si
no contáramos con la fortaleza del Señor? El problema está en que le
demos un significado que el contexto del versículo no resiste.

Leamos el pasaje en su contexto

Cuando vamos a interpretar un texto, resulta útil leerlo en varias
versiones de la Biblia y procurar observar los detalles. Una buena idea
es hacer lo que dice Ramesh Richard[1] cuando propone que todo texto
bíblico consta de "carne", "huesos" y "corazón". "Carne" se refiere a
la información que podemos extraer del texto, como autor, destinatarios, datos generales, etc. Los "huesos" se refieren a la estructura-
ción o puntos del texto, la manera en que está organizado y cómo
se presentan sus ideas. El "corazón" se refiere a determinar la idea
o verdad central del texto, porque todo texto tiene la idea central
o las ideas centrales que el autor concibió. Es en este último punto
que muchos creyentes han fallado al momento de aplicar Filipenses
4:13. Hicieron una mala aplicación porque primero hicieron una mala
interpretación.

---

[1] Ramesh Richard, *Siete pasos para la predicación expositiva* (Buenos Aires: FADEAC,
2002).

Entonces, ¿cuál es la interpretación correcta y qué es lo que Pablo quiere decir?

Filipenses 4:13 está dentro de un contexto marcado por los versículos anteriores y posteriores. Entonces, si leemos el contexto nos daremos cuenta de que Pablo está haciendo exhortaciones diversas a los hermanos de Filipos, entre ellas:

- A permanecer firmes (v. 1);
- A las hermanas Evodia y Síntique a ser de un mismo sentir, y a que su fiel compañero ayude a estas mujeres que combatieron por el evangelio (vv. 2-3);
- A regocijarse en el Señor, y ser bondadosos, y a orar en vez de afanarse y distraerse con cosas materiales (vv. 4-7);
- Además, amonesta a los destinatarios a pensar solo en lo que es digno de alabanza (vv. 8-9).

En los versículos siguientes (Fil. 4:10-18), el apóstol pasa de la exhortación a la gratitud. Estos versos, vistos de manera detallada, evidencian su confianza en el Señor y que, aunque agradece a los filipenses sus dádivas, la dependencia de Pablo sin lugar a dudas está en el Señor (vv. 10-13). También puede apreciarse su gozo y gratitud por el apoyo económico que recibió de los filipenses, y su confianza en el Dios amoroso y soberano que le ha permitido vivir en diferentes situaciones: algunas de abundancias y otras de escasez. Él confiesa que siempre se ha visto acompañado y sostenido, lo cual dio como resultado lecciones de dependencia en el Señor que él no habría de olvidar (Fil. 4:14-20).

La visita de Epafrodito, la compañía de Timoteo, y la amistad de tantos hermanos que iban a verlo jamás podrían fortalecer su espíritu como Cristo Jesús lo hacía. "Todo lo puedo en Cristo que me fortalece" no es un *mantra* que vamos a repetir como resultado de nuestra fe para no tener límites en las distintas circunstancias que nos toca vivir. Más bien es un testimonio personal del apóstol Pablo, que tiene como idea central la confianza y el gozo en un Dios bondadoso y soberano que lo llevó por caminos de abundancia y también de escasez (v. 12) pero que él *todo* lo podía (vivir en una situación o en la otra) porque Cristo lo fortalecía. Lo que este texto quiere enseñarnos es que el apóstol podía enfrentarse con cualquier situación relacionada con sus necesidades materiales y mantener siempre una actitud positiva y un espíritu de contentamiento que agradara a Dios.

Hoy en día, "todo lo puedo en Cristo que me fortalece" es más necesario que nunca, pues este es un tiempo de excesiva sobreestimación de lo material, de mensajes distorsionados que consideran los momentos de escasez económica como una maldición y no como un medio de gracia que Dios puede usar para llevarnos a la dependencia y al gozo. Este texto es una exhortación al contentamiento y a la fortaleza que recibimos de un Dios fiel, más allá de las circunstancias económicas en las que nos encontremos.

"Todo lo puedo en Cristo que me fortalece", tenga trabajo o no.

"Todo lo puedo en Cristo que me fortalece", en estos tiempos de economía mundial tambaleante.

"Todo lo puedo en Cristo que me fortalece", aunque la tierra no dé su fruto, ni haya vacas en los corrales.

5

Pide en el nombre de Jesús

NATHAN DÍAZ

*Y todo lo que pidan en Mi nombre, lo haré, para que el
Padre sea glorificado en el Hijo. Si Me piden algo en Mi
nombre, Yo lo haré (Juan 14:13-14).*

Un ateo me desafió una vez a explicarle cómo es que se puede confiar en la Biblia cuando está llena de promesas que obviamente no se cumplen. Él se refirió en aquella oportunidad a este pasaje de Juan, donde Cristo nos dice que hará lo que pidamos en Su nombre, puesto que era evidente que muchos cristianos pedían cosas en nombre de Jesús y no se cumplían.

¿Es cierto que Dios hace lo que sea que pidamos en el nombre de Jesús? Si no lo hace, parece estar mintiendo. Pero, como pasa con todo versículo de la Biblia, leer correctamente el contexto nos ayuda a aclarar el verdadero significado del texto. Si queremos saber si Dios hará lo que pedimos, debemos hacernos las siguientes preguntas.

1. ¿Será el Padre glorificado en el Hijo con mi petición?

Romanos 11:36 dice que todas las cosas son de Él, por Él y para Él. La manifestación de Su gloria es el propósito final y superior en todo lo que Dios hace. Por eso dice Juan 14:13: "...para que el Padre sea glorificado en el Hijo". Ese es el propósito por el cual Dios hace lo que pedimos.

Jesús nos dio un ejemplo muy claro de este tipo de peticiones que están motivadas por un deseo de la gloria de Dios. Cuando explicó el propósito de la muerte de Lázaro, Él dijo: "Esta enfermedad no es para muerte, sino para la gloria de Dios, para que el Hijo de Dios sea glorificado por medio de ella" (Juan 11:4). ¿Y qué vemos aquí? Que cuando Jesús oró para que Lázaro resucitara, ¡Dios contestó!

2. ¿En qué confío, en la sabiduría de Dios o en la mía?

Justo después de que Cristo dijo que contestaría las oraciones que hagamos en Su nombre está la promesa del Espíritu Santo. Jesús promete que no nos dejará huérfanos (Juan 14:18). Esta dependencia y guía del Espíritu es lo que debe regir nuestras peticiones. Dependemos de la guía del Dios sabio para tomar decisiones sabias y vivir correctamente la vida cristiana.

¿Sabemos en realidad qué es lo mejor para nosotros? Si en verdad consideramos que Dios es más sabio que nosotros, diremos junto con el apóstol Pablo: "De la misma manera, también el Espíritu nos ayuda en nuestra debilidad. No sabemos orar como debiéramos, pero el Espíritu mismo intercede *por nosotros* con gemidos indecibles. Y Aquél que escudriña los corazones sabe cuál es el sentir del Espíritu, porque Él intercede por los santos conforme a *la voluntad* de Dios" (Rom. 8:26-27).

Esto significa que al pedirle algo a Dios, debemos hacerlo en un espíritu de humildad y dependencia. Debemos procurar una actitud que demuestre fe: "A mí me gustaría que hicieras esto, pero sé que tú ves un panorama mucho más extenso y profundo que el que yo puedo ver. Por favor, haz lo que el Espíritu está intercediendo por mí ahora".

Ese es el tipo de oración que glorifica al Padre, el tipo de oración que muestra dependencia y confianza en Su soberanía y Su superioridad para conocer el mejor lugar al que nos puede llevar como hijos Suyos. Ese lugar podría ser la escasez económica, la enfermedad, o aun la muerte. ¿Por qué querríamos que Dios nos diera algo menos que lo mejor? Y solo Él sabe qué es realmente mejor.

3. ¿Quiero lo mismo que quiere Dios?

Hace poco realicé un estudio sobre el Padre Nuestro basado en una serie de mensajes de David Platt. En uno de los mensajes, el pastor Platt decía: "Desea lo que Dios desea, y luego pide lo que quieras". Me parece que allí está la verdadera clave de que una oración sea contestada. Entre más vayamos creciendo en santidad hacia ser más como Cristo en nuestra manera de pensar, más oraciones veremos contestadas. Por eso dice el versículo 15, justo después del texto que estamos considerando, "Si ustedes Me aman, guardarán Mis mandamientos". Nuestro amor a Dios siempre se verá reflejado en las cosas que deseamos, porque lo que deseamos es un reflejo de lo que valoramos. Jesús dice que el reflejo de nuestro amor por Él es cómo valoramos Sus mandamientos en nuestras vidas.

Este concepto lo vuelve a reforzar Juan en 15:16, pero ahora Sus mandamientos se convierten en fruto: "...y los designé para que vayan y den fruto, y que su fruto permanezca; para que todo lo que pidan al

Padre en Mi nombre se *lo* conceda". Dios quiere que llevemos fruto, por lo tanto, cada vez que pidamos llevar fruto y que ese fruto permanezca, no debemos tener la menor duda: Dios contestará esa oración.

Conclusión

La oración no es para que Dios se someta a nosotros, sino para que nosotros nos sometamos a Dios. Y esa es la verdadera fe. La que hace cosas sobrenaturales y mueve montañas. La que muestra que Dios hará todo aquello que lo glorifique. Y cada vez que pidamos que Jesús sea glorificado en la manera que Dios conteste nuestra oración, tengamos por seguro que lo hará, aunque signifique arrancar un monte de su lugar para echarlo al mar. Pidámosle a Dios llevar fruto para Su gloria. Solo Dios sabe en Su infinita sabiduría cómo y dónde lo hará. Pero sí, lo hará.

6

Cristo se hizo pobre para que fueras rico

CARLOS CONTRERAS

Porque conocen la gracia de nuestro Señor Jesucristo,
que siendo rico, sin embargo por amor a ustedes se
hizo pobre, para que por medio de Su pobreza ustedes
llegaran a ser ricos (2 Cor. 8:9).

"¡Dios quiere que seas rico!". De seguro oíste esta expresión. Quizás hasta has visto este versículo usado para explicar y justificar que la muerte de Cristo garantiza prosperidad económica. Y es que este es un clásico ejemplo de un versículo que es tomado para injertarle un significado que no le corresponde. Esa es una costumbre común cuando vamos a la Biblia para encontrar justificación a alguna de nuestras creencias. Debemos recordar que la Biblia no es un formulario ni un recetario adonde vamos para tratar de encontrar lo que queremos. La Biblia contiene lo que en realidad necesitamos, pero es ella misma la que nos lo revela, la que discierne nuestras almas y nos confronta con la verdad. Debemos venir a la Biblia para que sea ella la que nos hable, no para darle expresión a nuestras propias ideas o invenciones.

Este texto de 2 Corintios se usa mucho para promover el mal llamado "Evangelio de la Prosperidad". Digo mal llamado porque no es en verdad un evangelio. No son buenas noticias. Es una terrible distorsión del evangelio de Jesucristo, una deformación del asombroso mensaje de que Jesús vino a morir por nosotros para darnos vida en y con Él por toda la eternidad. Este "evangelio" rebaja esas buenas nuevas al cambiar el objetivo de la muerte de Jesucristo; ya no para llevarnos a Dios, sino para que tengamos una vida de prosperidad y holgura en este mundo. El verdadero evangelio nos anuncia que Cristo murió para darnos de Su vida abundante y para que la disfrutemos con Él por la eternidad. El falso evangelio te dice que debes buscar una vida "buena" en el aquí y el ahora, gozando de las riquezas de este mundo.

Algo mayor que dinero

El texto que estamos considerando no enseña que Cristo vino a la tierra para proveernos riqueza material. Tiene otro significado. Uno de mucho mayor importancia. 2 Corintios 8:9 inicia con el recordatorio a los corintios de que ya "conocen la gracia de nuestro Señor Jesucristo". Esa es la gracia de Dios en referencia al verdadero evangelio, la gracia manifestada en la iniciativa de Dios mismo en venir a rescatarnos de nuestra perdición. Ellos ya la conocen y deben recordarla siempre. Nunca debemos olvidar lo que Él hizo por nosotros. Ese acto de humillación y sacrificio voluntario con el fin de ofrecernos el perdón por nuestros pecados y una vida eterna completamente inmerecidos.

Si leemos el contexto del pasaje nos daremos cuenta de cuál es la razón de este versículo. Este fragmento es un paréntesis en un argumento de Pablo para con la iglesia en Corinto, llamándolos a que sean liberales y fieles en su promesa de dar de sus bienes materiales para aliviar la necesidad de la empobrecida iglesia en Jerusalén. El autor toma como ejemplo el sacrificio de nuestro Señor Jesucristo para demostrar que, si Él estuvo dispuesto a empobrecerse, los corintios, así como las iglesias de Macedonia (2 Cor. 8:2-3), también deberían estar dispuestos a dar con una riqueza de liberalidad. Los macedonios le suplicaron, a pesar de su pobreza material, que les concediera el privilegio de aportar para esa necesidad (2 Cor. 8:4), y Pablo quiere que los corintios también muestren esa misma disposición sacrificial. Todo el capítulo 8 de 2 Corintios no apunta a que Cristo murió para que los cristianos tengan más posesiones, sino para que den de lo que ya tienen.

Alguien mayor que las riquezas

Cuando Pablo nos habla de que Cristo se hizo pobre, está pensando en el ejemplo de vida que el mismo Señor nos dejó. Jesús se humilló a Sí mismo, despojándose de Sus prerrogativas divinas de gloria para tomar forma de siervo (Fil. 2:6-7). Un siervo que nació en un pesebre, creció como hijo de un carpintero, y, cuando salió a cumplir su ministerio, lo hizo sin tener un lugar en donde recostar su cabeza (Luc. 9:58). Cristo no vino para ser servido, sino para servir y para dar Su vida en rescate por muchos (Mat. 20:28). Cristo se empobreció porque Él era el precio a pagar por la salvación de nuestras almas. Se humilló hasta lo sumo, hasta el punto de morir desnudo, destrozado y consumido como un criminal maldito colgado de un madero (Gál. 3:13). Este es el pensamiento que consumía a Pablo: Su Rey y Salvador se había humillado de esta forma para ofrecernos, de manera gratuita, la gran riqueza de ser llamados Hijos de Dios y coherederos con Cristo.

Pero además, Pablo está pensando en el llamado que Cristo hizo a Sus discípulos a no vivir confiando en las riquezas materiales. Los llamó, y por ende a nosotros también, a nunca estar preocupados por nuestro sustento o vestimenta (Mat. 6:24-25), porque Él es capaz y suficiente para cuidar de nosotros. Nos alertó en contra de confiar y servir a las riquezas, pues son engañosas y destructivas (Mat. 13:22; 1 Tim. 6:17). De hecho, nos advirtió que a los que tienen riquezas les es muy difícil entrar en el reino de Dios (Mar. 10:23). El mismo Pablo nos explica en otro lugar que la raíz de todos los males es el amor al dinero, ya que tiene el poder de extraviar de la fe salvadora y hundir a los hombres en la perdición (1 Tim. 6:9-10).

Cristo también habló de las riquezas mundanas como injustas, y anticipó a Sus discípulos las riquezas verdaderas que habrían de recibir (Luc. 16:11). Por ello, nos llama como discípulos Suyos a hacer tesoro en los cielos, donde no hay ladrones ni polillas que lo destruyan, y lo hace en el contexto de estar aún dispuestos a despojarnos de las cosas materiales, siendo generosos con los pobres (Mat. 19:21; Luc. 12:33). Esto está en total oposición con un mensaje de enriquecimiento terrenal, y es coherente con lo que leemos en 2 Corintios 8:9. Cristo nunca afirmó que vino a morir para hacernos ricos materialmente. Al contrario, vino para hacernos libres de las riquezas materiales.

El problema de malinterpretar

Entonces, ¿por qué es tan peligroso que algunos tuerzan el significado de este pasaje? Porque rebaja la riqueza del significado del sacrificio de Cristo. Es una terrible depreciación del gran valor del sacrificio de nuestro Salvador. Es darle a la muerte del Santo Hijo de

Dios el despreciable valor de cosas temporales y vanas. Es decir que Cristo descendió del Cielo y se encarnó en el evento más significativo de la historia del hombre para que puedas tener un automóvil nuevo.

Jesús vino para ofrecer verdaderas riquezas espirituales. Vino para ofrecer riquezas de bondad, paciencia y compasión para aquellos que merecían Su justo juicio y condenación (Rom. 2:4). Vino para llamarnos a recibir de las riquezas de la gloria de Su herencia en los santos (Ef. 1:18), y a que vivamos por Su bondad manifestando continuamente evidencia de las sobreabundantes riquezas de Su gracia para con nosotros, Sus amados (Ef. 2:7). Son esas riquezas de Su gloria las que nos llenan de gozo inefable (1 Ped. 1:8) y nos fortalecen con Su poder en nuestro ser. ¿Qué mayor riqueza pudo haber mostrado Dios para con nosotros en que siendo aún pecadores seamos ahora llamados Hijos de Dios? (1 Jn. 3:1).

Perspectiva correcta

Pero entonces, ¿no es legítimo que una persona busque salir de su pobreza material? Creo sin lugar a dudas que es legítimo que se busque aplicar principios bíblicos, como el trabajo diligente, la frugalidad, y el ahorro. Y creo que Dios, por Su gracia, prosperará a esa persona. Pero el apóstol Santiago, al poner el ejemplo de los pobres, nos dice que Dios los escoge, pero no para enriquecerlos materialmente, sino para que sean ricos en la fe, como coherederos del reino (Sant. 2:5). También el autor de Hebreos nos recuerda el ejemplo de Moisés, que escogió identificarse con el penoso oprobio de Cristo antes que con las riquezas de los tesoros de Egipto (Heb. 11:24-26).

El creyente virtuoso y maduro debe buscar identificarse con los sufrimientos de Cristo antes que con los placeres y bienes que este mundo ofrece. Pablo y los apóstoles consideraban un privilegio que a los creyentes se les concediera participar de los sufrimientos de Cristo (Rom. 5:3; Fil. 1:29; 1 Ped. 4:13). La Biblia nos enseña que las tribulaciones de este mundo, incluyendo la pobreza, son oportunidades para crecer en piedad y para glorificar a nuestro Dios por medio de nuestra respuesta en fe y confianza de que es Él quien tiene cuidado de nosotros. Debemos procurar ser fieles en nuestro trabajo y aplicar principios bíblicos de mayordomía con los recursos que Él nos ha dado. Pero no por amor al dinero, sino por amor al Dador. Y aun esto, como Pablo instruyó a los corintios, es para abundar en dádivas a los necesitados, no para aumentar nuestras posesiones.

Conclusión

Este pasaje en 2 Corintios es un hermoso recordatorio de la magnanimidad del evangelio de Jesucristo. Es ese testimonio el que nos debe llamar de continuo a la liberalidad, a dar a otros de gracia de lo que por gracia hemos recibido. Pero también nos muestra que la Biblia nos llama específicamente a buscar de manera específica, no la riqueza material, sino la riqueza espiritual. Somos llamados a ser ricos en Cristo. A buscar la riqueza que procede de una verdadera y profunda comprensión en el conocimiento de la persona de Cristo (Col. 2:2). Él es, a fin de cuentas, nuestra máxima riqueza. Él es nuestro absoluto tesoro.

7

Instruye al niño en su camino y no se apartará de él

JOSÉ MERCADO

Instruye al niño en el camino que debe andar, y aun cuando sea viejo no se apartará de él (Prov. 22:6).

La gran mayoría de los padres cristianos tienen el clamor en su corazón de que sus hijos sirvan a Dios. Con buenas intenciones, muchos padres se aferran a este texto de Proverbios con la esperanza de ver a sus hijos crecer y que puedan permanecer en la senda de la justicia. Toman este verso como un ancla que les da esperanza en momentos de dificultad. Años después, vemos que se preguntan ¿por qué mi hijo se apartó del camino? Con tristeza, vemos que en ocasiones este pasaje parece no cumplirse en sus vidas. Todos aquellos que crecimos en la Iglesia sabemos de muchos amigos que ya no sirven a Dios, a pesar de ser hijos de cristianos. ¿Qué sucedió? ¿Dios no cumplió Su promesa? Es importante interpretar de forma adecuada Proverbios 22:6 para poder navegar en el difícil reto de la crianza de nuestros hijos.

El asunto de los géneros

Uno de los principales problemas al interpretar la Palabra es que muchos no toman en cuenta el género literario que están leyendo. La Biblia fue escrita por hombres inspirados por el Espíritu Santo. Esto no quiere decir que era necesariamente un dictado de Dios, pues Él usó las personalidades, experiencias y vidas de cada uno de los escritores para comunicar la verdad de Su plan de redención. De esta forma, Dios decidió compartir Su Palabra completamente inspirada por Él, a la vez que utilizó los géneros literarios para ayudarnos a interpretar el mensaje que cada pasaje quiere transmitirnos.

Cuando lees un libro que comienza diciendo "Érase una vez... " sabes que lo que estás a punto de leer es un cuento de hadas. Eso te dice que no es verídico, que tiene personajes que no son reales, y con frecuencia la historia tiene una moraleja. De la misma forma, cada género de la Biblia nos comparte claves para ayudarnos a interpretar el mensaje que está comunicando. Si queremos ser fieles a ese mensaje original inspirado por Dios, debemos tomar en cuenta el género literario.

En el caso del libro de los Proverbios, muchas veces las personas lo toman como un manual de promesas, como acontecimientos que siempre deben suceder. No obstante, el mismo libro nos dice cómo debe ser usado:

> Los proverbios de Salomón, hijo de David, rey de Israel: para aprender sabiduría e instrucción, para discernir dichos profundos, para recibir instrucción en sabia conducta, justicia, juicio y equidad; para dar a los simples prudencia, *y* a los jóvenes

conocimiento y discreción. El sabio oirá y crecerá
en conocimiento, y el inteligente adquirirá habilidad, para entender proverbio y metáfora, las palabras de los sabios y sus enigmas (Prov. 1:1-6).

Podemos ver que Salomón nos dice cómo usar este libro. Nos da
la llave hermenéutica. Es para crecer en sabiduría y para actuar con
prudencia. En ningún momento afirma que es un libro de promesas
que Dios va a cumplir. Proverbios está lleno de consejos que, si los
aplicamos, *usualmente* tienen el resultado esperado. El empleo de la
palabra usualmente quiere decir que no siempre se van a cumplir, y
este es el caso con el pasaje que estamos viendo.

Aprender de la instrucción

Entonces, si "Enseña al niño el camino en que debe andar" no es
una promesa sino un verso que comparte sabiduría, ¿qué debemos
aprender de él? Este pasaje debe llevarnos a reflexionar sobre la
pregunta "¿Cómo instruyo a mis hijos en el camino de Dios?".
Durante mucho tiempo los padres han pensado que la respuesta
es nada más que llevar a los hijos a la iglesia. No importa cómo
lo hagamos, con tal de cumplir con este objetivo, de ahí en adelante les dejamos al pastor y a sus miembros que lo instruyan por
nosotros. Esta no es una forma bíblica de instruir a nuestros hijos.
Aunque la comunidad de creyentes tienen el rol de ayudarnos a
educarlos en el temor de Dios, la responsabilidad de la instrucción
recae en los padres.

En lo personal, creo en la teología bíblica llamada "Teología del
Pacto". Sin entrar en detalles, considero que la disposición de Dios

es salvar a los hijos de creyentes que están en el pacto, y esta disposición es evidente al nacer ellos en una familia de creyentes. Nuestra esperanza nunca está en cómo nosotros instruimos a nuestros hijos, sino que debe estar en un Dios soberano que es el único que puede dar vida a un corazón muerto. Nosotros no tenemos que cargar el peso de que la salvación de los hijos depende de nosotros. Dios nos salvó a nosotros, y de esa misma forma puede salvar a nuestros hijos. A la vez, Dios usa a los padres como medio de gracia para que la verdad del evangelio sea predicada y modelada en los hijos, y les dé la salvación.

¿Cómo instruimos a nuestros hijos?

Predicarles el evangelio.

Desde pequeños debemos decirles la verdad de que son pecadores, pero que Cristo vino al mundo para salvar a los pecadores de sus pecados.

Llenarlos de la Palabra.

Hablar de la Biblia debe ser algo que caracterice nuestros hogares.

Modelarles el evangelio.

Como padres, nunca debemos presentarnos como seres perfectos que jamás pecamos. Nos relacionamos con ellos como pecadores que somos, dejándoles saber que si hay algo bueno en nosotros, es la gracia de Dios en nuestras vidas.

Cuidarnos de la hipocresía.

Si nuestra vida es diferente de lo que predicamos, esto va a tentar a nuestros hijos. La forma en que se relacionan los padres y cómo tratan a sus hijos es crucial para proteger el evangelio.

Disciplinarlos.

Esto incluye instruirlos y corregirlos de acuerdo con la Palabra de Dios en las conductas que son contrarias al evangelio en sus vidas.

Velar por sus corazones.

Estamos más interesados en qué motiva sus corazones que en hacerles actuar de una forma que nos complace.

Expresarles nuestro amor.

Ellos siempre deben estar conscientes de nuestro amor y aceptación. Así como Dios nos ama, debemos amar a nuestros hijos.

Conclusión

Aunque Proverbios 22:6 no es una promesa, nos apunta a la sabiduría que necesitamos en la difícil tarea de criar a los hijos. Nuestra confianza no está en nosotros: está en Dios, nuestro único Salvador. Con esta confianza, podemos trabajar en ser fieles al llamado de instruirlos, para que Dios use esto como medio de gracia en la vida de ellos, para Su gloria.

8

Cree en Cristo y serás salvo

MATTHEW HALL

...Que si confiesas con tu boca a Jesús por Señor, y crees en tu corazón que Dios Lo resucitó de entre los muertos, serás salvo (Rom. 10:9).

Estoy convencido de que hay pocas promesas más hermosas y que provean más paz que la que el apóstol Pablo presenta en Romanos 10:9. Hay una profunda simplicidad en ella: confiesa a Jesús como Señor, cree en Su resurrección con tu corazón, y serás salvo.

El pueblo de Dios está compuesto por aquellos que confían en las buenas nuevas de que la salvación es solo por gracia mediante la fe en Cristo. Mientras los sistemas falsos añaden ciertas obras para ganar o merecer la salvación, el evangelio de Cristo es escandaloso: es Otro el que cumple la ley a la perfección y quien ganó la salvación en nombre de todos los que confían en Él como su sustituto. No podemos hacer nada para ganar nuestra salvación. Al contrario, nuestra única esperanza es que esa "justicia ajena" sea acreditada a nuestra cuenta.

Es la naturaleza simple y escandalosa del evangelio lo que nos da esperanza y seguridad. De no ser por el evangelio, nunca podríamos tener la garantía de saber si por fin hicimos lo suficiente para ganar-nos el favor de Dios. ¡Gracias a Dios por la justicia imputada de Cristo y Su perfecta obediencia!

Así que, si Romanos 10:9 nos dice la verdad del evangelio, ¿por qué tantos cristianos (incluso pastores) parecen estar tan confundidos por este versículo? Una vez más, es necesario conocer el contexto para entender el texto. En base a la totalidad de la revelación de Dios en la Escritura, hay dos cosas que podemos concluir con certeza que este texto no está diciendo.

1) Pablo no está sugiriendo que somos salvos por nuestras obras u oraciones.

Algunos cristianos han tomado este versículo para sugerir que solo recitar una oración es lo que salva a la gente. En otras palabras, si podemos hacer que la gente rece la "oración del pecador", entonces podemos asegurarles que son salvas.

Eso está lejos de la doctrina bíblica de la conversión. La Palabra de Dios deja en claro que somos salvos solo por fe. Nuestras buenas obras no nos ganan nada delante de Dios. De hecho, Isaías 64:6 dice que son como trapos de inmundicia. Si el acto verbal de rezar una oración fuera lo que nos salvara, sería una forma de justicia por obras. Llegaríamos a la conclusión de que el factor determinante de nuestra salvación sería haber "rezado la oración". Pero la cuestión clave en el evangelio es la fe.

Por supuesto, es muy natural y apropiado que cuando Dios con-cede la fe y el arrepentimiento a un pecador, eso se haga evidente a través de una oración. Esto es, en parte, lo que Pablo está queriendo decir en este mismo versículo. Pero eso es bastante diferente a decirle a alguien que la oración en sí es lo que lo salva. Aquello es un "evangelio" de abracadabra, no el evangelio de Cristo.

2) Pablo no está diciendo que las buenas obras no tienen importancia.

Toda la Carta a los Romanos es clara. Somos justificados –declarados justos– sobre la base de la fe, no por las obras. La ley –el conjunto de mandamientos que el Antiguo Testamento ordenaba que el pueblo cumpliera– es incapaz de salvar a nadie, y es que la intención de Dios nunca fue esa, sino mostrarnos nuestra necesidad de misericordia y de una justicia que no es nuestra (Rom. 3:19-24).

Así que algunos podrían concluir que este versículo transmite la idea de que tomar una decisión inicial de seguir Jesús es todo lo que importa. "Confiésalo como salvador y listo: serás salvo". Esto sugiere que la autoridad de Cristo como Salvador puede estar divorciada de Su autoridad como Señor. Pero ni en este verso ni en ningún otro lugar de las Escrituras hay una categoría para un cristiano que vive igual que aquellos en el mundo.

¿Cómo somos salvos?

Entonces, ¿qué está diciendo Pablo? Nota que este versículo es parte de la carta de Pablo a los cristianos de Roma, a quienes les asegura que el evangelio es para judíos y para gentiles; por la fe, aparte de la ley, y a través de la buena voluntad soberana de Dios, a fin de formar un pueblo para Sí mismo. Estas son buenas noticias. Todos estábamos muertos en nuestros pecados. La ley no fue capaz de salvar a nadie. Y en la carta, el apóstol se enfrenta a un desafío teológico increíble.

¿Cómo es que el evangelio viene a "gentiles que no iban tras la justicia", pero que Israel "que persigue una ley que llevaría a la justicia" no tuvo éxito en llegar a esa ley? Por un lado, se pone de manifiesto en el capítulo 9 que esto se debe por completo a la elección libre y soberana de Dios. Pero la buena noticia es que Dios salva a todos los que invocan a Cristo, judío o gentil, porque la justicia que es por la fe es la que da vida (Rom. 10:5-6).

¿Y cómo luce la fe cuando Dios por gracia la otorga a un pecador? Es espectacularmente simple. Se trata de una confesión de fe y una creencia, una confianza en la obra salvífica de Jesús y Su tumba vacía. Ese es el punto de Romanos 10:9. No hay nadie, sin importar la raza, la clase social, la etnia o el género, que esté demasiado lejos para ser reconciliado con Dios.

Como Pablo aclara más adelante en Romanos y en el resto de sus epístolas, nuestra fe por fuerza dará frutos. O, como dijo Martín Lutero: "Somos salvos por la fe sola, pero la fe que salva no está sola". La fe salvadora siempre se manifestará mediante buenas obras en las vidas del pueblo de Dios. Sí, vamos a ser imperfectos y tropezaremos con el pecado. Pero la vida de alguien que ha confesado a Cristo como Señor y ha creído en Él es una vida que también exhibirá el fruto del Espíritu. Esta es la razón por la que solo un par de capítulos más adelante, Pablo da una lista bastante explícita de mandamientos y expectativas de lo que debe caracterizar a un cristiano.

Conclusión

Si eres cristiano, es por la simple promesa del evangelio de Jesucristo. Ni tú ni yo hicimos nada para contribuir a nuestra salvación o para merecerla. Por el contrario, es un don gratuito de Dios. ¡Gracias a

Dios por esa buena noticia! Pero recuerda la exhortación del mismo apóstol Pablo "ocúpense en su salvación con temor y temblor" (Fil. 2:12). Esto es lo que significa ser un discípulo, salvo por gracia y llamado a seguir a Cristo como maestro. Gracia y misericordia indescriptibles, que nos llaman a una vida que dé testimonio del reinado de Cristo sobre el universo.

9

Dios es amor

ENRIQUE ORIOLO

El que no ama no conoce a Dios, porque Dios es amor
(1 Jn. 4:8).

"Yo no creo en el infierno porque Dios es amor".

"Si Dios es bueno y es amor, ¿cómo no me va a perdonar?".

"Dios me ama y sabe que hago lo mejor que puedo: Él es amor".

¿Escuchaste alguna vez una de estas frases? Seguro que sí. Yo las escuché. No recuerdo haberlas dicho, pero de seguro he pensado cosas similares. Crecí como un católico romano que procuraba cumplir todo lo que tenía que cumplir: me confesaba cada dos meses, iba a misa todos los domingos, tomaba la eucaristía. Yo era más religioso que mis compañeros de clase, que mis amigos del barrio. Si a eso le sumamos que ¡Dios es amor!, ¡ya está! ¿Qué más necesito?

De plano debo decirlo: Dios es amor, y Dios ama de un modo increíble. Negar tal cosa sería negar la Biblia. Lo importante es ver el resto de la panorámica sobre esta idea y este texto de 1 Juan 4:8, que también se presenta unos versículos más abajo: "Y nosotros hemos llegado a conocer y hemos creído el amor que Dios tiene para nosotros.

Dios es amor, y el que permanece en amor permanece en Dios y Dios permanece en él" (1 Jn. 4:16). Dios es amor, pero... ¿es solo eso?

El panorama en la Biblia

En su Primera Epístola, Juan está interesado en traernos seguridad y convicción a nosotros, los cristianos. Seguridad sobre nuestra vida en Cristo y convicción sobre la verdad que hemos oído desde el principio. Así leemos: "Estas cosas les he escrito a ustedes que creen en el nombre del Hijo de Dios, para que sepan que tienen vida eterna" (1 Jn. 5:13). También nos dijo antes: "No les he escrito porque ignoren la verdad, sino porque la conocen y porque ninguna mentira procede de la verdad" (1 Jn. 2:21) y "Les he escrito estas cosas respecto a los que están tratando de engañarlos" (1 Jn. 2:26).

Los falsos maestros estaban introduciendo sus herejías en la iglesia, y Juan advierte al pueblo de Dios de que ellos ya conocen la verdad. Es por eso que en los primeros versículos de la carta Juan utiliza expresiones como: "hemos oído... hemos visto... hemos contemplado... han palpado nuestras manos... damos testimonio...". Estos términos son intencionales: están hablando del que existía desde el principio y del que estaba con el Padre y se manifestó: Jesucristo.

Entender el amor

En medio de los marcados contrastes entre el mundo y la iglesia, entre los hijos de Satanás y los hijos de Dios, entre la luz y las tinieblas, entre el amor y el odio, Juan coloca allí nuestro texto: "Dios es amor". El amor es un tema recurrente en las cartas de Juan, y para poder entender lo que él nos está diciendo, nuestro concepto de amor debe ser el mismo concepto que maneja Juan al escribir. El mismo apóstol Juan nos dejó registrado que Jesús dijo en Su ministerio terrenal que no hay mayor amor que dar la vida por sus amigos (Juan 15:13). Así se mostró el amor de Dios: por medio del sacrificio sustitutorio de Cristo en la cruz del Calvario: "En esto se manifestó el amor de Dios en nosotros: en que Dios ha enviado a Su Hijo unigénito (único) al mundo para que vivamos por *medio de* Él" (1 Jn. 4:9). El Hijo unigénito del Padre murió para que nosotros vivamos por medio de Él y podamos ser llamados hijos de Dios.

"Miren cuán gran amor nos ha otorgado el Padre: que seamos llamados hijos de Dios. Y *eso* somos" (1 Jn. 3:1). "En esto conocemos el amor: en que Él puso Su vida por nosotros" (1 Jn. 3:16). Si comprendemos esto podemos ver que no estamos hablando de un amor poético, de fantasía. De un amor que tiene ojos ciegos y que no toma en cuenta nuestras acciones porque "el amor es más fuerte". El amor de Dios por nosotros ha costado la vida de Jesucristo. No es un juego. Si dos veces se dice que Dios es amor, dos veces se dice que Dios es justo, y se nos dice como algo que debemos saber: "Si saben que Él es justo, saben también que todo el que hace justicia es nacido de Él" (1 Jn. 2:29); "Hijos míos, que nadie los engañe. El que practica la justicia es justo, así como Él es justo" (1 Jn. 3:7).

Amor y justicia

La justicia de Dios requiere que el culpable reciba su castigo (comp. Ezeq. 18:20; Ex. 34:7), y Dios no puede ir en contra de sí mismo. Su amor no puede ir en contra de Su justicia. Dios ama al hombre, pero el hombre se rebeló contra Él, se volvió Su enemigo y cambió la gloria de Dios por la adoración de ídolos. En Su amor, Dios quiere otorgar Su perdón. En Su justicia, Él quiere castigar al culpable. Es aquí donde el evangelio brilla más fuerte: Dios es justo, entonces no te puede perdonar solo porque te ama o porque es amor. De hecho, Dios es amor, por lo que no quiere dejarte en tu pecado. Él debe hacer que ese pecado sea borrado de tu cuenta.

Dios no podía perdonarme por el hecho de que yo era más religioso que el resto de mis compañeros, ni porque yo cumplía ciertas reglas religiosas, porque por las obras ningún hombre puede ser hecho justo (Rom. 3:20). Dios tuvo que remover el pecado de mi cuenta, tuvo que satisfacer la ira que estaba sobre mí, y ejecutar el justo juicio que me esperaba. ¿Y cómo Dios fue amor y justo al mismo tiempo? Cuando Jesucristo, que vivió una vida sin pecado, fue a la cruz a morir como un pecador. El pecado, la ira y el justo juicio que estaban a mi nombre fueron pasados a Su cuenta; y Su vida perfecta, sin pecado y justa, fue aplicada a mi cuenta.

El Hijo unigénito de Dios tuvo que morir para que yo pueda formar parte de Su familia. Si perdemos a Dios el justo, perdemos a Dios como amor, y nos quedamos con un recorte fotográfico que distorsiona el panorama. Si unimos la justicia y el amor de Dios, nos encontramos con una cruz. Y es desde la cruz que entendemos que Dios es amor.

Conclusión

¿Cómo entendemos que Dios es amor? Mirando hacia la cruz, la mayor entrega, la mayor expresión de amor, el dar la vida por otros. Es en el evangelio donde vemos al Dios que es amor. ¿Recuerdas Juan 3:16? De tal manera amó Dios al mundo que entregó. Dios es amor, y el amor de Dios se entiende en el evangelio.

10

Ojo por ojo

JUAN SÁNCHEZ

Pero si hubiera algún otro *daño, entonces pondrás* como castigo, *vida por vida, ojo por ojo, diente por diente, mano por mano, pie por pie, quemadura por quemadura, herida por herida, golpe por golpe (Éx. 21:23-25).*

¿Alguna vez has pensado por qué las películas de revancha son tan populares? Esas como *Gladiador, Corazón valiente, Búsqueda implacable*. Creo que estas películas son populares porque, en el fondo, cada uno de nosotros tiene un deseo innato por la justicia. Ahora bien, debido a nuestra naturaleza pecaminosa, el deseo por la justicia puede conducirnos con facilidad a la revancha, y esto nos puede llevar hacia un ciclo interminable de venganza. Dios, nuestro Creador, está consciente de esta realidad. Es por eso que en este texto de Éxodo 21, Él proveyó un estándar de justicia que pone límite a la sed de venganza.

El contexto del Antiguo Testamento: El pacto mosaico

Cuando Dios llevó a Israel al Monte Sinaí y les reveló los términos de Su pacto, en Éxodo 19-24, Él en primer lugar resumió Sus expectativas en diez palabras, lo que conocemos como los Diez Mandamientos (Éx. 20:1-17). Luego, Dios explicó con gran detalle lo que esperaba de Su pueblo Israel (Éx. 20:22-22:1). Uno de los principios que Dios explica es la ley de la justicia equitativa. Conocemos este principio como, "ojo por ojo", y también lo encontramos en Levítico 24:20 y Deuteronomio 19:21.

Por desgracia, esta ley de justicia equitativa ha sido aplicada y entendida de forma errónea. En vez de servir como la base de la justicia, ha sido utilizada como la base de la venganza. Jesús expone la mal aplicación que los fariseos hacían de este principio, en Mateo 5:38. Los fariseos habían pervertido este principio al usarlo como el fundamento de la venganza personal: "Si me haces X cosa a mí, ¡entonces tengo el derecho de hacerte X cosa a ti!". Cuando el principio se entiende y aplica de forma errónea, puede convertirse en una excusa para demandar nuestro derecho personal para hacerles a otros lo que entendemos que ellos nos han hecho en primer lugar.

El principio del Antiguo Testamento: Ojo por ojo

El contexto específico de la ley de la justicia equitativa en Éxodo 21:23-25 concierne a unos hombres involucrados en un altercado físico y que, por accidente, hieren a una mujer encinta. Si la mujer y el bebé resultaban ilesos, el hombre que la hirió debía pagar una multa propuesta por su marido y determinada por un juez (v. 22). No obstante, si había daños, ya sea contra la mujer o contra el bebé o contra ambos, entonces el pago era (v. 23):

- Vida por vida
- Ojo por ojo
- Diente por diente
- Mano por mano
- Pie por pie
- Quemadura por quemadura
- Herida por herida
- Golpe por golpe

Es evidente que la intención de la ley es proveer justicia equitativa. En términos modernos, podríamos decir que el punto de la ley es asegurarse de que el castigo sea adecuado al crimen. Tal principio tiene el propósito de proveer justicia, tanto para el inocente como para el culpable. Por ejemplo, en el caso de una mujer que pierde a su bebé por causa de la riña de dos hombres, el esposo puede ser tentado a establecer una multa exorbitante. O si la parte culpable es muy rica, puede evadir la justicia al pagar una multa sin que afecte su bolsillo. La ley de la justicia equitativa toma el veredicto de las manos de las partes involucradas y la pone en las manos de un tercero: un juez. Aunque el marido proponga una multa, el juez determina la cantidad.

El principio para hoy: perdón y tolerancia

El principio de la justicia equitativa (ojo por ojo) no es la base para ejecutar la venganza, sino una guía para llevar a cabo la justicia equitativa. Este principio quita la justicia de nuestras manos y la pone en las manos de un tercero juez, quien ha de asegurarse de que el castigo sea adecuado a la transgresión. Tal principio protege a la víctima de buscar revancha, ya que asegura que la justicia se cumplirá. Y también protege a la parte culpable, ya que asegura que el castigo será adecuado al crimen: ni más, ni menos.

No podemos cerrar aquí. El principio de la justicia equitativa expone el hecho de que todos nosotros hemos ofendido a un Dios santo y que nuestro castigo debe ser adecuado a nuestra transgresión. La paga por pecar en contra de un Dios santo es la pena de muerte. Pero el evangelio nos recuerda que Jesús, la única persona inocente y sin pecado, pagó la penalidad por nuestro pecado (vida por vida) al sufrir y morir en la cruz como un criminal. Todo aquel que reconoce su pecado y culpabilidad puede renunciar a su pecado y volverse a Cristo con fe para recibir el perdón por sus transgresiones. Todo aquel que se arrepiente de sus pecados y cree en Jesucristo experimenta la realidad de la satisfacción de la justicia de Dios en la muerte de Cristo.

Conclusión

Debido a que hemos sido perdonados, nosotros también podemos vivir una vida caracterizada por el perdón hacia otros. En otras palabras, la justicia equitativa de Dios al castigar nuestros pecados en Jesús nos libera de buscar venganza contra aquellos que pecan contra nosotros (Mat. 5:38-42). No necesitamos devolver mal por mal o injuria por injuria; al contrario, somos llamados a bendecir a aquellos que nos persiguen, demostrando así que somos hijos de Dios, que recibiremos Su herencia por venir (1 Ped. 3:8-17).

11

Atar al enemigo

GERSON MOREY

Yo te daré las llaves del reino de los cielos; y lo que ates
en la tierra, será atado en los cielos; y lo que desates en la
tierra, será desatado en los cielos (Mat. 16:19).

En verdad les digo, que todo lo que ustedes aten en la
tierra, será atado en el cielo; y todo lo que desaten en la
tierra, será desatado en el cielo (Mat. 18:18).

En nuestros días nos encontramos una y otra vez con un cristianismo que resalta las capacidades del hombre al punto de convertirlo casi en una deidad. A tal efecto, la iglesia ha malinterpretado el hecho de que el hombre fue creado "a semejanza de Dios", y a partir de ahí ha enseñado que el hombre, en cierta medida, puede hacer lo que Dios hace.

En ese sentido, una de las enseñanzas que está muy arraigada en los círculos cristianos es que los creyentes también podemos declarar y mandar con autoridad, así como Dios lo hace. Mejor dicho, que nuestras palabras tienen tanto poder como las palabras de Dios.

Dicha autoridad, dicen, incluye un poder que los creyentes tenemos para "atar al diablo y sus demonios". La justificación bíblica para esta práctica es tomada de dos textos del Evangelio de Mateo, y en ambos casos Jesús les está enseñando a Sus discípulos algunos aspectos de la autoridad que la Iglesia tendría en su misión en la tierra.

Atar, desatar y el evangelio

El primer texto lo encontramos en Mateo 16, cuando Jesús les está preguntando a Sus discípulos: "Y ustedes, ¿quién dicen que soy Yo?" (Mat. 16:15). Pedro fue el único que respondió, diciendo: "Tú eres el Cristo (el Mesías), el Hijo del Dios viviente" (v. 16). El Señor anuncia que Su Iglesia será fundada sobre esta declaración, y es en este contexto que le dice a Pedro que le dará las llaves del reino y que lo que ate y desate en la tierra será atado y desatado en el cielo.

La referencia inmediata de este texto aplicaba al apóstol Pedro y luego a los otros discípulos, quienes fueron los pioneros que "abrieron" el acceso al reino, a través de la proclamación del evangelio. Su predicación hizo posible que tanto judíos como gentiles tuvieran la oportunidad de ser parte del reino de los cielos y recibir sus bendiciones.

Sin embargo, en su aplicación más amplia, esta autoridad "de atar y desatar" quedaba extendida a toda la Iglesia en su misión evangelizadora. En el cumplimiento de la Gran Comisión, la Iglesia de Jesucristo puede asegurar las bendiciones de acceso al reino o puede advertir de juicio y condenación a los hombres, según ellos respondan. Por esta razón, debemos recordar que cuando el creyente predica las buenas nuevas, puede darles seguridad de perdón de pecados a quienes se arrepienten, y aun advertir de juicio a quienes rechazan el mensaje del evangelio. Esa es la autoridad para atar y desatar que vemos en Mateo 16.

Atar, desatar y la disciplina

Ahora, el otro texto que nos enseña sobre esto de atar y desatar está en Mateo 18, y otra vez Jesús les está enseñando a sus discípulos diciendo:

> En verdad les digo, que todo lo que ustedes aten en
> la tierra, será atado en el cielo; y todo lo que desaten
> en la tierra, será desatado en el cielo (Mat. 18:18).

En esta oportunidad, el tema que el Señor está discutiendo es la disciplina eclesiástica. Jesús les está recordando a los discípulos la responsabilidad que la Iglesia tiene de ejercer disciplina a quien rehúsa ser corregido en vez de buscar arrepentimiento por un acto pecaminoso. Eso lo podemos ver por los versículos que anteceden:

> Si tu hermano peca, ve y repréndelo a solas; si te
> escucha, has ganado a tu hermano. Pero si no *te*
> escucha, lleva contigo a uno o a dos más, para que
> TODA PALABRA SEA CONFIRMADA POR BOCA DE
> DOS O TRES TESTIGOS. Y si rehúsa escucharlos, dilo
> a la iglesia; y si también rehúsa escuchar a la iglesia,
> sea para ti como el Gentil (el pagano) y el recauda-
> dor de impuestos (Mat. 18:15-17).

Cuando alguien ha cometido algún pecado, el deber de la iglesia es restaurarlo, y los creyentes que ejerzan la disciplina deben procurar ganar al hermano. La meta es hacerle ver su pecado y llevarlo a buscar el perdón. Pero si en una instancia íntima, la persona que pecó se resiste, debemos llamar a un par de testigos para concederle una nueva oportunidad. Si todavía no hay arrepentimiento, el otro peldaño en la escalera de la restauración es decirlo en público a la iglesia. Si el hermano no acepta la disciplina, la cuarta y última medida será tenerlo "por gentil y publicano", o más bien, expulsarlo de la iglesia, tal como lo había demandado el apóstol Pablo a los corintios cuando uno de sus miembros estaba en abierta desobediencia a las Escrituras, practicando un pecado sexual (1 Cor. 5:13).

En este contexto, "y lo que ates en la tierra, será atado en los cielos; y lo que desates en la tierra, será desatado en los cielos" se refiere al respaldo que el cielo otorga cuando la iglesia cumple su labor y procura la santidad entre sus miembros. Cuando ejercemos bien la autoridad para disciplinar en la tierra, el cielo aprueba la disciplina.

Conclusión

Pensar que tenemos la necesidad de "atar y desatar" al diablo es un argumento que no se ajusta al testimonio de las Escrituras en los versículos comúnmente utilizados para sostener tal idea. Lo que es más, pensar de esta manera desvía la atención de la iglesia. Los pasajes de Mateo 16 y 18 que nos hablan de atar se refieren de manera clara al evangelizar y a la disciplina en la iglesia. Los creyentes no tenemos que enfrascarnos en una "batalla campal" contra el diablo y sus demonios, ni tampoco "atarlos" en el nombre de Jesús. Por un lado, porque Satanás, ya fue atado y derrotado hace 2000 años por un Hombre más fuerte que él: Jesús de Nazaret (Mat. 12:29). Además, porque la relativa influencia que el diablo pueda tener hoy día siempre estará sujeta a los límites que Dios ha establecido en Su soberanía.

En medio de la guerra espiritual —que es real y no ignoramos— el llamado que tenemos en la Escritura es a resistir y estar firmes (Ef. 6:11,13; Sant. 4:7). No tenemos que atar al diablo porque toda su obra está bajo el permiso y control soberano de Dios, cuya soberanía y amor hacia nosotros deben constituirse en la base de nuestra confianza para evangelizar, y para ejercer la disciplina de la iglesia cuando sea necesario.

12

Serás salvo tú y tu casa

DANIEL PUERTO

*Ellos respondieron: "Cree en el Señor Jesús, y serás salvo,
tú y toda tu casa" (Hech. 16:31).*

En una reunión de oración un tiempo atrás, una hermana pidió que
la acompañáramos pidiendo a Dios por la salvación de sus familiares. Si mal no recuerdo, ella mencionó a su padre, sus hermanos y
tíos. Nosotros le prometimos que oraríamos en ese momento por
la salvación de su familia. Pero antes de comenzar a orar, ella nos
dijo: "Yo tengo fe que Dios salvará a mis familiares porque en su
Palabra dice: 'Cree en el Señor Jesucristo, y serás salvo, tú y tu casa'.
Yo confío en las promesas de mi Dios". Por supuesto, ella se estaba
refiriendo a Hechos 16:31. Ahora bien, si esta es una promesa, como
ella pensaba, entonces ¡se le debe una explicación a muchos cristianos!
Muchos de nuestros hermanos y hermanas han orado toda su vida por
la conversión de un familiar, y sin embargo nunca llega. Entonces,
¿qué ha pasado?

¿Cuál es el contexto del pasaje?

Lo dicho por Pablo en Hechos 16:31 acontece en medio de su encarcelamiento junto a Silas, poco después de haber sido azotados. Ellos habían sido puestos en el calabozo, y mientras oraban y cantaban himnos a Dios: "De repente se produjo un gran terremoto, de tal manera que los cimientos de la cárcel fueron sacudidos. Al instante se abrieron todas las puertas y las cadenas de todos se soltaron" (16:26).

De acuerdo con la ley romana, si un guardia perdía a un prisionero, él recibía el mismo castigo que el gobierno había determinado para el delincuente. Al ver toda las puertas abiertas, el carcelero entró en un estado de pánico, al punto de buscar su espada para quitarse la vida. Los gritos de Pablo evitaron su suicidio, al explicarle que todos los presos seguían dentro de la cárcel.

Luego de tan emocionante escena, el carcelero preguntó a los misioneros: "Señores, ¿qué debo hacer para ser salvo?" (16:30). La respuesta de Pablo y Silas fue la proverbial expresión "Cree en el Señor Jesucristo y serás salvo tú y *toda* tu casa". Como la señora en la reunión de oración, muchos cristianos entendieron estas palabras como una promesa directa de parte de Dios para ellos mismos. Ellos vieron en este versículo una razón para creer que sus familiares no creyentes algún día, tarde o temprano, llegarán a creer en Cristo como Salvador.

Historias y enseñanzas

¿Es Hechos 16:31 una promesa de Dios acerca de la salvación de nuestros familiares? En resumidas cuentas, no.

Una regla importante que debemos seguir al estudiar la Biblia es interpretar las narraciones históricas a la luz de los textos didácticos, es decir, interpretar las historias en base a las enseñanzas. "El término *didáctico* viene de la palabra griega que significa enseñar o instruir. La literatura didáctica enseña o instruye".[1] Hablando en términos generales, los Evangelios y el libro de los Hechos son en gran parte narraciones históricas; mientras que las cartas de Pablo, Pedro, Juan, etc. son textos didácticos.

Los Reformadores del siglo XVI tenían como principio hermenéutico que las Epístolas interpretan los Evangelios, en lugar de que los Evangelios interpreten las Epístolas.[2] No podemos sacar nuestra teología de narraciones históricas, ignorando la enseñanza que con claridad podemos leer en los pasajes didácticos.

El escritor español José M. Martínez explica de manera contundente que "la atribución de carácter normativo a un hecho determinado debe basarse en otros textos del Nuevo Testamento que la justifiquen… Sin el debido apoyo del resto del Nuevo Testamento, no debe generalizarse ninguna experiencia personal o práctica eclesiástica y propugnar su repetición como si fuese exigible a todo cristiano o a toda iglesia local. Ello sería una ligereza poco recomendable".[3]

En Hechos 16:31 Dios no enseña que mi familia recibe salvación automáticamente después de que yo soy salvo. Tampoco enseña que Dios me prometió que los miembros de mi familia serán salvos si yo comprendí el evangelio y recibo el regalo de la salvación. De acuerdo con el mensaje completo del Nuevo Testamento, los miembros de la familia del carcelero recibirían salvación si escuchaban el mensaje y eran objeto de la obra regeneradora del Espíritu Santo. Como enseña el capítulo 10 de esta misma obra, para que ellos creyeran

---

[1]   R. C. Sproul, *Knowing Scripture* (Downers Grove: InterVarsity Press, 2009). Edición para Kindle, loc. 1013.

[2]   Ibid., loc. 1022.

[3]   José M. Martínez, *Hermenéutica Bíblica* (Barcelona: Libros CLIE, 1984), 479.

en Cristo como Salvador, el evangelio tenía que llegar a sus oídos (Rom. 10:13-17) y el Espíritu Santo tenía que hacer Su obra de salvación (Juan 3:1-8). Y esto mismo sucedió, pues los versículos siguientes narran que ellos escucharon la Palabra, creyeron y fueron bautizados con gozo (Hech. 16:32-34).

Sí, Pablo le dijo al carcelero de Filipo que su familia sería salva si él creía en el evangelio. Pero eso fue el apóstol Pablo al carcelero de Filipo. Una promesa particular, dada en el tiempo: no una promesa que yo pueda dar a quien yo quiera. No hay ninguna enseñanza en la Escritura que confirme que mi conversión va a dar como resultado la conversión de mis familiares. Es una hermosa historia, no una enseñanza eterna. Lo que sí se nos enseña con toda claridad en la Escritura es la disposición de Dios para salvar a cada individuo que crea en Jesús (Rom. 10:9).

Conclusión

Para que los miembros de mi familia que no son salvos lleguen a recibir el regalo de la vida eterna, el mensaje del evangelio debe llegar a ellos y el Espíritu Santo debe alumbrar su entendimiento y hacerlos nacer de nuevo. Como creyente, oro por la salvación de aquellos familiares y amigos que no recibieron el regalo de la vida eterna. Sin embargo, pensar que en Hechos 16:31 encuentro una promesa de Dios para la salvación de mi familia es poner en boca de Dios lo que Él nunca dijo. No esperemos que cumpla lo que Él no ha prometido. Tampoco dejemos de predicar a quienes amamos. ¡Nuestro Dios se goza en salvar!

13

En Cristo no hay hombre ni mujer

PATRICIA NAMNÚN

No hay Judío ni Griego; no hay esclavo ni libre; no hay
hombre ni mujer, porque todos son uno en Cristo Jesús
(Gál. 3:28).

Gálatas 3:28 es uno de esos pasajes que se ha interpretado de diversas formas en diversos momentos de la historia de la Iglesia. Por ejemplo, tiempo atrás, algunos entendían que en este pasaje el apóstol Pablo establecía la abolición de la esclavitud al decir que en Cristo no hay esclavo ni libre.[1] En nuestros días, la discusión sobre este pasaje ya no gira en torno a la esclavitud, sino en torno a la diferencia de roles entre hombre y mujer. De hecho, este mismo verso se usa cada vez más para justificar la homosexualidad.

Los igualitaristas, aquellos que creen que el hombre y la mujer son iguales no solo en dignidad sino también en sus roles, consideran

---

[1] Byron Barlowe, *"Slavery, William Wilberforce and the Film 'Amazing Grace'"*, [Esclavitud, William Wilberforce y el filme "Amazing Grace"], 18 de junio de 2007, visto el 10 de diciembre de 2015, https://www.probe.org/slavery-william-wilberforce-and-the-film-amazing-grace/.

este pasaje de Gálatas como "La carta magna de la humanidad, el gran capítulo de la igualdad cristiana",[2] "El texto socialmente más explosivo en la Biblia",[3] y aun "La proclamación de emancipación de la mujer".[4] Argumentan que Gálatas 3:28 es una especie de llave que permite interpretar los pasajes relacionados con el género que se encuentran en el Nuevo Testamento, entendiendo que elimina toda barrera social entre el hombre y la mujer, proclamando la igualdad de roles entre ambos. Mary Kassian resume esta postura:

> De acuerdo a los feministas, Gálatas 3:28 enseña que Dios ha creado en Cristo un nuevo orden completo en las relaciones. La manera de ver la jerarquía en las relaciones sociales es producto del antiguo orden derivado de la caída. Los feministas insisten en que las distinciones sociales entre hombre y mujer no deben existir más. Para los feministas bíblicos, igualdad significa la abolición de todos los roles de género en la sociedad, la iglesia y en el hogar.[5]

Como vemos, este texto se utiliza para enarbolar la bandera del feminismo y "abolir" la diferencia de roles entre hombre y mujer. Pero más que traer nuestras ideas a la Escritura, veamos qué es lo que el Espíritu de Dios nos dice a través de Pablo.

---

[2]   Paul K. Jewett, *Man as Male and Female: A Study in Sexual Relationships from a Theological Point of View* (Grand Rapids: Eerdmans, 1975), 142.
[3]   Klyne R. Snodgrass, "The Ordination of Women-Thirteen Years Later: Do We Really Value the Ministry of Women?" *Covenant Quarterly* 48/3 (1990), 34.
[4]   Ben Witherington, III, "Rite and Rights for Women-Galatians 3:28", *New Testament Studies* 27/5 (1981), 602.
[5]   Mary A. Kassian, *Women, Creation, and The Fall* (Nashville: Crossway Books, 1990), 155.

Gracia y fe

El tema general de la Epístola a los Gálatas es la justificación por gracia a través de la fe. En el momento en el que Pablo escribe esta carta, la iglesia en Galacia estaba siendo influenciada por falsos maestros, a quienes Pablo llama "algunos que los perturban" (Gál. 1:7). Estos perturbadores estaban convenciendo a los gálatas de un falso evangelio que les demandaba someterse a toda la ley mosaica –en particular al requerimiento de la circuncisión– antes de que pudieran convertirse en cristianos. Estos falsos maestros les estaban exigiendo las obras de la ley, y muchos de los gálatas eran persuadidos por esas falsas enseñanzas. Dada esta circunstancia, Pablo escribe en defensa de la justificación por la fe, advirtiéndoles de las consecuencias de abandonar la doctrina que les había sido enseñada: el evangelio verdadero.

Gálatas 3 gira en torno del contexto de la carta. Pablo comienza este capítulo llamando insensatos a los gálatas (Gál. 3:1) por haberse dejado fascinar por estas enseñanzas que ponían las obras de la ley por encima de la fe, y por estar tratando de terminar en la carne habiendo comenzado por el Espíritu (Gál. 3:3).

A lo largo de este capítulo, Pablo les deja claro a sus lectores que la ley vino para ser un guía para conducirnos a Cristo a fin de ser justificados por la fe, y no por las obras de la ley (Gál. 3:24). Pero al momento de llegar la fe, ya no estamos bajo el guía (la ley) pues somos hechos hijos de Dios mediante la fe, y esta fe puesta de manera exclusiva en Cristo Jesús (Gál. 3:25-26). Entonces, en este contexto de la fe y la ley, encontramos el versículo 28: *"No hay Judío ni Griego; no hay esclavo ni libre; no hay hombre ni mujer, porque todos son uno en Cristo Jesús".*

Ver el pasaje completo deja en evidencia que Pablo no está hablando de igualdad de roles: está hablando de salvación. La idea central en el pasaje de Gálatas 3:28 no es igualdad de roles en Cristo, sino unión en Cristo. El doctor y comentarista Thomas Schreiner dice lo siguiente:

> Pablo mismo nunca entendió Gálatas 3:28 como cancelación de todas las distinciones. Él continuaba creyendo que había diferencias entre judíos y griegos, de lo contrario el argumento de Romanos 9-11 es superfluo. Él continuaba creyendo que había diferencias entre esclavos y amos, de lo contrario su consejo a ambos sería contradictorio (Efesios 6:5-9; Colosenses 3:22-41). Él continuaba creyendo que había diferencias entre hombres y mujeres. De otra manera su acusación contra la homosexualidad es inconsistente (Romanos 1:26-27), y su mandato a los esposos y esposas incomprensible (Efesios 5:22-33; Colosenses 3:18 -19)... El valor y la dignidad de todo ser humano es proclamado por Pablo, pero este verso no debe ser usado en defensa de ideologías modernas. Debemos escuchar las palabras de Pablo, aunque sean extrañas para nosotros.[6]

Diversos, pero unidos en Él

La muerte de Cristo ha traído la era de un Nuevo Pacto, uno que no requiere las obras de la ley para nuestra salvación. Proclamar la necesidad de obras para poder ser salvos es negar el corazón mismo del

---

[6] Thomas R. Schreiner, *Paul, Apostle of God's Glory in Christ: A Pauline Theology* (Downers Grove: InterVarsity, 2001), 402.

evangelio, que es la justificación solo por fe y no por cumplir las obras de la ley. Ese es el mensaje central de Gálatas 3 y de la Palabra misma:

> Sin embargo, sabiendo que el hombre no es justificado por las obras de *la* Ley, sino mediante la fe en Cristo Jesús, también nosotros hemos creído en Cristo Jesús, para que seamos justificados por la fe en Cristo, y no por las obras de *la* Ley. Puesto que por las obras de *la* Ley nadie será justificado (Gál. 2:16).

De ninguna manera Gálatas 3:28 hace referencia a la igualdad de roles o a la manera en la que ciertos grupos deben actuar. El capítulo 3 de Gálatas es un recordatorio de que nuestra salvación depende única y exclusivamente de la obra de Cristo, no la nuestra.

Conclusión

El concepto que expresa Pablo en este texto es que todos somos justificados de la misma manera: por gracia, a través de la fe. Sin lugar a dudas, todos somos uno en Cristo Jesús. Pero Dios no hace a un lado la diferencia entre hombre y mujer, sino que establece la unidad en Cristo. Gálatas 3:28 enarbola la bandera de la unidad en Él en medio de la diversidad de roles. A través de Cristo, todos somos hechos hijos de Dios, judíos y griegos; esclavos y libres; hombres y mujeres. Todos, así diferentes como somos, tenemos salvación y comunión en Uno solo: Cristo Jesús.

14

Dios no te dará más de lo que puedes soportar

*No les ha sobrevenido ninguna tentación que no sea
común a los hombres. Fiel es Dios, que no permitirá que
ustedes sean tentados más allá de lo que pueden soportar,
sino que con la tentación proveerá también la vía de
escape, a fin de que puedan resistirla (1 Cor. 10:13).*

"Dios nunca te dará más de lo que puedes soportar". Creo que
todos hemos escuchado esta frase en algún momento, por lo general, en medio del sufrimiento. De hecho, muchos han abrazado este
concepto dando por sentado que Dios les quitará el sufrimiento o el
dolor cuando lleguen al punto donde ya no lo puedan soportar más.
¿Qué es lo que nos está diciendo la Biblia aquí?

Malinterpretar este versículo abre la puerta a dos grandes erro-
res. Primero, podemos caer en el orgullo. Nos consideramos más
fuertes de lo que somos porque tenemos en nosotros mismos la gran
habilidad de poder soportar cualquier sufrimiento, aún más de lo que

puedan muchos otros cristianos. Por otro lado, podemos llegar a definir lo que somos capaces de "soportar" en base a nuestras emociones o nuestras propias fuerzas. Nos convencemos de la falsa esperanza de que Dios nunca dejará que pasemos por algo que afectará nuestra salud, nuestra familia, nuestras finanzas, etc.

Fortaleza contra la tentación

Para entender este versículo iniciemos preguntándonos, ¿a qué se refiere Pablo al usar la palabra tentación?

Esta pregunta se puede contestar al ver el contexto del versículo. Vale la pena recordar una vez más lo importante que es entender cada versículo dentro de su propio contexto. Los versículos no son encantamientos mágicos o hechizos que podemos usar para mejorar una situación. Cada versículo surge de un argumento que se está desarrollando en las páginas de las Escrituras.

En los versículos anteriores al texto que estamos viendo, Pablo resume parte de la historia de Israel. Él dice en el versículo 5: "Sin embargo, Dios no se agradó de la mayor parte de ellos, y por eso quedaron tendidos en el desierto". Luego continúa explicando por qué es que Dios no se agradó de la mayor parte de ellos. Pablo explica lo que sucedió para dar un ejemplo, "a fin de que no codiciemos lo malo, como ellos *lo* codiciaron" (v. 6).

Después de esa introducción, Pablo da una serie de mandamientos o advertencias que tienen que ver con el pecado en particular:
- v. 7 "No sean, *pues*, idólatras, como *fueron* algunos de ellos…"
- v. 8 "Ni forniquemos, como algunos de ellos fornicaron…"
- v. 9 "Ni provoquemos al Señor, como algunos de ellos Lo provocaron…"

- v. 10 "Ni murmuren, como algunos de ellos murmuraron…"

Lo que queda claro es que el pueblo de Israel había rechazado la roca de la que habían bebido. Ellos habían rechazado el pacto que Dios había guardado con fidelidad, y buscaron satisfacer sus antojos carnales con cosas terrenales.

Después de hablar con tanta claridad sobre cómo fue que los israelitas cayeron en toda forma de pecado, Pablo otra vez explica en 1 Corintios 10:11 que eso sucedió como un ejemplo para nosotros, para que podamos enfrentar la tentación de una manera diferente de los demás. Y luego da una seria advertencia en el versículo 12: "Por tanto, el que cree que está firme, tenga cuidado, no sea que caiga".

De manera explícita, Pablo está diciendo que el que piensa que con sus propias fuerzas puede estar firme contra el pecado debe tener cuidado de no caer. Podría inferirse que es solo cuestión de tiempo hasta que caiga. Quizás uno puede luchar contra la tentación durante un tiempo, pero si está dependiendo de sus propias fuerzas, el corazón humano siempre caerá en la tentación.

Los corintios —al igual que los israelitas— estaban enfrentando mucha idolatría. Y Pablo está usando la experiencia de Israel para llamar la atención de los corintios sobre el hecho de que ellos no tienen en sí mismos la fuerza para enfrentar el pecado, pues para ello se requiere una fuerza sobrenatural. Y es en ese contexto que Pablo escribe la promesa tan bella del versículo 13.

Entender el pasaje línea por línea

No les ha sobrevenido ninguna tentación que no sea común a los hombres. Es posible que todos caigamos en la trampa de pensar que lo que nosotros estamos enfrentando es único. Sin embargo, Pablo inicia este versículo explicando que la tentación a la idolatría es común a todos, como ya lo había demostrado en los versículos anteriores. Lo que los corintios estaban enfrentando no fue algún ataque particularmente difícil. La tentación de pecar, de ofrecer sacrificio a los ídolos en vez de a Dios es una lucha diaria.

Fiel es Dios, que no permitirá que ustedes sean tentados más allá de lo que pueden soportar... Primero, es importante reconocer que todo el contexto de este pasaje se refiere a la tentación hacia el pecado. Se refiere a la tentación de rechazar a Cristo y buscar satisfacer nuestros antojos carnales con cosas terrenales en vez de dejar que Cristo sea suficiente para nosotros. A pesar de lo que se suele decir, el enfoque no es el sufrimiento.

Segundo, Pablo arraiga la promesa de cuánto seremos tentados no en nuestra fuerza, sino en la fidelidad de Dios. Sí, Pablo dice que no seremos tentados más allá de lo que podemos soportar, pero inicia esa misma frase diciendo que Dios es fiel. ¿Fiel a hacer qué? Tal vez unos dirían que Él es fiel a no dejar que seamos tentados más allá de nuestra capacidad. Sin embargo, yo creo que Dios es fiel en cumplir con todo lo que Él ha prometido cumplir, que nos da toda la fuerza necesaria para soportar la tentación. Es decir que nuestra fuerza para soportar la tentación viene directo de la fidelidad de Dios.

En Romanos Pablo explica que Dios ya nos libertó del poder del pecado. Lo que Pablo quiere decir en este versículo es que todo el poder, toda la fuerza para combatir el pecado ya nos lo ha dado Dios en Cristo. Nosotros podemos soportar la tentación porque Dios es fiel en cumplir con todo lo que ha prometido, no porque nosotros somos fuertes. Él nos dará la gracia para decir "no" al pecado (Tito 2:11-12). Él obrará en nosotros para llevar a cabo nuestra salvación (Fil. 2:12-13). En el evangelio, Él nos dio todo el poder para la salvación, no solo de la pena del pecado, sino también por encima del poder del pecado (Rom. 1:16, 1 Cor. 1:18). Dios es fiel, y por Su fidelidad todo lo que necesitamos para soportar la tentación está disponible para nosotros.

...sino que con la tentación proveerá también la vía de escape, a fin de que puedan resistirla. Y más importante que todo eso, Dios siempre provee una salida. Él proveyó la salida de la pena del pecado en la cruz. Él proveyó la salida del poder del pecado en la cruz. Y Él proveyó Su Espíritu que obra en nosotros, llevando a cabo la santificación en nuestro corazón. Eso significa que en cualquier momento de tentación, todo lo necesario está disponible.

Conclusión

Serás tentado más de lo que puedes soportar con tus propias fuerzas, pero nunca serás tentado más de lo que la fidelidad de Dios puede soportar. Él siempre cumplirá Sus promesas. Dios hará en ti todo lo necesario. Te dará siempre el poder para decir "¡No!" a la tentación. Si caemos, no es porque no lo pudimos soportar: es porque nosotros, al igual que los israelitas, buscamos satisfacer nuestros antojos carnales con otras cosas terrenales que no son Cristo.

15

Si somos infieles, Dios permanece fiel

SUGEL MICHELÉN

> *Palabra fiel es ésta: Que si morimos con Él, también*
> *viviremos con Él; si perseveramos, también reinaremos*
> *con Él; si Lo negamos, Él también nos negará; si somos*
> *infieles (incrédulos), Él permanece fiel, pues no puede*
> *negarse a sí mismo (2 Tim. 2:11-13).*

En 2 Timoteo 2:13 encontramos unas palabras que, para muchos, representan una de las grandes promesas de la Biblia. De manera equivocada, ellos entienden que no importa cuán infieles lleguemos a ser, nuestro Dios permanece fiel. Su amor es absolutamente incondicional y, por lo tanto, no importa lo que hagamos o dejemos de hacer, Él continuará bendiciéndonos y cuidando de nosotros, como lo haría con el más fiel de Sus hijos.

"Si somos infieles (incrédulos), Él permanece fiel". Observar esta afirmación de manera aislada puede llevarnos a concluir que, en efecto, esta es una hermosa promesa. Sin embargo, cuando leemos el texto en su contexto nos damos cuenta de que en realidad no es una promesa, sino más bien una solemne advertencia.

El contexto inmediato

¿Cuál es el contexto de este pasaje? Pablo está alentando a su hijo en la fe, Timoteo, a que siga adelante haciendo la obra del ministerio a pesar de las dificultades que seguramente encontraría en el camino. Él le recuerda cuatro cosas:

- Que servimos a un Mesías victorioso que murió y resucitó (2 Tim. 2:8).
- Que el mundo puede perseguir a los cristianos, pero no puede detener el avance del evangelio (2 Tim. 2:9; Pablo estaba en la cárcel, pero la Palabra de Dios no está presa).
- Que Dios ha decretado salvar a los escogidos por medio de la predicación del evangelio (2 Tim. 2:10).
- Y que Él es fiel a Sus promesas, lo mismo que a Sus advertencias (2 Tim. 2:11-13).

Es en este contexto que aparece la declaración que estamos considerando aquí. Nuestro Dios es fiel a Su Palabra, porque Él no puede negarse a sí mismo. Por lo tanto, podemos estar seguros de que si somos muertos con Cristo, también viviremos con Él. Por supuesto, eso no quiere decir que la única forma de salvarse es muriendo como mártires por nuestra fe. Pablo parece estar usando esa expresión en el mismo sentido de 1 Corintios 15:31, donde dice que él muere cada día por causa del Señor. También nos dice en 2 Corintios 4:10 que él lleva siempre en su cuerpo "por todas partes la muerte de Jesús, para que también la vida de Jesús se manifieste en nuestro cuerpo".

El llamado de Cristo a los suyos es un llamado a la muerte, a la muerte del "yo" y de nuestra propia seguridad, porque es un llamado a seguirlo a Él. Todo aquel que de verdad va camino al cielo debe transitar por la misma senda que Él transitó; y ese camino, antes de llegar a la gloria, primero pasa por la cruz.

A esto también alude Pablo en la primera parte del versículo 12, al decir que "Si perseveramos, también reinaremos con Él". La vida cristiana conlleva un caminar. Conlleva perseverancia. Nadie puede andar diciendo que es un verdadero cristiano si no está dispuesto a someterse a la voluntad de Dios. No somos salvos por obedecer a Dios, ni por hacer buenas obras; pero todos aquellos que han sido salvados por gracia, por medio de la fe, muestran la realidad de la gracia y de la fe a través de su obediencia y de sus buenas obras a lo largo de su vida, hasta Su regreso o hasta que Él nos llame al hogar.

Promesas y advertencias

La fidelidad de Dios a Su Palabra opera también en el sentido contrario, dice Pablo a partir de la segunda mitad del versículo 12. Si negamos al Señor, "Él también nos negará; Si somos infieles (incrédulos), Él permanece fiel, pues no puede negarse Él mismo". El apóstol nos dice aquí que el Señor es fiel a Su advertencia de que Él negará a los que lo nieguen. En otras palabras, si el Señor dejara de cumplir cualquiera de Sus promesas, estaría dejando de ser un Dios fiel. Pero lo mismo sucedería si dejara de cumplir alguna de Sus advertencias.

El Señor Jesucristo fue muy claro al respecto. Vemos en Mateo 10:32-33: "Por tanto, todo el que Me confiese delante de los hombres, Yo también lo confesaré delante de Mi Padre que está en los cielos. Pero cualquiera que Me niegue delante de los hombres, Yo también lo negaré delante de Mi Padre que está en los cielos". El Señor es fiel en cumplir Sus promesas: al morir con Él, viviremos con Él; al perseverar, reinaremos. Del mismo modo, Él es fiel en cumplir Sus advertencias: si lo negamos, Él también nos negará, pues Él no se negará a sí mismo.

Conclusión

Este no es el lugar para discutir la doctrina de la perseverancia de los santos, pero algo es claro en las Escrituras: la única forma de saber que una persona está siendo preservada por Dios para salvación es si la persona está perseverando. Si se aparta de manera definitiva de la fe que profesa, esa es una prueba inequívoca de que nunca fue creyente (comp. Mat. 7:21-23; 1 Jn. 2:19).

Esto debía animar a Timoteo, y a todos nosotros, a no descuidarnos. La salvación es segura para el que la tiene. Ningún verdadero creyente se perderá. Pero la única forma de confirmar la veracidad de nuestra fe es perseverando hasta el fin. Que la advertencia de 2 Timoteo 2:13 nos motive a la piedad tanto como las promesas de los versículos anteriores. En lo uno y en lo otro, Dios es fiel.

16

El conocimiento envanece

JAIRO NAMNÚN

En cuanto a lo sacrificado a los ídolos, sabemos que todos
tenemos conocimiento. El conocimiento envanece, pero
el amor edifica. Si alguien cree que sabe algo, no ha
aprendido todavía como debe saber; pero si alguien ama a
Dios, ése es conocido por Él (1 Cor. 8:1-3).

Recuerdo con mucha nitidez la primera vez que me encontré de frente con esto de que "el conocimiento envanece". Estaba conversando emocionado con un pastor, comentándole cuánto estaba aprendiendo a través de un programa de televisión cristiano. Allí podía ver cómo se desmenuzaba cada versículo, se traían a colación asuntos importantes del contexto histórico del pasaje, y se analizaba cada palabra para poder entender mejor su significado. Yo estaba extasiado por todo lo que estaba aprendiendo, y quería comunicarle mi gozo a este pastor, con el deseo de que pudiera implementarlo en su congregación. Él no estaba igual de emocionado. Más bien, me llevó a 1 Corintios 8 y me dejó ver que tanto conocimiento no me serviría de mucho. Yo me quedé aturdido. ¿Será que todo este conocimiento que me hacía sentir tan bien solo me servía para envanecerme?

Luego de aquella experiencia de hace tantos años, he escuchado este texto sacado de su contexto en docenas de ocasiones. Muchas veces lo usan los pastores que, bien intencionados, no quieren que sus ovejas vayan detrás del conocimiento a expensas del bien de su alma. Una vez supe de alguien que no quería que sus hijos hicieran demasiado esfuerzo en la universidad porque no quería que se envanecieran. En muchas de las iglesias contemporáneas, el conocimiento está en segundo plano detrás de la experiencia, y pareciera que no son pocos los que van detrás de sentir más que de pensar. Piensan, como dice el dicho, que "una persona con una experiencia nunca está a la merced de alguien con un argumento".

No obstante, hay algo que debe quedar claro: la marca del creyente genuino es una vida transformada (Mat. 7:16), que manifiesta el fruto del Espíritu (Gál. 5:22-23). Obtener conocimiento no es la meta: aun los demonios conocen la sana doctrina (Sant. 2:19). Pero, ¿no se supone que debemos amar a Dios con toda nuestra mente? Por esa razón es necesario que entendamos qué nos está diciendo Dios a través de este pasaje, a fin de poder aplicarlo correctamente a nuestras vidas.

Lo que no dice: El conocimiento es malo

Pablo no puede estar diciendo que el conocimiento es malo en sí mismo. La razón por la que no puede decirlo es que Pablo conoce bien el Antiguo Testamento, y sabe que en Oseas Dios dice que se deleita más en que lo conozcan a Él que en los holocaustos (Os. 6:6), y que Su pueblo era destruido por falta de conocimiento (Os. 4:6). Pablo conoce el libro de Proverbios, con los diferentes llamados que hace a buscar la sabiduría y el conocimiento. Y Pablo también sabe cómo se habla bien de los hijos de Isacar, puesto que eran "expertos en discernir los tiempos, con conocimiento..." (1 Crón. 12:32).

A lo largo de las Escrituras, y a lo largo de la historia de la Iglesia, podemos ver que Dios usa una y otra vez a personas de mucho conocimiento. Eso incluye al mismo Pablo, quien fue capaz de presentar una defensa de la fe ante los filósofos de su tiempo, aun citando a poetas no tan conocidos (Hech. 17); y quien conocía al menos el hebreo (Hech. 26:14) y el griego (Hech. 21:37), y con toda probabilidad hablaba arameo y posiblemente latín. Pablo también era habilidoso en su trabajo de hacer tiendas. Debido a la forma en que se manejaba en diferentes culturas, nos queda la impresión de que el apóstol era un hombre entendido en los tiempos.

Además, es evidente que Pablo tenía un amplio manejo del Antiguo Testamento. En sus últimos momentos, él deseaba seguir escudriñando las Escrituras (2 Tim. 4:13). Él instruyó a su discípulo a que conociera "con precisión" la Biblia (2 Tim. 2:15). Pablo elogió a los romanos por estar llenos de todo conocimiento (Rom. 15:14), y oraba por que el amor de los filipenses abundara en todo conocimiento (Fil. 1:9).

Por lo que podemos ver en la Escritura, abundar en conocimiento es una bendición, no un problema. Y de manera particular, conocer a Dios es un privilegio para los cristianos, y ese conocimiento solo se obtiene en la persona de Jesús (Juan 1:18), a través de las Escrituras (Juan 5:39).

Lo que sí dice: El conocimiento no nos hace superiores

Por todo el contexto de la carta, es evidente que la iglesia en Corinto tenía una tendencia a la división. Vemos que algunos decían que eran de Pablo, otros de Apolos, otros de Pedro, y aun algunos decían que eran de Cristo (1 Cor. 1:12). Esta misma tendencia a la división se manifiesta en este capítulo, pero ahora entre los que se consideraban más espirituales que los demás.

1 Corintios 8:1 inicia haciendo referencia a "lo sacrificado a los ídolos". En los tiempos de esta carta, la carne más barata se vendía en el contexto religioso. Corinto era una ciudad muy mística, y los templos eran lugares de mucho comercio y movimiento. Se creía que los seres espirituales perversos que querían poseer a los seres humanos entraban en la comida, para luego poseer a la persona que ingiriese el alimento. Lo habitual era, entonces, sacrificar el alimento a algún ídolo, y esto se hacía comúnmente en los templos. Esta parece ser la carne a la que Pablo se refiere en el pasaje, carne que había sido ofrecida a dioses falsos que ahora llegaba a las manos del cristiano común y corriente.

Algunos entre los corintios habían entendido lo absurdo de todo esto, al saber que "un ídolo no es nada" (1 Cor. 8:4). Este conocimiento "elevado" era correcto. Era lo que debían pensar. Sin embargo, el pasaje nos deja ver que algunos entre los corintios, teniendo el conocimiento real, no estaban aplicándolo como debían. Su ortodoxia no los estaba llevando a una *ortopraxia*. Pareciera ser que los que poseían aquel conocimiento elevado se envanecieron, considerando como inferiores a los que no lo poseían. Por eso, Pablo les deja ver que "ni somos menos si no comemos, ni *somos* más si comemos" (1 Cor. 8:8).

El pasaje también nos muestra algo interesante en el versículo 2, y es que el orgullo envanecido se hace evidente en la autoconfianza. Mientras más conocemos al Dios de la Escritura y la Escritura del Dios vivo, mientras más entendemos la mente de Dios, más nos damos cuenta de cuán superiores son los pensamientos de Dios a los nuestros.

Aquel que más conoce de la Palabra más se da cuenta de cuánto le falta por conocer. Por tanto, aquel que piensa que conoce todo lo que tiene que saber en realidad demuestra cuánto le falta por conocer.

Conocimiento correcto

El conocimiento que necesitamos es un conocimiento como el de Dios. El cristiano vive su vida buscando ser más como Él. Cristo Jesús, nuestro Salvador, ha sido el hombre más sabio que ha pasado por la tierra, y también fue el hombre más humilde que alguna vez haya existido. Estando ahí en la creación del mundo, Él disfrutaba pasar tiempo con los niños. Sosteniendo el universo por la Palabra de Su poder, Él pasaba tiempo con hombres y mujeres de reputaciones dudosas. Siendo tanto superior a nosotros, Él dio Su vida por ti y por mí.

Jesús ejemplifica que tener conocimiento no siempre significa envanecernos. Que es posible crecer en nuestro intelecto y a la vez crecer en nuestro amor por los demás. De hecho, esta es la vida cristiana: conocer a nuestro Dios cada vez más y, al conocerlo a Él, amar más a los que son creados a Su imagen. Esto era lo que habían perdido los corintios. Su conocimiento no se estaba traduciendo en amor, lo cual demostraba que no habían entendido correctamente. Y si les pasó a nuestros hermanos en Corinto, nos puede pasar a nosotros también.

Conclusión

¿Qué tal estás con tu conocimiento? Aquello que estás aprendiendo de la Palabra, o en la universidad o donde sea, ¿cómo te está sirviendo para amar a los demás? ¿Cómo lo estás poniendo en práctica en tu iglesia local? Si a medida que estás creciendo en tu conocimiento, te vas envaneciendo y te estás sintiendo superior a tus hermanos, entonces algo anda mal. Pero si el conocimiento que estás adquiriendo te lleva a amar más a Dios y a mostrar ese amor al amar más a tus hermanos, entonces eres conocido por Él (1 Cor. 8:3). Y eso, amado hermano, es el deseo de todo creyente.

> *Así dice el Señor:*
> *"No se gloríe el sabio de su sabiduría,*
> *Ni se gloríe el poderoso de su poder,*
> *Ni el rico se gloríe de su riqueza;*
> *Pero si alguien se gloría, gloríese de esto:*
> ***De que Me entiende y Me conoce***
> *Pues Yo soy el Señor que hago misericordia,*
> *Derecho y justicia en la tierra,*
> *Porque en estas cosas Me complazco" (Jer. 9:23-24).*

17

Traed los diezmos al alfolí

GREG TRAVIS

"Traigan todo el diezmo al alfolí, para que haya alimento en Mi casa; y pónganme ahora a prueba en esto;" dice el SEÑOR de los ejércitos "si no les abro las ventanas de los cielos, y derramo para ustedes bendición hasta que sobreabunde. Por ustedes reprenderé al devorador, para que no les destruya los frutos del suelo, ni su vid en el campo sea estéril," dice el SEÑOR de los ejércitos (Mal. 3:10-11).

Durante mis primeros años como misionero en Argentina aprendí mucho acerca de la gran escasez de sana enseñanza en las iglesias locales. Recuerdo que cada domingo pasaba la misma persona de siempre a hablar de la ofrenda, haciendo una especie de mini-sermón. Recuerdo cuando dijo algo así como: "Reprendemos al devorador y declaramos prosperidad y trabajo". Este hombre estaba haciendo una conexión directa entre la ofrenda y la prosperidad económica de las personas. ¿Te suena familiar?

Me di cuenta de que en ese momento él estaba citando Malaquías 3:11. Este pasaje se suele usar para decir que Dios nos bendice cuando ofrendamos y reprende todo aquello que impide nuestra prosperidad económica. En esencia, lo que se enseña es que ofrendar y diezmar es un buen negocio, una buena inversión. Yo doy, y como resultado mi economía va a ir mejor.

No a nosotros, pero para nosotros

Alguien dijo que la Biblia no nos fue escrita a nosotros, sino para nosotros. Quizás hayas escuchado la historia del hombre que pedía que Dios le hable a través de la Biblia abriéndola al azar. Después de hacer su oración, voltea las hojas al azar, pone su dedo y llega a este pasaje: "Y arrojando las monedas de plata en el santuario, Judas se marchó; y fue y se ahorcó" (Mat. 27:5). Intenta de nuevo, cierra los ojos, y cuando los abre, lee así: "Ve, y haz tú lo mismo" (Luc. 10:37). No lo puede creer, pero intenta una tercera vez y lee: "Y lo que vas a hacer, hazlo pronto" (Juan 13:27). Es un ejemplo exagerado del peligro de divorciar el pasaje de su contexto e intentar aplicarlo sin más a nuestra vida. Pero es eso mismo lo que se hace a menudo.

Es de vital importancia entender el mensaje que fue revelado en su contexto original antes de que intentemos entender cómo aplicarlo hoy. Necesitamos comprender qué es lo que Dios estaba diciendo originalmente en el libro de Malaquías antes de que podamos entender qué es lo que Dios nos quiere decir hoy a nosotros. Quisiera ofrecer tres observaciones contextuales importantes para entender este pasaje, y después concluir con tres pensamientos a modo de aplicación.

Observar el contexto

1. Contexto histórico.

Malaquías se ubica unos cuatrocientos años antes del nacimiento de Cristo. Es un tiempo en que los judíos están de regreso en su tierra (bajo dominio persa). Hace más de un siglo Dios había usado a personas como Esdras, Hageo y Zacarías para reedificar a un pueblo que había estado cautivo durante setenta años en la nación de Babilonia. Pero para cuando llegamos al tiempo de Malaquías, encontramos una nación que había caído en la mediocridad, la apatía y la desobediencia. Es en este contexto histórico que se escribe el libro.

2. Contexto teológico.

El mensaje de Malaquías 3:10-11 fue dado en primera instancia a la nación de Israel, que era una teocracia. Dios había revelado en Deuteronomio 28 que había bendiciones muy específicas por obedecer y maldiciones concretas por desobedecer la ley mosaica. Una de las áreas de desobediencia era la de los diezmos. El resultado de no dar como correspondía según la ley mosaica era que Dios mismo podía intervenir en el clima, a tal punto que no habría buena cosecha (la frase "abro las ventanas de los cielos" se refiere a una lluvia de bendición tanto literal como figurada).

Malaquías 3:9 nos dice que toda la nación estaba maldita. Las cosas no les estaban yendo bien como nación por desobedecer el pacto mosaico. En el Libro de Hageo pasa algo similar: el pueblo había dejado de construir el templo y vivían muy cómodos en sus hogares. Dios les muestra cómo les iba mal por tener prioridades equivocadas. Cuando la nación se arrepiente, Dios empieza a bendecirlos.

3. Contexto gramatical.

Los diezmos de que se habla acá afectaban directamente a quienes servían en el templo. Era en esencia la comida para los sacerdotes y levitas. La reprensión del devorador tenía que ver con las plagas que afectaban la cosecha. La plaga era una forma de juicio en el Antiguo Testamento (como podemos ver, por ejemplo, en el libro de Joel). Dios iba a detener esto si la nación se arrepentía y obedecía.

Aplicar el texto

1. La teología de la prosperidad.

Me indigna el evangelio de la prosperidad. Distorsiona el evangelio. "Utiliza" a Dios para lograr fines egoístas. Este pasaje se ha usado para motivar a las personas mediante la culpa o con promesas falsas para que ofrenden. Muchas personas rechazan el verdadero evangelio por haber estado expuestas a este mensaje. Explicar esto a otros nos permite corregir falsas percepciones del verdadero evangelio, y nos permite entender que Malaquías 3 tenía un contexto muy diferente del nuestro.

2. La cantidad que damos.

No somos Israel. No somos una nación teocrática. No todo lo que Dios le dijo a Israel se aplica directamente a nosotros. El Nuevo Testamento no habla de un diezmo, sino de ofrendar según cada uno haya prosperado (1 Cor. 16:2). El 10% es una buena guía (como lo es un día de descanso en la semana); pero es un piso, no un techo. Y el énfasis de dar en el Nuevo Testamento es la actitud del corazón.

3. La motivación por la cual damos.

Jesucristo se dio a Sí mismo por nosotros, y Su sacrificio debería ser nuestra motivación al dar. Cuando damos, estamos respondiendo con gratitud a Su entrega por nosotros. Además, estamos expresando nuestra confianza en Dios y reconociendo que todo lo que tenemos es Suyo.

Conclusión

Agustín de Hipona dijo que lo que en verdad importa no es tanto lo que el hombre posee sino lo que lo posee al hombre. El uso del dinero y nuestra disposición a dar indican si el dinero es nuestro amo o nuestro siervo. Ofrendemos con liberalidad a nuestro Dios, sin esperar nada a cambio, sino con gratitud por todo lo que Él hizo en Cristo Jesús, y como muestra de nuestra confianza en Él.

Sobre los autores

Andrés Birch 🐦 @AJBirch
Andrés Birch es un misionero británico afincado en España desde 1983. En la actualidad es pastor de la Iglesia Bautista Reformada, en Palma de Mallorca, España.

Justin Burkholder 🐦 @jlburkholder
Justin Burkholder, su esposa Jenny y su familia sirven como misioneros en Guatemala con TEAM (*The Evangelical Alliance Mission*). En la actualidad, forma parte del equipo pastoral de la Iglesia Reforma, en la Ciudad de Guatemala.

Carlos Contreras 🐦 @PastorCarloz
Carlos Contreras es pastor en la Iglesia Cristiana Gracia Soberana de Ciudad Juárez, México y anfitrión de la conferencia para pastores y líderes Fieles a Su Llamado. Está casado con María Eugenia (Kena) Flores, con quien ha tenido cuatro hijos.

Nathan Díaz 🐦 @ClasAradio
Nathan Díaz es pastor de enseñanza en la Iglesia Evangélica Cuajimalpa en la Ciudad de México, y productor del programa de radio "Clasificación A" que se transmite a lo largo del mundo hispanohablante. Estudió Biblia y teología en el Instituto Bíblico Moody de Chicago. Él y su esposa Cristin tienen tres hijos.

Matthew Hall 🐦 @MatthewJHall
Matthew J. Hall (Ph.D., Universidad de Kentucky) es vicepresidente de servicios académicos en el Seminario Teológico Bautista del Sur en Louisville, Kentucky, donde también es profesor asistente de Historia de la Iglesia.

José Mercado
José Mercado es oriundo de Puerto Rico. Graduado de Ingeniería Industrial, renunció a su carrera de consultoría en el año 2006 para ingresar al colegio de pastores de Sovereign Grace Churches. En la actualidad está completando un grado en Divinidad en el Southern Baptist Theological Seminary. Es el pastor principal de la Iglesia Gracia Soberana, en Gaithersburg, Maryland. Está casado con Kathy Mercado y juntos tienen dos hijos.

Sugel Michelén 🐦 @symichelen
Sugel Michelén (MTS) ha sido durante más de 30 años uno de los pastores de Iglesia Bíblica del Señor Jesucristo, en República Dominicana, donde tiene la responsabilidad de predicar con regularidad la Palabra de Dios en el día del Señor. Es autor de varios libros, incluyendo *Palabras al cansado, Hacia una educación auténticamente cristiana* y más recientemente *De parte de Dios y delante de Dios,* una guía de predicación expositiva. El pastor Michelén y su esposa Gloria tienen 3 hijos y 4 nietos.

Steven Morales 🐦 @stevenmorales
Steven Morales es editor asociado en Coalición por el Evangelio. También se desempeña como uno de los pastores en Iglesia Reforma, en la Ciudad de Guatemala. Está casado con Gabriela.

Gerson Morey 🐦 @gersonmorey
Gerson Morey es pastor en la Iglesia Día de Adoración, en el Sur de la Florida y autor del blog cristiano El Teclado de Gerson. Está casado con Aidee y tienen tres hijos.

Jairo Namnún 🐦 @jnamnun
Jairo se desempeña como director editorial para Coalición por el Evangelio y está encargado de idear y supervisar el contenido del ministerio. Recientemente se reincorporó al personal de la Iglesia Bautista Internacional, en República Dominicana, donde sirve como líder de jóvenes, luego de completar su Maestría en Estudios Teológicos en el Southern Baptist Theological Seminary en Louisville, Kentucky. Está casado con Patricia.

Patricia Namnún 🐦 @patynamnun
Patricia es coordinadora de iniciativas femeninas de Coalición por el Evangelio. Es graduada en ministerio del Instituto de esposas de seminaristas del Southern Baptist Theological Seminary. Además es encargada administrativa del Instituto Integridad y Sabiduría, en República Dominicana.

Miguel Núñez 🐦 @PastorMNunez
Miguel Núñez (M.D., D.Min.) se desempeña como pastor titular de la Iglesia Bautista Internacional (IBI), en Santo Domingo, República Dominicana, y es el presidente y fundador del Ministerio Integridad y Sabiduría, que tiene como visión impactar la generación de hoy con la revelación de Dios en el mundo hispanohablante. Además es el presidente del Instituto Integridad y Sabiduría donde también forma parte del equipo docente.

Enrique Oriolo 🐦 @enriqueoriolo

Enrique Oriolo es el coordinador creativo de Coalición por el Evangelio, y supervisa toda el área de diseño y redes sociales del ministerio. Es miembro de la Iglesia Bíblica de City Bell en Argentina, y cofundador del ministerio Soldados de Jesucristo. Es graduado del Centro de Capacitación Bíblica para Pastores (CCBP), en City Bell. Está casado con Tamara y juntos tienen dos hijas.

Daniel Puerto 🐦 @danielpuerto51

J. Daniel Puerto es pastor de la Iglesia Bautista La Nueva Esperanza, en Tampa, Florida. Estudió en el Instituto Bíblico Río Grande y está cursando una maestría en el Southeastern Baptist Theological Seminary. Está casado con Claudia y tienen una hija.

Juan Sánchez 🐦 @manorjuan

Juan Sanchez (Ph.D.) es el pastor principal de High Pointe Baptist Church en Austin, Texas, y miembro fundador del consejo directivo de Coalición por el Evangelio.

Otto Sánchez 🐦 @PastorOttoS

Otto Sánchez es pastor de la Iglesia Bautista Ozama (IBO), en Santo Domingo, República Dominicana. Además es director del Seminario Teológico Bautista Dominicano. Está casado con Susana Almánzar, y tienen dos hijas.

Greg Travis

Greg Travis creció en México y Argentina como hijo de misioneros. Obtuvo su maestría en el Seminario Teológico de Dallas. En la actualidad es misionero y pastor de la Iglesia Bíblica de City Bell, Argentina, y sirve en la capacitación de líderes y pastores. Está casado con Caro, y juntos tienen tres hijos.

COALICIÓN POR EL EVANGELIO es una hermandad de iglesias y pastores comprometidos con promover el evangelio y las doctrinas de la gracia en el mundo hispanohablante, enfocar nuestra fe en la persona de Jesucristo, y reformar nuestras prácticas conforme a las Escrituras. Logramos estos propósitos a través de diversas iniciativas, incluyendo eventos y publicaciones. La mayor parte de nuestro contenido es publicado en www.coalicionporelevangelio.org, pero a la vez nos unimos a los esfuerzos de casas editoriales para producir y colaborar en una línea de libros que representen estos ideales. Cuando un libro lleva el logo de Coalición, usted puede confiar en que fue escrito, editado y publicado con el firme propósito de exaltar la verdad de Dios y el evangelio de Jesucristo.

TGC | COALICIÓN